A SPECIAL NOTE
ON
HURRICANE FLOYD AND THE ABACOS

The rebuilding began the day after Hurricane Floyd hit the Abacos on September 14th, 1999. Considered by many old-timers to be even worse than the devastating Hurricane of 1932. Floyd arrived bringing winds of between 140 and 155 mph, with the eye passing directly over the central Abacos. No settlement escaped damage, though miraculously only one life was lost on Grand Bahama. As is usual in hurricanes, the greatest damage was done by the storm surge and accompanying flooding. The following is a brief outline of the damages Floyd brought upon the Abacos.

On Great Abaco, from Coopers Town to Crown Haven, most buildings were destroyed, as were the docks. The people began living out of tents for the duration of the reconstruction.

Green Turtle Cay suffered both flooding, due to Floyd's storm surge, as well as a tornado, and both the Green Turtle Club and Bluff House were damaged extensively.

Treasure Cay suffered a lot of damage and flooding due to a reported 15' tidal surge. On Great Guana Cay damage was moderate. The Guana Beach Resort dock was destroyed, and the cliff near Nippers suffered some damage. Man-O-War Cay suffered a minimum of damage. The docks were undamaged and there were few cases of structural damage.

Elbow Cay was effectively cut in two near White Sound (with the loss of several houses) though the island is once again one cay. Most of the homes on high ground and around the harbour fared well though a lot of the boats in the harbour suffered damage.

Most of the docks in Marsh Harbour suffered damage and one boat wound up on the road. Several warehouses suffered damage.

As of press time I have heard unsubstantiated reports that the Johnston Foundry and Pete's Pub were destroyed at Little Harbour. Cherokee Sound survived fairly intact though some trees were down and a few older houses wrecked. In Spring City most of the houses were destroyed, but in White Town, the buildings remained intact. At Casaurina Point, Nettie Symonette's Different of Abaco suffered little damage.

At Sandy Point flooding did the most damage; the docks survived, but a few homes were lost and many roofs were damaged. The sea wall that protects the road was broached and residents had to use boats to reach the mainland. In the Bight of Abaco, Mores Island lost ten homes as well as a church in Hard Bargain. The Prime Minister said that Mores Island was one of the most heavily hit places in Abaco. At Crossing Rocks most of the homes were damaged. Disney Cruise Lines and American Bridge sent in the Big Red Boat with water and emergency supplies for Sandy Point, Mores Island, and Crossing Rocks.

As you cruise through the Abacos, please bear in mind the effects of Hurricane Floyd upon what appears in this guide. All of the soundings in this guide were taken prior to Floyd, and from all indications the routes appear unchanged. But remember to trust your eyes and your depth sounder if in doubt. The fine people of Abaco are now in the process of rebuilding and I am told most repairs are expected to be complete before the new millenium. A few of the businesses mentioned in this guide will have likely changed by the time you cruise these islands; some were destroyed entirely by Floyd and may not be rebuilt. The Abacos are still one of the finest cruising grounds in the world, and this will remain so. However, a few shore-side inconveniences may be suffered by visiting yachtsmen, but they are nothing compared to the inconveniences Floyd brought to the people who live in these lovely islands. Before you know it the Abacos will have recovered and everyone will be talking about Floyd, the hurricane of 1999.

The Abaco Guide

A Cruising Guide

to the

Northern Bahamas

Published in the USA by Seaworthy Publications, Inc., 507 Sunrise Drive, Port Washington, Wisconsin 53074, phone (262) 268-9250, fax (262) 268-9208, e-mail publisher@seaworthy.com, web pages www.seaworthy.com.

CAUTION: The charts in this publication are intended as supplements for NOAA, DMA, or British Admiralty charts and no warranties are either expressed or implied as to the usability of the information contained herein. The Author and Publisher take no responsibility for their misuse.

A publication like this is actually the result of a blending of many people's knowledge and experiences. I would like to take this opportunity to thank the following for their help in this effort: Capt. Lee Bakewell on the S/V *Winterlude* for his help with the programming; John DeCarion of the S/V *Packadreams*; Andy Lowe and Star Droshine of the S/V *Moria*; Mimi Rehor; Linda Turner, WD4OCI, and her later husband Ron, KA4FNP, S/V *Moon Shadow*, for their help and friendship over the years; Hugh Verkerk of the S/V *Trekker*; Ed Wagner of the M/V *Gambier*; Carolyn Wardle for her help with the section on ham radio and weather broadcasts, and let us not forget her tireless efforts on the Bahamas Weather Net which benefits all mariners plying these waters. Last but not least, I would like to thank my publisher, Joe Janson, for making this work possible. If there is anybody that I have neglected to mention here, rest assured that it is an oversight and I sincerely apologize.

Cover design and artwork by **Jack Blackman**. An Abaco montage featuring Hole in the Wall Light, New Plymouth, Hope Town, Elbow Cay Light. Biographical information about Jack can be found on the page just after the index.

Other books by Stephen J. Pavlidis:
 A Cruising Guide to the Exuma Cays Land and Sea Park; with Ray Darville, ISBN 0-9638306
 The Exuma Guide, A Cruising Guide to the Exuma Cays; ISBN 0-9639566-1-2
 On and Off the Beaten Path, A Guide to the Central and Southern Bahamas; ISBN 0-9639566-9-8
 The Turks and Caicos Guide; ISBN 1-892399-01-6

You can visit Steve's web site at: www.islandhopping.com

 Library of Congress Cataloging-in-Publication Data

Pavlidis, Stephen J.
    The Abaco Guide : a cruising guide to the Northern Bahamas including Grand Bahama,
    the Bight of Abaco, and the Abacos / by Stephen J. Pavlidis.
      p. cm.
    Includes bibliographical references.
    ISBN 1-892399-02-4 (alk. paper)
      1. Pilot Guides--Bahamas--Abacos. 2. Pilot Guides--Bahamas--Grand Bahama. I. Title.

VK973.B3 P38 2000
623.89'297296--dc21

                                                          99-046516

The Abaco Guide

A Cruising Guide to the Northern Bahamas

Including

Grand Bahama
The Bight of Abaco
and the Abacos

Stephen J. Pavlidis

Seaworthy Publications, Inc.

Port Washington, Wisconsin

Contents

<u>Dedication</u>

For Kelly,
My first and only mate:

For you have endured all the hardships
that these books have brought,
hard work,
bad weather,
rough seas,
boredom,
long hours,
moods,
and yet your complaints were few…
far fewer than mine.
Without your support
so much of this was not possible.
You deserve as much credit as I for these publications.

With all my love.

Pav

INTRODUCTION

My first cruise to The Bahamas took me to the Abacos back in 1988. In the almost dozen years since then I've seen quite a few changes come over these lovely cays. It's amazing what can happen in a decade in these supposedly slow-moving islands. Creating this guide was a bit of a homecoming to me, to waters and people that are near and dear to my heart.

Back then a major cruise ship stop over was being created on Great Guana Cay. Today that site is just a memory, a few run down huts and a still usable dock. Meanwhile, Disney has constructed a fantasy island at Castaway Cay, previously known as Gorda Cay, which is expected to bring visitors by the millions to Abaco shores.

People were up in arms over the proposals for a "Grabaco" Bridge, linking Abaco with Grand Bahama Island, an often discussed and often cussed controversy. Today certain interests are intent on placing lit pilings across the Little Bahama Bank from Indian Cay Channel to Great Sale Cay and beyond to Angelfish Point.

The *Tiki Hut* in Marsh Harbour was just opening up at Earl Albury's *Triple J Marina*. Today the *Tiki Hut* has moved over to *Harbour View Marina* and the *Triple J Marina* has new owners. Back then Marsh Harbour had one traffic light…today they are bracing for an addition of five new lights. Back then Jack Tar Village was in its declining years while today Old Bahama Bay is renovating West End Point on Grand Bahama and things are looking up for the economy of West End.

A decade ago, Charlie Murphy, the scruffy, lovable Commodore of the *RMHYC* (*Royal Marsh Harbour Yacht Club*) taught celestial navigation classes in Marsh Harbour. Today Charlie has moved back to Canada, but those same stars I shot then still sit in the night sky over Abaco. Charlie had a wonderful nonsensical ditty that went: *The rain she pours, the wind she roars, but you'll never drown, in Abaco Sound, if you don't go near the water.*

Back then Spanish Cay was bypassed; today it is a major stopover in its own right. Back then sea life was much poorer in Abaco in places; today the reefs are rebounding a bit and manatees have been spotted in Man-O-War and Hope Town.

Time was that there were always rumors of *Customs* officials charging exorbitant fees when clearing in. Today there is a new flat fee of $100 that covers *Customs* and *Immigration* charges as well as transportation fees and a fishing license.

Change can be both good and bad, and with that in mind let me remind readers that there is a lot that hasn't changed in these islands. Hope Town lighthouse is still a friendly beacon on a dark night and a great spot to catch an unrivaled view of the Hub of Abaco. The fishing is still great, both offshore and inshore. The dolphins still come to White Sand Ridge every May/June to mate. *Pete's Pub* is still the place to be and Milo still holds court on Guana Cay.

But enough reminiscing, let's move on and see what's new in the Northern Bahamas. In this publication veteran cruisers will find all of their favorite anchorages sounded and charted (in color you'll notice!), and even the oldest Abaco hand might discover a couple of new anchorages and passages that have never been shown anywhere else; for instance, the excellent hurricane hole at Snake Cay. I will show you a new route into the Bight of Abaco from the north, a sort of Northwest Passage if you will, that allows vessels with drafts of over 5' to round West End Point on Little Abaco at MLW.

I've sounded the Bight of Abaco and included that area and Grand Bahama as well. Here you'll find the first ever charts of Mores Island and the first correct and up-to-date charts on the rest of the Bight.

Because so many cruisers now must maintain a connection to the information superhighway, I've added a new section on e-mail, Bahamas web sites, and Internet access options while in The Bahamas for those that need to be in touch.

Stephen J. Pavlidis
S/V *IV Play*
Savannah, Georgia

THE BASICS

ANCHORING

Just as important as getting your vessel moving and keeping her heading along your chosen courseline quickly and efficiently is the fine art of keeping your vessel from moving. Anchor choice is basically a personal preference. Some skippers prefer CQRs, while others swear by a Bruce or a Danforth. Of the "Big Three" you will find that a Danforth holds as well or better than a CQR or Bruce in sandy bottoms while the CQR or Bruce is preferred when anchoring in rocky bottoms. Whatever your choice of anchor, you must deploy your anchor correctly and with sufficient scope to hold you when the tide changes, if a front approaches, or if a squall should blow through at 2:00am (which seems to be the time they choose to blow through). Your anchor should have a length of chain (at least 15') shackled to your anchor to keep your rode from chafing against coral or rocks and to create a catenary curve that helps absorb shock loads while lowering the angle of pull on your anchor. Too high an angle may cause your anchor to pull up and out of the bottom. Some cruisers prefer all chain rodes with a nylon snubber to absorb the shock loads. This is an excellent arrangement but a windlass may be needed unless you prefer the workout involved with hauling in the chain and anchor every time you move.

In many of the lee side anchorages in the northern Bahamas you will find that you can lie quite comfortably to only one anchor. When setting your anchor do not just drop it and let your rode run out, piling itself on top of your anchor. Lower your anchor to the bottom and deploy the rode as you fall back with the current or wind until you have at least a 5:1 scope out, 7:1 is preferable but not always possible. When calculating the amount of scope required, be sure to allow for high tide as well as the height of your anchor roller or fairlead above the water. Without being precise, you can figure on a 2'-3½' tidal rise in The Northern Bahamas although occasionally you may find a 4' rise such as during spring tides, a little more during a full moon and a little less with no moon. When you have secured your rode, back down with the engine at about ½ throttle to set the anchor. If you have not succeeded in securing your anchor, try again. To check the set it is best to dive on your anchors or at the very least, look at their set through a glass bottom bucket from your dinghy. You may find that you will have to set them by hand, especially in rocky areas.

Some of the anchorages in the Bahamas are swept by swift tidal currents, sometimes as strong as 2.5 knots. To avoid bumping into your neighbor in the middle of the night, or putting your vessel on the rocks or the beach, two anchors, such as in a Bahamian moor, are required. Although one anchor may be fine if you have the swinging room, when the tide changes it may pull out and fail to reset. Sometimes these anchorages can be crowded and while you may swing wide on your one anchor and not find yourself endangered by the rocks or the beach, you and your neighbor may go bump in the night because his two anchors have kept him in one spot. If unsure the best thing to do is follow the lead of those boats that are there before you. Conversely, if you arrive at an anchorage and everyone is on one anchor and you choose to set two, do so outside the swing radius of the other boats. If you are riding on one anchor and find that you are lying to the wind but that the swell is rolling you, position another anchor at an angle off the stern so as to align your bow into the swell making for a more comfortable night. A better idea is to set a bridle. Run a line from your anchor rode at least half your waterline length from your bow and lead it back to a winch through a block near your stern. You can then winch in the line to change the angle your boat lies to the swells.

To set a Bahamian moor you must first decide where you wish for your vessel to settle. You will lay out two anchors, one up-current and one down-current of that spot which will keep you swinging in a small circle. Head into the current to where you will drop your first anchor and set it properly. Let out as much scope as you can, setting your anchor on the way by snubbing it, until you are at the spot where you are to drop your down-current anchor. If the wind has pushed you to one side or the other of the tidal stream, you will have to power up to the position where you will set your second anchor. Lower your second anchor and pull your vessel back up current on your first rode, paying out the rode for the second anchor and snubbing it as you maneuver back up current to your chosen spot. You may want to dive on your anchors to check their set. Keeping your rodes tight will keep you swinging in a tighter circle. Check your anchor rodes daily as they will twist together and make it extremely difficult to undo them in an emergency. You can also set your up-current anchor and settle back to where you wish to lie and then dinghy your second anchor out down current. The only problem with this is that you must make sure your down-current anchor has set well before the tide changes.

In some tight anchorages you will be unable to set your anchors 180° apart. An alternative is to set them 90° apart in a "Y" configuration perpendicular to the wind. A skipper with a large swing radius in very tight quarters is apt to find out what his neighbors think of his anchoring technique as soon as the wind shifts. Responsible anchoring cannot be overstressed.

Always set an anchor light. Some cruisers feel this is unimportant in some of the more isolated anchorages. What they probably do not understand is that many locals run these islands at all hours of the night, even on moonless nights, and an anchor light protects your vessel as well as theirs.

Never anchor in coral, even with your dinghy anchor. An anchor can do a great deal of damage to a very fragile ecosystem that will take years to recover if it is to recover at all. Besides, sand holds so much better anyway.

In summer months and on into the early fall, or when there is no wind, you may wish to anchor a good distance from shore to keep away from the relentless biting insects. Cays with a lot of vegetation or mangroves will have a higher concentration of biting insects.

Proper anchoring etiquette should by practiced at all times. For instance, if the anchorage is wide and roomy and only one boat is at anchor, don't anchor right on top of them, give your neighbor a little breathing room and some solitude. You would probably appreciate the same consideration should the situation be reversed. All too often cruisers exhibit a herding instinct where they seek the comfort of other nearby cruisers, anchoring much too close at times. Many boaters, after a long, hard day in rough seas or bad weather, anxiously await the peace and tranquillity of a calm anchorage. The last thing they want is noise and wake. If you have a dog aboard that loves to bark, be considerate of your neighbors who don't wish to hear him. They do have that right. PWC's can be a lot of fun, but only when you're astride one. Many cruisers have little tolerance for the incessant buzzing back and forth of high-speed jet skis. It is a good show of manners to slowly leave the anchorage where you can have your high-speed fun and games and not disturb anyone. If at all possible, try not to run your generators at sunset or after dark. At sunset, many cruisers are sitting in their cockpits enjoying cocktails and watching the sun go down and don't want a generator disturbing their soft conversations. Many powerboats use a lot of electricity by running all sorts of lights at night. Some will leave on huge floodlights for one reason or another with no idea of the amount of glare and light it produces in nearby cockpits to other boaters. This is not an incrimination of all powerboaters, only the careless few. The vast majority of powerboaters are very considerate and professional and do not approve of their noisy, blinding, cousins. Courtesy shown is usually courtesy returned.

CHARTERING

There are quite a few companies and individuals running charters in the Abacos. *Florida Yacht Charters & Sales,* located at Boat Harbour Marina in Marsh Harbour, offers what they call a "true Out Island adventure" aboard their fleet of new air-conditioned *Hunter* sailboats, *Mainship* trawlers and cruising catamarans, either as bareboat or with a captain. You can call *FYC* at 642-367-4853 or check out their web site at: http://www.floridayacht.com. You can e-mail them at boat@floridayacht.com for more information.

The Moorings, located at the *Conch Inn Marina* in Marsh Harbour offers monohulls from 35'-46' and catamarans from 37'-45'. Contact them at 800-535-7289 or 727-535-1446.

Abaco Bahamas Charters, the oldest bareboat company in Abaco, operates a fleet of monohull sailboats out of Hope Town. They can be reached at 800-626-5690 or you can visit their website at http://www.abacocharters.com. Their e-mail address is info@abacocharters.com.

Also in Hope Town, *Lighthouse Charters* offers bareboat or captained sailing charters (catamarans) by the day or by the week. You can reach them at 242-366-0172.

Sail Abaco offers *PDQ* catamarans exclusively and can be reached at 242-366-0172. Their website is at http://www.sailabaco.com and their e-mail is charters@sailabaco.com.

There are over a dozen boat rental businesses in Abaco that have boats ranging from 19 to 26 feet available on a daily or weekly basis. For more info on small boat rentals, see the text for each island or check out *Appendix C: Service Facilities*.

Students wishing to do research in the northern Bahamas should contact Nicolas and Dragan Popov of *Island Expeditions School at Sea* at P.O. Box CB11934, Love Beach #4C, Nassau, N.P., The Bahamas, 242-327-8659. *Island Expeditions* has several sailing trips each year through the Exumas, the southern Bahamas, and the Turks and Caicos on the way to the Silver Banks as part of a humpback whale study program as well as trips to Abaco in May to swim with the dolphins on the White Sand Ridge.

CLOTHING

If you are heading to the northern Bahamas you will enter a sub-tropical climate where the theme for clothing is light. You will most likely live in shorts and T-shirts (if that much). Long pants and sturdy, comfortable shoes are preferred when hiking for protection from the bush and the rugged terrain. Long sleeved shirts (or old cotton pajamas) and wide brimmed hats are important in keeping the sun off you. Polarized sunglasses (essential for piloting) and suntan lotion (suntan oil tends to leave a long lasting greasy smear all over everything) should be included in your gear. In winter months it is advisable to bring something warm to wear, especially in the evenings. Winter in the Northern Bahamas is very similar to winter in central Florida. Freeport actually once reported snowflakes a few years ago. Long pants and sweaters are usually adequate and a light jacket would be a good idea as some frontal passages will occasionally drop the temperature to 50° F and even lower in extreme conditions.

As is the norm anywhere in The Bahamas, beachwear is not acceptable in town. Men should wear shirts and women should not wear bathing suits except when on the beach, at a pool, or a beach side bar.

CURRENCY

The legally acceptable currency of The Bahamas is the Bahamian dollar whose value is on par with the American dollar which is readily acceptable throughout the islands. Bahamian money comes in 1¢, 5¢, 10¢, 25¢, $1, $3, $5, $10, $20, $50, and $100 denominations.

CUSTOMS AND IMMIGRATION

Abaco/Grand Bahama Ports of Entry:
GRAND BAHAMA: West End (Old Bahama Bay Marina), Lucaya (Port Lucaya Village, Lucayan Marina).
ABACO: Walker's Cay, Spanish Cay, Green Turtle Cay, Marsh Harbour.

All vessels entering Bahamian waters must clear in with *Customs* and *Immigration* officials at the nearest port of entry listed above. Failure to report within 24 hours may subject you to a penalty and make you liable for confiscation and forfeiture of your vessel. When approaching your selected port of entry be sure to fly your yellow "Q" flag. Tie up to a dock or marina and await the officials if directed. In places like Bimini (where the dockmasters will usually have the necessary forms for you) or Green Turtle Cay, only the captain of the vessel may go ashore to arrange clearance and no other shore contact is permitted until pratique is granted. Some of the marinas that you use may levy a charge for using their dock, Cat Cay in particular. If they do not charge you, good manners suggest that you at least make a fuel purchase. Most southbound vessels usually clear in long before reaching the outer islands while those northbound skippers have a choice of ports of entry.

There is a new fee structure for vessels clearing into The Bahamas, a flat rate of $100. This covers all *Customs* and *Immigration* charges as well as transportation fees and it includes a fishing license. U.S. citizens need proof of citizenship, a passport (not required) or Voter Registration Card. Canadian and British visitors also do not need passports. Visas are not required for visitors from the U.S., Canada, and persons from any British Commonwealth country. If you are flying in and returning by way of a boat in transit you need some proof that you are able to leave the country. It is suggested that you purchase a round trip ticket and leave the return reservation open. When you return aboard your boat you may then cash in your unused ticket or use it for a future flight. Check with the airline when buying your ticket as to their policy in this matter.

If yours is a pleasure vessel with no dutiable cargo, the captain will fill out a *Maritime Declaration of Health*, *Inwards Report* for pleasure vessels, and a crew list. Do not mistakenly call your crew "passengers" or it may be interpreted that you are running a charter. An *International Marine Declaration of Health* in duplicate will be accepted in lieu of a *Bill of Health* from vessels arriving in The Bahamas. Smallpox vaccination certificates and cholera inoculation certificates are required only if the vessel is arriving directly from an infected area.

Each crewmember will fill out and sign an *Immigration* Card. You will be asked to keep the small tab off the card and return it by mail after you leave The Bahamas. You can ask for and receive a stay of up to eight months however some *Immigration* officials will only give three or four months for reasons that are clear only to them. This is an inconsistency that one sees every now and then as you talk to different cruisers and find out about their clearing-in adventure. An *Immigration* official in Nassau explained that it is up to the individual officer to determine how long a stay to permit. If you have guests flying in they also must have a return trip ticket and proof of citizenship.

The captain will be issued a Cruising Permit (Transire) for the vessel that is valid for up to 12 months. This permit must be presented to any *Customs* official or other proper officer (if requested) while in The Bahamas. If you wish to keep your vessel in Bahamian waters for longer than one year without paying import duties, special arrangements must be made with *Customs*. The owner may extend the one year stay for up to three years by paying a fee of $500 per year after the first year. Import duties are now 7.5% for vessels of 30'-100' while vessels less than 30' are charged 22.5%. Spare parts for installation aboard your vessel are duty-free. If the parts are imported as cargo they are subject to a 6% duty.

If you have pets on board they must have an import permit. An application for the permit may be requested by writing to the Director of the Department of Agriculture, P.O. Box N-3704, Nassau, Bahamas (242-325-7413, fax # 242-325-3960). Return the completed application with a $10.00 fee in the form of a Postal Money Order or International Money Order payable to the Public Treasury. This will hasten the process of obtaining your permit although you should allow three to four weeks processing time. Rabies certificates are required of all animals over three months old and must be more than 10 days but less than 9 months old and should be presented when you clear *Customs* and *Immigration*.

Non-residents of The Bahamas entering aboard a foreign vessel are not required to obtain permits nor pay duties on firearms during their visit to the islands. This exemption is for three months following the arrival of the vessel at a designated port of entry. After three months a certificate must be obtained from the Commissioner of Police. All firearms must be kept safe from theft under lock and key and be declared on your cruising permit with an accurate count of all ammunition. Firearms may not be used in Bahamian waters nor taken ashore. Hunters should contact the Department of Agriculture and Fisheries in Nassau for information on hunting in The Bahamas. Completely forbidden are tear gas pens, military arms such as artillery, flame-throwers, machine guns, and automatic weapons. Exempt are toy guns, dummy firearms, flare guns, and spear guns designed for underwater use.

Certain items may be brought in duty-free including personal effects such as wearing apparel, ship's stores, 1 quart of alcoholic beverage, 1 quart of wine, 1 pound in weight of tobacco or 200 cigarettes or 50 cigars. As soon as the captain has cleared *Customs*, you may take down your yellow "Q" flag and replace it with the Bahamian courtesy flag.

American flag vessels are not required to obtain clearance when departing U.S. ports. If you are clearing back into the United States you must, upon entry, call the U.S. Customs Service to clear in. You are required to go to a nearby telephone immediately upon arrival and dock nearby. You can dial 1-800-432-1216, 1-800-458-4239, or 1-800-451-0393 to get a Customs Agent on the line to arrange clearance. When you have Customs on the phone you will need to give them your vessel's name and registration number, the owner's name, the Captain's name and date of birth, all passenger names and date of births, a list of all foreign ports visited and the duration of your stay there, a list of guns aboard, the total value of all purchases, and your Customs User Fee decal number if one has been issued, and whether you have anything to declare (total of all purchases, fresh fruit, vegetables, or meat). If you do not have a decal you may be directed to the nearest U.S. Customs station to purchase one within 48 hours. Decals may be purchased prior to departing on your voyage by ordering an application (Customs Form #339) and submitting the completed application with a $25.00 fee (Money Order or check drawn on U.S. bank) to U.S. Customs Service, National Finance Center, P.O. Box 198151, Atlanta, Georgia 30384.

Each resident of the United States, including minors, may take home duty-free purchases up to $600 U.S. if they have been outside the U.S. for more than 48 hours and have not taken this exemption in 30 days. This includes up to 2 liters of liquor per person over 21 provided that one liter is manufactured in The Bahamas or a member of the Caribbean Basin Initiative (CBI). A family may pool their exemptions. Articles of up to $1000 in excess of the duty-free $600 allowance are assessed at a flat rate of 10%. For example, a family of four may bring back up to $2400 worth of duty-free goods. If they were to bring back $6400 worth of goods, they would have to pay a duty of $400 on the $4000 above the duty-free allowance. This flat rate may only be used once every 30 days. If the returning U.S. resident is not entitled to the duty-free allowance because of the 30 day or 48 hour restrictions, they may still bring back $25 worth of personal or household items. This exemption may not be pooled. Antiques are admitted to the U.S. duty-free if they are over 100 years old. The Bahamian store selling the antique should provide you with a form indicating the value and certifying the age of the object. Importation of fruits, plants, meats, poultry, and diary products is generally prohibited. More than $10,000 in U.S. or foreign coin, currency, traveler's checks, money orders, and negotiable instruments or investment securities in bearer form must be reported to Customs. Importation of Bahamian tortoise or turtle shell goods is prohibited. Many medicines purchased over the counter in The Bahamas such as *222*, a codeine-aspirin-caffeine compound, are not allowed entry. Although you can buy Cuban cigars in Nassau, enjoy them on your cruise and do not attempt to bring them back into the U.S. The U.S. Customs Service frowns on Americans spending money on Cuban products. Hopefully that will change in time.

Any number of gifts may be sent to the U.S. from The Bahamas and the recipient will pay no duty provided that the gift is worth U.S. $50 or less. If the value is over U.S. $50, duty and tax is charged on the full value. The following regulations must be complied with. Only $50 worth of gifts may be received by the U.S. addressee in one day. The value of the gifts must be clearly written on the package as well as the words "Unsolicited Gift." No alcoholic beverages or tobacco may be sent. Perfume with value of more than $5 may not be sent. Persons in the U.S. are not allowed to send money to The Bahamas for gifts to be shipped to them duty-free, the gifts must be unsolicited. Persons may not mail a gift addressed to themselves. For more information, contact the U.S. Customs Service before you leave or call them in Nassau at 242-327-7126.

Canadian residents may take advantage of three categories of duty-free exemption. If you have been out of Canada for 24 hours, you may make a verbal declaration to claim a CDN$20 duty-free allowance any number of times per year. This exemption does not include alcohol or tobacco. If you have been out of the country for 48 hours, any number of times per year, a written declaration must be made and you may claim a CDN$100 allowance. This allowance can include up to 200 cigarettes, 50 cigars, or 2 lbs. of tobacco, and 1.1 liters of alcohol per person. If you have been out of Canada for over 7 days, you may make a written declaration and claim a CDN$300 exemption including the above mentioned amounts of tobacco and alcohol. After a trip abroad for 48 hours or more you are entitled to a special 20% tax rate on goods valued up to CDN$300 over and above the CDN$100 and CDN$300 personal exemption. For importation of tobacco the claimant must be 16 years of age. For alcohol, the claimant must have attained the legal age prescribed by the laws of the provincial or territorial authority at the point of entry.

Unsolicited gifts may be sent to Canada duty-free as long as they are valued under CDN$400 and do not contain alcoholic beverages, tobacco products, or advertising matter. If the value is above CDN$400 the recipient must pay regular duty and tax on the excess amount.

THE DEFENCE FORCE

The Royal Bahamas Defence Force came into existence officially on March 31, 1980. Their duties include defending The Bahamas, stopping drug smuggling, illegal immigration, poaching, and to provide assistance to mariners whenever and wherever they can. They have a fleet of 26 coastal and inshore patrol craft along with 2 aircraft. The Defence Force has over 850 personnel including 65 officers and 74 women.

I have been associated with a number of Defence Force personnel through my efforts at Exuma Park and I have developed a healthy respect for these men and women. Every officer and seaman that I have met has been highly intelligent, articulate, dedicated, and very professional in regards to their duties. These are not the thugs and hoodlums that so many cruisers have come to fear over the last few years. As late as 1991, horror stories were coming out of Nassau concerning improprieties during routine boardings. The Defence Force has taken corrective steps and reports of trouble caused by boarding parties are almost non-existent now. What complaints I have heard I have found to have two sides, and quite often cruisers take the boaters side instinctively while giving no thought to the other side of the coin. There is no reason to dread the gray boats as they approach. The Defence Force has a very difficult job to do and it often becomes necessary for them to board private pleasure vessels in routine searches. The boarding party will do everything they can to be polite and professional, however, due to the violent nature of the criminals they seek, standard procedure is to be armed. Unfortunately, in the process of protecting themselves, they inadvertently intimidate cruisers. Please do not be alarmed if a crewman bearing an automatic weapon stays in your cockpit while the officer conducts a search below decks in your presence. If you are boarded you will be asked to sign a statement saying that the search was carried out politely and in the presence of the owner or skipper. I have been boarded and found the boarding officer and crew to be courteous and professional. It is not unusual for the Defence Force to enter an anchorage and board all the vessels anchored there. Normally they will not board a vessel that is unoccupied, preferring to keep an eye out for your return.

Cruisers often ask, "Why single me out, why search my boat?" "What are they looking for?" Besides the obvious problem with drugs, The Bahamas has problems with people smuggling illegal weapons and ammunition into the country. With single bullets selling for $5 and more on the street in Nassau, a boater could fatten his or her cruising kitty very easily. You must keep accurate records on all your weapons and ammunition and make sure you record them on your cruising permit when you check in.

The Defence Force also must defend the richness of the marine fisheries in The Bahamas. It is not unknown for a boat to cross over from the states without a permit and fill up its freezers with Bahamian caught fish, conch, and lobster. In 1997, a boat from south Florida was boarded upon its return to Florida and the owners and crew arrested and charged under the Lacy Act. The Defence Force, if they board your vessel, will probably want to see your fishing permit and ask you whether you have any fish aboard. For most cruisers this does not pose a problem. If, however, you have 100 dolphin aboard, you will find yourself in a world of well deserved trouble. You might have a better understanding of what the Defence Force goes through if you learn about the four Defence Force Marines who died a decade ago when

Cuban MIGs sank their boat after the rest of the crew boarded Cuban fishing boats illegally operating in Bahamian waters along the southern edge of the Great Bahama Bank. This is serious business.

DINGHY SAFETY

Most cruisers spent a considerable amount of time in their dinghies exploring the waters and islands in the vicinity of their anchorage. It is not unknown for a dinghy engine to fail or a skipper to run out of gas miles away from the mother vessel. For this reason I urge boaters to carry some simple survival gear in their dinghies and to check their gas every time they get in their dink to go anywhere. First, I would recommend a handheld VHF radio for obvious reasons. If there are any other boats around this may be your best chance for getting some assistance. Oars and a good anchor with plenty of line is also high on the list. I do not mean one of those small three pound anchors with thirty feet of line that is only used on the beach to keep your dinghy from drifting away. It may pay to sacrifice the onboard room and use a substantial anchor with a couple of feet of chain and at least 100' of line. Just as you would go oversize on your mother vessel do the same with your dinghy. If you are being blown away from land, a good anchor and plenty of line gives you a good chance of staying put where someone may find you. Next, a dinghy should have a supply of flares. In The Bahamas I learned a trick from the locals there who often carry a large coffee can with a rag soaked in oil lying in the bottom. If they get in trouble lighting the rag will produce an abundant amount of smoke which can be seen from quite a distance. A dinghy should be equipped with survival water, a bottle or some small packages manufactured by a company called DATREX. It would be a good idea to throw in a few MRE's. These are the modern, tastier version of the K-rations which our armed forces survived on for years. Each MRE also contains vital survival components such as matches and toilet paper. Another handy item that does not take up much room is a foil survival blanket. They really work and take up as much space as a couple of packs of cigarettes.

Please don't laugh at these suggestions. I have seen people forced to spend a night or two in a dinghy and these few items would have made their experience much more pleasant if not entirely unnecessary. I have run out of gas and used flares to attract some local attention even though one of my boat mates was ready to dive in and swim for the nearest island to fetch some help. Now, I never leave in my dinghy without my little survival bag stashed away in the dink. It doesn't take much effort to prepare a small bag for your dinghy and it will be worth its weight in gold should you need it.

DIVING

From shallow water reef dives to deep water wall drop-offs, the diving in The Bahamas is as good as it gets any-where and much better than most places. You don't need scuba equipment to enjoy the undersea delights that are available, many reefs lie in less than 30' and are easily accessible to those with snorkels, dinghies, and curiosity.

Although the waters in The Bahamas are crystal clear and the obstructions plainly visible in the ambient light, divers must take proper precautions when diving in areas of current. Experienced divers are well aware of this but it must be stated for novices and snorkelers. Tidal fluctuations can produce strong currents which must be taken into account when diving. Waves breaking over and around inshore reefs can create strong surges which can push or pull you into some very sharp coral. For safety's sake, only experienced divers should penetrate wrecks and caves. And while we're on the subject of wrecks, divers will want to check out the wreck of the *San Jacinto*, the first U.S. steamship, that sank in 1865 near Green Turtle Cay. Another interesting dive is the Union warship *Adirondack* which sank on the reef near Man-O-War Cay in 1862.

In Abaco, Fowl Cay and the Pelican National Park are underwater preserves and are protected by the Bahamas National Trust. They offer some of the finest shallow water diving in the entire Caribbean.

E-MAIL IN THE ABACOS

More and more cruisers these days are relying on their computers, e-mail, and the Internet to stay in touch. The folks in the Abacos are already hip to this and have had e-mail service into and out of the Abacos available for some time now.

Every morning on the VHF, the Cruiser's Net offers e-mail announcements and where to pick up and send e-mail from the Abacos. Check with the net for the latest word on e-mail, but for now, as of this writing several places throughout the Hub of Abaco offer e-mail services. The folks that offer these services ask that you follow a few simple guidelines. Please refrain from frivolous and/or lengthy messages and NO attachments please.

In Marsh Harbour, *Sapodilly's Bar and Grill* will send and receive e-mail for you. To receive e-mail via *Sapodilly's* have the e-mail addressed to sapodilly@oii.net and put your boat's name in the subject field. Incoming e-mail is posted on the bulletin board by the bar on the deck.

Over on Man-O-War Cay, *Man-O-War Marina* has now taken over the job of forwarding e-mail to cruisers that may not be in Marsh Harbour. To receive your e-mail via *Man-O-War Marina* have it addressed to cruisers@oii.net with the boat's name in the subject field. *Man-O-War Marina* will announce any mail they are holding during the "Announcements" portion of the Cruisers Net immediately following the weather. *Man-O-War Marina* has a strong signal and they are sometimes heard as far north as Allan's-Pensacola and beyond. If you miss the morning *Cruisers Net* you can still check on your e-mail by calling *Man-O-War Marina* on VHF ch.16. In Hope Town, *Club Soleil* offers e-mail service. Have your e-mail addressed to cruisers@clubsoleil.com with your boat's name in the subject field. For Northern Abaco, *Fox Town Texaco* and the *Tangelo Hotel* have volunteered to broadcast the weather and announce waiting e-mail each morning on the VHF.

For those cruisers who wish to send their own e-mail, there are several possibilities. You can take your laptop into the local *Batelco* office and make arrangements to use their phone lines for your own Internet access. Some *Batelco* offices do not provide this service so you'll have to check first. Several businesses allow the use of their phone lines for e-mail access; The *Conch Inn Marina* in Marsh Harbour will allow their guests to hook into their phone lines for Internet service. Be sure to bring with you a phone line with a standard RJ11 connector.

Acoustic couplers are popular items with some cruisers. These allow you to hook up your computer directly to any pay phone in the Bahamas to access the net. The only problem you might run into is that the ambient noise can be a factor in making and maintaining a connection. There's a nifty little item out now called *Pocketmail*, a self-contained portable e-mail device. These are very popular with boaters who don't have computers or Internet access. They range in price from $99 to $199 and the service itself is $9.99 per month.

Be advised that there are no 800 numbers in Abaco for stateside service providers in The Bahamas. All calls to *AOL*, *CompuServe*, *Prodigy* and other ISP's have to be made as an international long distance call. The costs are approximately $1 a minute direct dial calls, and $3-$7 a minute for credit card or operator assisted calls. *AOL* and *CompuServe* users can now check their e-mail through any Internet connection directly from the http://www.aol.com website using *Netscape* or *Microsoft Internet Explorer*. *AOL* has a new number in Nassau at 243-325-7004. Even for subscribers of other ISP's there is no longer any need to configure an e-mail program (*Microsoft Outlook Express, Netscape Mail, Eudora*, etc.) to check your e-mail account. *Yahoo, Hotmail* and others now let you get mail from your "POP" account using your browser.

If you want to access the Internet directly here on Abaco, you have to deal with *BatelNet*, the only Internet service provider on Abaco with local phone number access. You can visit *BatelNet's* website: http://www.batelnet.bs/.

There is a new ISP coming to Abaco, the Internet service of *100JAMZ*, an FM station with studios in Nassau. *100JAMZ* has a remote transmitter in Marsh Harbour that uses a satellite bounce to connect their studio with the Abaco transmitter. *100JAMZ* is also licensed to serve the internet in the Bahamas and this service should be available by mid-1999. Short-term visitors wanting Internet access may purchase a *Net Card* for $25 for 8 hours of Internet access. These cards are to be available at shops and marinas all over Abaco. This service will be available as a local phone call from anywhere on Abaco.

If you need computer supplies, repairs, or if you're simply having trouble accessing your account, see the folks at *Abacom, Ltd.*, the owners of oii.net. They're located in downtown Marsh Harbour and their phone number is 242-367-3475 and their webmaster can be reached in Treasure Cay at 242-365-8800.

Bahamas Web Sites:

URL	Website
http://www.oii.net/oii.html	Abaco community message board
http://www.greatabacobeach.com	Abaco Beach Resort
http://www.abacolife.com	Abaco Life magazine
http://www.abacoinn.com	The Abaco Inn
http://www.abacos.com/aoc/location.html	The Abaco Ocean Club
http://www.oii.net/alburysferry	Albury's Ferry
http://www.interknowledge.com/bahamas/bshome01.htm	Bahamas home page
http://www.bahamas.com	Bahamas Ministry of Tourism
http://www.bahamas-on-line.com	Bahamas online dot com

http://www.bahamasvg.com	Bahamas vacation guide
http://oii.net/BluffHouse	Bluff House on Green Turtle Cay
http://www.internetfl.com/abaco.html	Dive Abaco
http://www.deepwatercay.com	The Deep Water Cay Bonefishing Club
http://www.greenturtleclub.com	The Green Turtle Club
http://www.guanabeach.com	The Guana Beach Resort
http://www.bahamasvg.com/pedalpaddle.html	Kayak/bike tours in Nassau
http://www.oii.net/radioabaco	Radio Abaco
http://www.scubabimini.com	Scuba Bimini and Chub Cay
http://www.smallhope.com	Small Hope Bay Lodge on Andros
http://www.stanielcay.com/	The Staniel Cay Yacht Club
http://www.treasurecay.com	The Treasure Cay Resort
http://www.nws.fsu.edu/B/buoy?spgf1	Current weather-West End, GB

FERRIES

In the area of the "hub of Abaco," the waters between Guana Cay, Marsh Harbour, and Hope Town, you'll find a mode of transportation that is unique in The Bahamas...the ferry.

Abaco Island Transportation offers ferries from Guana Cay to Marsh Harbour at 0800, 1500, and at 1700. Return trips from Marsh Harbour to Guana Cay run at 0900, 1200, 1600, and 1800. The rates are $6 one way and $12 round trip. You can purchase 10 passes for $50, a savings of $10.

The *Green Turtle Ferry* runs from Green Turtle to Treasure Cay at 0800, 1330, and 1500 and returns from Treasure Cay to Green Turtle at 1030, 1430, and 1615. Rates are $7 per person to New Plymouth and $8 per person to White Sound. Round trips on the same day cost $11 per person to New Plymouth and $13 to White Sound. The *Green Turtle Ferry* also has special charter runs from Green Turtle to Treasure Cay at 0915, 1115, and at 1215. Return charters from Treasure Cay to Green Turtle are at 0945 and at 1445. Rates are $35 for 1-2 people and $40 for 3-5 people.

Albury's Ferry Service is probably the busiest ferry in the hub. *Albury's* has daily ferries from Marsh Harbour to Man-O-War at 1030 and 1600 daily and from Man-O-War to Marsh Harbour at 0800 and 1330 daily. *Albury's* also leaves Hope Town for Marsh Harbour at 0800, 1130, 1330, and 1600 and returns from Marsh Harbour to Hope Town at 1030, 1215, and 1600 daily. On Mondays, Wednesdays, and Fridays *Albury's* has a special ferry that leaves Man-O-War at 1130 and returns from Marsh Harbour at 1215. On all weekdays except holidays *Albury's* runs from Marsh Harbour's *Union Jack Dock* to Scotland and Guana Cays at 0730 and leaves from Marsh Harbour's *Union Jack Dock* and *Conch Inn* at 1100 and 1530. *Albury's* returns to the *Union Jack Dock* and the *Conch Inn* at 0900, 1215, and 1645. For the Scotland Cay service *Albury's Ferry* requests that you notify them ahead of time. All fees are collected on board and are $8, with children only $4. Same day round trips are $12, and children only $6. Any stops outside the main harbor will be a minimum charge of two persons while two persons or over will remain at the regular charge. *Albury's* also has special charter ferries available any time during daylight hours. A one-way ferry from Marsh Harbour to Hope Town or Man-O-War is $50 for 1-4 passengers or $10 each for 5 or more. If leaving before 0700 or arriving back after 1900 the fees are $70 for 1-4 passengers or $15 per person for 5 or more. A one-way from Marsh Harbour to Guana Cay is $80 for 1-6 passengers or $12 per person for 7 or more. If leaving before 0700 or arriving after 1900 the fees will be $95 for 1-6 persons or $15 each for 7 or more passengers. You can also arrange for a sightseeing tour by contacting *Albury's Ferry*.

FISHING

Fishing in The Bahamas is hard to beat. While trolling offshore you are likely to hook a dolphin, wahoo, or tuna, all excellent eating. Trolling on the banks you will usually catch a barracuda although it is possible to bring up a snapper, jack, or grouper. Bonefish can be found in the tidal flats scattered throughout the islands.

Grand Bahama is home to the *Bahamas National Bonefish Championships* while the Abacos are home to several fishing tournaments throughout the year. Marsh Harbour, Green Turtle Cay, Walker's Cay, and Treasure Cay all host several tournaments such as the *Bertram Hatteras Shootout*, the *Annual Treasure Cay Billfish Tournament*, the *Penny Turtle Annual Billfish Tournament*, the *Bahamas Billfish Tournament*, and the *Annual CABO Challenge*.

There are restricted areas in the Abacos where fishing is not allowed. The Pelican Cay Park and the Fowl Cay Preserve are two areas in central Abaco where this would apply. No marine resource (fish, shells, rocks, seaweed; take

Photo by Nicolas Popov.

Abaco hogfish bound for the dinner table.

nothing but photographs, leave nothing but footprints) may be taken from these park areas. The marine parks do not have signs so it is wise to give them a wide berth so there is no question as to your location.

The back of your fishing permit will have a brief (but incomplete) description of the fishing regulations in The Bahamas. Only six lines are permitted in the water at one time unless you have paid for a commercial permit (very expensive). SCUBA is illegal for the taking of marine life and an air compressor such as a Third Lung or similar type of apparatus, must have a permit issued by the Minister of Agriculture. Spearguns are illegal for fishing in The Bahamas and are illegal to have aboard. You may only use a Hawaiian Sling or pole spear for spearfishing. It is illegal to use bleach, firearms, or explosives for fishing. Spearfishing is illegal within one mile of New Providence and within 200 yards of any family island (defined as any cay with a residence). The capture of bonefish by net is illegal as is their purchase or sale. Conch, with a daily limit of 10 per person, may not be taken if they do not have a well formed, flared lip. Possession of a hawksbill turtle is prohibited. The minimum size for a green turtle is 24" and for a loggerhead, 30". The bag limit for kingfish, dolphin, and wahoo is a maximum combination of 6 fish per person aboard.

Crawfish, the spiny lobster that is such a treat as well as being a large part of the economy for local fishermen, has a closed season from April 1-August 1. The minimum limits are a carapace length of 3 3/8" and a 6" tail length. It is illegal to posses a berried (egg-laying) female or to remove the eggs from a female. You may not take any corals while in The Bahamas.

In the Out Islands there are far fewer jobs than there are people looking for jobs. The people here must eke out a living the best way they can. Remember that when you are fishing. Please catch just enough to eat and maybe put some away for tomorrow. So often cruisers come through this area with huge freezers just waiting to be filled to the brim to help their owners offset vacation costs. If you over-fish an area you may be taking food out of the mouths of children. To protect the livelihood of the people of The Bahamas, some of the richer fishing spots will not be mentioned in this guide.

Conch can usually be found on the bottom in beds of sea grass, or soft corals, where they prefer to feed. They are usually in areas with a swift current such as in the cuts between cays. The conch that you don't plan to eat right away can be left in a dive bag hanging in the water or may be put on a stringer. Punch or drill a small hole in the lip of the conch shell and string four or five together and set them on the bottom, they won't go far. After you clean the conch, save the tough orange colored skin and put it in your freezer for later, it is an excellent fish bait and a small piece of it should be placed on all lures to give them an attractive aroma to fish.

The reefs in The Bahamas can provide you with a plentiful supply of fish such as grouper, snapper, hogfish, turbots (trigger fish), and grunts. How many you can get is dependent on your skill with the spear. Groupers are especially wary and prefer holes to hide in. When near cays, the drop-offs are excellent for game and food fish. You may find yourself hooking a dolphin, wahoo, shark, kingfish, or tuna.

Crawfish, the clawless spiny lobster, is the principal delicacy that most cruisers search very hard for and which are getting increasingly difficult to find. They prefer to hide during the day under ledges, and rocks, and in holes where the only visible sign of them will be a pair of antennae resembling some sort of sea fan jutting out from their hiding spot. If you are fortunate enough to spear a few, and they are large enough, do not overlook the succulent meat in the base of the antennae and in the legs. So many cruisers ignore these pieces and just take the tail. Watch a Bahamian as they prepare a lobster, very little goes to waste.

FLIGHTS

Flying in and out of the northern Bahamas poses little problem (just remember that there is a $15 departure tax if you leave by air). On Grand Bahama, *Freeport International Airport* (242-352-6020) has daily flights from New York, Miami, Ft. Lauderdale, Palm Beach and Nassau as well as *American Eagle* (800-433-7300) flights from Miami, *Bahamasair* (242-352-8341, 800-222-4262) flights from Miami and Ft. Lauderdale; and *8u* (800-231-0586). Canadians can try *Conquest* from Toronto at 800-722-0860. *Delta/Comair* (800-221-1212, 242-352-3070) has flights from Ft. Lauderdale and Orlando, while *Gulfstream* (242-352-6447) and *Laker Airlines* (305-653-9471, 242-352-3389) both offer flights from Florida. You can reach *Taino Airlines* at 242-352-8885 and *Bahamas Trans Air* at 242-352-5569.

In Abaco, *Continental/Gulfstream*, services Marsh Harbour and Treasure Cay and can be reached at 242-367-3415. Island Express services all parts of the Bahamas and can be reached at 242-367-3597 and *American Eagle Airlines* can be reached at 242-367-2231 while *Bahamasair* can be reached at 242-367-2095.

In Abaco, besides the major airlines there are several smaller, private carriers such as *Reliable Air Service* (242-333-2444, 954-359-8266). *Reliable* has been flying from Ft. Lauderdale to Treasure Cay since 1954 and carries passengers as well as freight. *Abaco Air* (242-367-2266 and VHF ch. 72 in Marsh Harbour), offers charter service to the entire Bahamas and Florida. *Cherokee Air* also handles charters in and around the Abacos and can be reached at 242-367-2089. *Vintage Props and Jets* has daily flights from Marsh Harbour and Treasure Cay to Orlando and Daytona Beach. *Vintage* can be reached at 800-952-0275 or 904-423-1773. *Major's Air Services* covers both Abaco and Grand Bahama and can be reached at 242-352-5778.

GARBAGE

When I first began cruising I had this naive idea that all cruisers lived in a certain symbiosis with nature. My bubble finally burst with the bitter realization that many cruisers were infinitely worse than common litterbugs. So often they have the attitude of "out of sight, out of mind". I sometimes wonder if they believe in supernatural beings, hoping that if they dump their trash somewhere imaginary garbage fairies will come along and take care of the disposal problems for them. One cruiser leaves a few bags of garbage in some secluded (or not so secluded) spot and the next cruiser says "My, what a good spot for a garbage dump. Ethel, bring the garbage, I've found the dump!" This is why you often go ashore on otherwise deserted islands and find bags and piles of bags of garbage. Nothing is worse than entering paradise only to discover some lazy, ignorant, slob of a cruiser (no, I have not been too harsh on this type of person, I can still think of plenty of other adjectives without having to consult a thesaurus) has dumped his or her bags of garbage in the bushes. Please do not add to this problem. Remember that your garbage attracts all kinds of foul creatures such as rats and other ignorant, careless cruisers.

Nobody likes storing bags of smelly garbage aboard but if you cannot find a settlement nearby to take your garbage for free, you will have to make an allowance in your budget to pay for the local garbage disposal service. If you are nowhere near a garbage facility you should stow your trash aboard separated into three groups for easier disposal. First cans and bottles (wash them first to remove any smells while being stored), then into another container stow the organic stuff such as food scraps, rinds, and eggshells, and finally paper and plastic trash. Your food scraps, you can store them in a large coffee can with a lid, should be thrown overboard daily on an outgoing tide. The paper and plastic should be burned completely when necessary and the ashes buried deep and not on the beach. Cans and bottles should be punctured or broken and dumped overboard in very deep water at least a few miles offshore. Cut off both ends of the cans and break the bottles overboard as you sink them. If you cannot implement a garbage disposal policy aboard your vessel, stay home, don't come to these beautiful islands. Do not abuse what we all use.

GPS

The accuracy of LORAN east of West End, Grand Bahama should be viewed as suspect at best. In the search for reliable positioning, more and more skippers are turning to that electronic marvel called GPS as their main source of navigational data. It is a truly remarkable system offering very accurate positioning around the clock anywhere in the world. Nowadays anyone with $100 can become an instant navigator.

The GPS waypoints listed in this guide are for general usage only. I do not intend for you to follow a string of waypoints to an anchorage. Instead, I will bring you to the general area where you can pilot your way in the rest of the way. Do not attempt to maneuver your vessel from waypoint to waypoint without a constant lookout. The GPS is truly a marvel but I have yet to find one that will locate and steer around a coral head or sandbar. Any skipper who attempts to navigate a tricky channel by using only GPS waypoints deserves whatever ill fortune befalls them. The inherent error in such waypoints due to the Selective Availability (SA) of the system is too great to make such dangerous routes viable. I repeat: use these waypoints only as a guideline, trust your eyes and your depthsounder!

GPS datum used is WGS 84. Skippers with DGPS capability tell me that they receive excellent reception in the northern Bahamas from the continental United States beacons but that they tend to fade out in the southern Bahamas.

CELESTIAL NAVIGATION AND CHARLIE MURPHY

When a skipper leaves the deep waters of the Atlantic Ocean and embarks upon a voyage on the shallow banks of The Bahamas, they leave behind them the normal deep-water navigational methods that they used to get themselves to The Bahamas in the first place. In its place they begin to learn the art of eyeball navigation.

For the most part, the waters of The Bahamas are crystal clear, there is no runoff from the islands to cloud the waters, no muddy rivers emptying unto the banks. It's not unusual to see every aspect of the bottom in 60' of water on a calm day. Some folks are quite unnerved by this. They think nothing of puttering along on the ICW in 8' of murky, black water, but all of a sudden that same 8' in The Bahamas reveals rocks and heads that, although deep and posing no hazard to navigation, make the normally reserved skipper slow down and wildly dodge objects far below his keel. Time and miles soon teach the nervous navigator the differences between water color and the corresponding depth, and between the ripples on the surface and the hidden danger lying just under the surface that you can't see because of the sun's glare. Before too long the neophyte eyeball navigators are testing the limits of their newfound abilities, seeing just how far they can go in that pale green water before bumping, how close to the beach they can anchor, how far up inside the little cove they can tuck. The next thing you know some of them are moving around on full moon nights when the sandbars and heads show up as clearly as they do in the daytime.

When I first came to The Bahamas I had little or no deep-water skills to leave behind but unlike most people, I was able to adjust very quickly to eyeball navigation. I was fortunate in that everything just looked right to me. The learning curve was almost vertical as I immediately found exactly in what shade of water my 5' draft would run aground. Soon, the delicate hues between 4' and 6' deep stood out like black and white and I realized I would not be happy until I could discern the subtle difference between 4' 11" and 5' 1" of water. After more than a decade I'm still trying to hone my skills as the bottom of my keel stays free of lasting growth. I learned to appreciate polarized sunglasses and I came to hate cloudy days when the sun would play hide and seek, as would the rocks and sandbanks. My only real problems in navigating were in learning the deep-water methods that I had neglected in getting to The Bahamas.

When I first started cruising, I purchased a sextant and several books on celestial navigation and like so many others, I mistakenly thought I could teach myself while underway. At this time there was no GPS, and LORAN was iffy the further you ventured from Florida. I couldn't make heads or tails of celestial though I loved having a sextant to play with and enjoyed pulling it out and looking like I knew what I was doing. I had the tools and the books, but no practical experience, in short, I needed professional help.

Celestial navigation requires the ability to count and a little basic geometry. Every sextant sight reduction is essentially solving a right triangle. The formulas for solving problems such as bearings and distances off, cross track error, vectors, amd course over ground, were taught to me in one form or another back in high school. However, when I began navigating my own vessel from point A to point B, my 10th grade geometry class took on an entirely new meaning.

While struggling through nine months of Mrs. Barbara Carter's geometry class I felt that there was no way on God's green Earth that I would ever need to know this stuff to help me get through life. It was actually on God's blue earth, the sea, where I found myself needing the wisdom Mrs. Carter attempted to impart to me, lo those many years ago. For instance, in crossing the Gulf Stream from south Florida to The Bahamas, the navigator must solve a triangle, to be more specific, a plane oblique triangle. It is a vector problem in which you know only one angle and the length of two sides. It's fairly simply to do with just a pencil, a ruler, and a pair of dividers or a drafting compass. Trying to figure it out mathematically however is a "whole 'nother can of worms." Sines, cosines, sine law. Gawd help me Mrs. Carter. If I had known then what I know now, I would not have forgotten now what I learned then.

Many years later, my celestial navigation mentor, Charlie Murphy of Marsh Harbour, Abaco, re-introduced me to the world of geometric equations. Charlie and Barbara would have gotten along famously if they had ever met. They both had keen intellectual minds, a good insight into the psychology of people who are trying to learn something, and me for a student. Charlie was able to take the basic geometric foundation that was laid by Mrs. Carter and build a strong framework of celestial ability upon it. Ahh, Charlie. If all the nuns, priests, and lay teachers that I had over the years could have had just a smidgen of your charisma I might have savored my school years more, I might not have missed so much school, and I might have even done my homework more often. Well, maybe not the homework.

Charlie Murphy, the long time Commodore of the *Royal Marsh Harbour Yacht Club*, used to teach celestial navigation classes in Marsh Harbour for next to nothing. It was the best bargain I ever stumbled across. It was only $10 for the two-week hands-on course, which included a huge notebook of forms and miscellaneous information. Charlie's only rule was that you had to leave his blankety-blank beer alone. Charlie Murphy just plain enjoyed sharing his knowledge with us pseudo-navigators, some of whom did not know which end of a sextant to look into even though we all seemed to have one on board, and turning out confident, competent navigators, most of whom would never again take a sight. He tempered his celestial course with a great deal of common sense and spiced it with some knowledge he picked up as a spotter for artillery in the Canadian Army. He taught us how a one-eyed, one-handed man could estimate angles. Try this as an experiment. Using either hand, make a fist and hold it out at arms length. Unfold and spread out the thumb and little finger and sight down your arm. For general purposes, the span of distance between the tip of your thumb and the tip of your little finger held out at arm's length is approximately 20°. If you make a fist, the span between the knuckle on your first finger and your pinky is approximately 5° while the span between the knuckle of your first finger and the middle finger is about 2°. If you measure the distance between *Polaris* and the horizon with this method you will be very close to your actual latitude. In fact, with this method, along with a chronometer and a means of measuring precise high noon (perhaps a sextant?) to acquire longitude, you can navigate anywhere on the planet.

Charlie led us in classroom studies, actual shots onboard one of our boats while underway, walks on the beach to measure the vertical angle of the Hope Town Lighthouse, and then he sent us home to try our skills at dusk with star sights. One night I was shooting a star that I thought I had identified correctly. I reduced the sight, plotted it, and was patting myself on the back when its LOP intersected in a nice small triangle with my previous shots of *Polaris* and *Vega*. It was only after this that I noticed my star had moved. I discovered my star was actually a masthead light.

In the 10 years since taking Charlie's course, I have taken maybe, oh, a couple of hundred shots. I have not crossed oceans and therefore had no real need for celestial, but I thank my navigational stars that I had the good fortune to meet Charlie Murphy. The coming of the GPS age was long awaited by mariners, and it has indeed made accurate and safe navigation possible with the touch of a button. I for one, love it. Unfortunately, we have lost something in the process. Today any skipper with a hundred dollars can purchase a GPS and become an instant navigator who can expertly recite his cross track error, course over ground, speed over ground, bearing and distance to the next waypoint, and GMT in an instant. But just ask this navigational wizard how to advance an LOP, or find *Dubhe* in the night sky, or derive latitude from *Polaris*. Many navigators-in-a-box cannot. With the exception of naval officers and some professional mariners, celestial navigation is fast becoming a forgotten art, much as learning Morse Code is to fledgling ham radio operators. But like Morse Code, celestial navigation should be mandatory, especially for all skippers transiting large bodies of water. In an emergency situation Morse Code on a simple carrier wave can use less power and get through more radio interference than standard sideband voice transmissions. If the box fails, and it will, celestial will get you home.

Celestial navigation, for some unknown reason, creates a learning block in even the most intelligent skippers. Overcoming this block is often times more difficult than ingesting the knowledge that is offered. Physically taking a sight on a moving boat is relatively easy to master. Practice, practice, practice, and you'll soon instinctively know when you've taken a good sight. The rest is simple math. All the unknowns are in a couple of books that will set you back a few dollars. Keeping your head straight while actually working the math one step at a time is the hardest part and where most navigators screw up. You have to double-check every step and you cannot forget a thing. Celestial is a little like doing math homework four or five times a day except that your grade is extremely important and vitally connected to your health and well being. Failure is not acceptable and you <u>must</u> do your homework.

There is no excuse for venturing upon the open ocean without knowing celestial and any skipper with only a GPS or three and no means of taking celestial sights is, pardon me if I offend anybody, a fool. It's like driving cross-country in a car with no spare. If you're not living right you may find yourself looking around wondering which way you have to walk to get to the nearest service station.

Fortunately celestial navigation is not really needed in The Bahamas; distances are short between the cays and eyeball navigation just about covers it all, especially with GPS. Even on the longer runs, just a compass course and a little knowledge of the currents will get you within sight of your landfall, but it's still nice to know you can do it if you have to. Charlie Murphy has moved back to Canada from Marsh Harbour and he is sorely missed. But there are quite a few celestial navigation courses around and learning celestial is no more difficult than a little high school geometry and we all know how easy high school geometry was don't we Mrs. Carter? Now if I could just find a use for that calculus course…

HAM RADIO

All amateur radio operators will need a Bahamas Reciprocal license (C6A) to operate legally in the waters of The Bahamas.

The Bahamas does not have a third-party agreement with the United States, this means that you cannot make a phone patch from The Bahamas to the U.S. If you head offshore three miles you will be in international waters and can make a phone patch from there without using your C6A, you will be MM2 (Maritime Mobile) once you are three miles out.

The following is a listing of ham nets you may wish to participate in during your Abaco cruise.

NET NAME	FREQUENCY KHz	TIME
Waterway Net	7268	0745-0845 ET
Computer Net	7268	0900 ET-Fridays
Tech Net	7268	0900 ET- Sundays
CW Net-slow	7128	0630 ET-Mon., Wed., and Fri.
CW Net-fast	7128	0630 ET-Tues., Thurs., Sat., and Sun.
Bahamas Weather Net	3696	0720 ET
Bah. Amat. Radio Soc.	3696	0830 ET-Sundays
Intercontinental Net	14300-14316 (changes often)	1100 UTC
Maritime Mobile Net	14300-14316 (changes often)	After Intercon. until around 0200 UTC
Caribbean Net	7230 (changes often)	1100-1200 UTC
Hurricane Watch Net	14325, 14275, 14175	When needed

HOLIDAYS

The following public holidays are observed in The Bahamas:

New Year's Day-January 1
Good Friday
Easter Sunday
Easter Monday
Whit Monday-six weeks after Easter
Labour Day-first Friday in June
Independence Day-July 10
Emancipation Day-first Monday in August
Discovery Day-October 12
Christmas Day-December 25
Boxing Day-December 26

Holidays that fall on Sunday are always observed on Monday. Holidays which fall on Saturday are also usually observed on Monday. Bahamians are very religious people so expect stores and services to be closed on Sundays as well as on Holidays. Some businesses may be open all day on Saturday but may close for a half day on Wednesdays. A must see is the Junkanoo Parade that begins about 4:00am on Boxing Day and New Years Day in Nassau and Freeport.

HURRICANE HOLES

To begin with, there is <u>no such thing</u> as a truly safe hurricane hole, in fact, the term hurricane hole itself is quite misleading. I believe that given a strong enough hurricane, any harbour, hole, or creek can be devastated, as was proven during Hurricane Floyd in 1999 with it's 155+ knot winds. Keep this in mind as the places that I am going to recommend offer the best protection and, under most circumstances, give you a better than average chance of surviving a hurricane, but are by no means "safe" in the true meaning of the word. Although you may feel quite safe in your chosen hole remember that no hurricane hole comes with a guarantee. Many factors will contribute to your survival. The physical location and protection the hole offers is your primary line of defense. But hand in hand with that is the way you secure your vessel, the tidal surge, other vessels around you, and the path and strength of the hurricane. Allow yourself plenty of time to get to your chosen location and to get settled. Only a fool would attempt to race a hurricane.

If you are going to be cruising in the Northern Bahamas from June through November, hurricane season, you'll want to know where the hurricane holes are, what you can expect when you get there, and how far you are away from your first choice at all times. Personally, this skipper prefers a narrow, deep, mangrove lined creek but if one isn't available I'll search for something equally suitable. Some holes are better than others but like the old adage advises, *"Any port in a storm."* With that in mind let me offer a few of the places where I would consider seeking shelter in the event of a hurricane. Bear in mind that if you ask ten different skippers what they look for in a hurricane hole you're likely to get ten different answers. Some of these holes may not meet your requirements. I offer them only for your consideration when seeking safety for your vessel. The final decision is yours and yours alone. For the best information concerning hurricane holes always check with the locals. They'll know the best spots.

Abaco offers quite a few decent hurricane holes. The best protection lies in places like Treasure Cay where you can anchor in the narrow creeks surrounding the marina complex. There is a man-made canal complex called Leisure Lee lying just south of Treasure Cay on Great Abaco. Here you will find excellent protection from seas in 8' but you will have to tie off to the trees along the shore as the entire complex is dredged and the holding is not good. Green Turtle Cay offers White Sound and Black Sound. I much prefer White Sound though there is a bit more fetch for seas to build up. Black Sound, though smaller, has a grassy bottom and a few concrete mooring blocks scattered about. At Man-O- War you can choose either anchorage. Just to the south on Elbow Cay, Hope Town Harbour boasts very good protection. Bear in mind that boats here were damaged by Hurricane Floyd in 1999. Although most boats anchored here survived Floyd, many were damaged by other boats in this crowded harbour. If you arrive early enough, and your draft is shallow enough, you may be able to work you way up the creek for better protection. There is an old hurricane chain stretched across the harbour that you may be able to secure your vessel to. Ask any local where to find the chain. Just a few miles away lies Marsh Harbour with that wonderful sand/mud bottom that anchors so love. The holding here is great but the harbour is open to the west for a fetch of over a mile. For small shallow draft (3') monohull vessels there is a small creek on the eastern side of the harbour just to the east of the *Conch Inn Marina*. Get there early. Farther south you might consider Little Harbour though it is open to the north with a 3' bar across the mouth. Between Marsh Harbour and Little Harbour lies Snake Cay which has excellent protection in its mangrove lined creeks. In the more northern Abacos you can try Hurricane Hole on the southeast end of Allan's-Pensacola Cay. Here excellent protection can be found in 6'-8' of water but the bar at the entrance will only allow about 4' at high water. Small shallow draft vessels can work themselves well up into the creeks at Double Breasted Cay if unable to get to better protection to the south. The harbour at Grand Cay may also be a consideration if caught unaware by a fast approaching storm.

MEDICAL EMERGENCIES

Most of the major settlements in the island have government clinics and Grand Bahama itself has several hospitals: *Rand Memorial Hospital* (242-352-6735), *Sunrise Medical Center*(242-373-3333), *Port Lucaya Medical Center* (242-373-1711), and the *Lucayan Medical Center East* (242-352-7400) and *West* (242-352-7288). If you need dental work try the Dental Centre at 242-352-4552. At Eight Mile Rock is the *ABC Health-World Holistic Clinic* at 242-352-2222. If you need the services of a vet on Grand Bahama you can call Dr. Bater or Dr. Rich at 242-352-6521 or try Dr. Hanna at 242-352-9511. If you need an ambulance while on Grand Bahama, call 242-352-2689.

You'll find government run clinics on almost all of the inhabited islands of the Abacos. They are usually staffed by a competent nurse with a doctor making regular visits. In Marsh Harbour you have the choice of visiting either Dr. Lundy or Dr. Boyce, both have very well equipped offices in downtown Marsh Harbour. The *Agape Family Dental Centre*, 242-367-4355, is a few blocks south of the traffic light (beware, there may be more than one traffic light by the time you get to Marsh Harbour). For prescriptions try either the *Chemist Shoppe* or *Lowe's Pharmacy*.

On Great Abaco you'll find the very professional *Trauma One* ambulance team who have been providing emergency service to Abaco residents and visitors for no fee, they are supported entirely by contributions. *Trauma One* has been operating since September of 1995 and your help is needed. Donations may be sent to *Trauma One*, P.O. Box AB 20594, Marsh Harbour. All contributions are recorded and acknowledged. If you need a dentist while at Treasure Cay, call Dr. Spencer at 242-365-8625.

PHONING HOME

Batelco handles all phone communications in the islands of The Bahamas and can easily be found in the outer island by walking to the base of the *Batelco* tower where you'll usually find their office. On Grand Bahama *Batelco* can be reached at 352-3500. If you need information dial 916, if you need time try 917, and if you need weather try 915.

PROVISIONING

The Abacos and Grand Bahama are blessed with good, well-stocked grocery stores with prices higher than stateside, sometimes twice as much. Milk, cigarettes, and beer will be wallet busters while rum and local produce and poultry may be a bit more economical. You'll also find different items here than you'll find in Florida…New Zealand, Irish, or Canadian butter at the same prices as margarine back home. New Zealand mutton is also another nice treat if you can find it.

If you have the room, you can stock your boat till the waterline is low, this will save you money in provisioning, but you'll spend more on fuel. Unless you're on a tight budge just make sure you have enough to get you to where you're going so you don't run out of food halfway across the bank. As far as engine spares and boat gear goes, it's best to buy your supplies in the States and bring them with you. You'll not only save money, but time as well; the items will need to be brought in, an expensive and often time-consuming ordeal.

Paper products, beer, cigarettes, all should be brought from home, but don't fret the produce, it's fairly easy to find fresh fruits and veggies in the northern Bahamas. Don't forget sun screen and bug sprays!

TIDES AND CURRENTS

The islands of The Bahamas are affected by the west setting North Equatorial Current on both their northern and southern extremities. After entering the Caribbean the North Equatorial Current splits into two branches, the northern branch flowing northeast of The Turks and Caicos and The Bahamas as the Antilles Current with an average velocity of approximately ½ knot. To a lesser extent the Antilles Current also flows through the Old Bahama Channel along the northern coast of Cuba. The more southern branch of the North Equatorial Current makes its way around the Caribbean and the Gulf of Mexico and enters the Straits of Florida as the Gulf Stream with an average velocity of approximately 2.5 knots in a northward direction. Once north of The Bahamas the stronger Gulf Stream merges with the weaker Antilles Current and bears off north and northeastward across the North Atlantic.

Where the shallow banks drop off to deeper ocean waters the tidal currents flow in and out the passes and cuts sometimes reaching 2-4 knots in strength and even more in a few of the more narrow passes. Some cuts may be impassable in adverse wind conditions or in heavy swells that may exist with or without any wind. Even in moderate conditions, onshore winds against an outgoing tide can create very rough conditions.

As a rule of thumb you can estimate the tidal rise and fall to be about 2'- 4' at most times with a mean rise of 2.6'. Neap tides, those after the first and last quarter of the moon, rise approximately ½' less, while tides after new and full moons rise approximately ½' more. During Spring tides, when the moon is nearest the Earth, the range is increased by another ½'. Cruising through The Bahamas during Spring full moon tides will give you some of the lowest lows and highest highs. It is quite easy to run aground at this time on some routes. Boats with drafts of 5' have reportedly run aground in what is normally a 6' depth at low water during this time. To receive tidal information while in The Bahamas see the section *Weather*.

When attempting to predict the state of tide at any time other than at slack tide, you can use the *Rule of Twelfths* for a generally reliable accuracy. To do this take the amount of tidal fluctuation and divide it into twelfths. For example, if high tide in Nassau is expected to be 3.0' and the low water datum is 0.0', the tidal fluctuation is 3', and each twelfth is 0.25' or 3". To predict the state of tide at different times you can use the *Rule of Twelfths* in the following table. The table is merely to demonstrate a point and uses an imaginary charted high tide of 3'. Always consult your chart tables or listen for tide information broadcasts and calculate accordingly.

TIME OF LOW WATER	TIDE DATUM-0 FEET
1 hour after low, add 1/12	¼ foot above datum-3"
2 hours after low, add 3/12	¾ feet above datum-9"
3 hours after low, add 6/12	1½ feet above datum-18"
4 hours after low, add 9/12	2¼ feet above datum-27"
5 hours after low, add 11/12	2¾ feet above datum-33"
6 hours after low, add 12/12	High Water-3'*

Caution: assumes a 3' tidal fluctuation as an example.

Chart tables give the times and heights of high and low water but not the time of the turning of the tide or slack water. Usually there is little difference between the times of high and low water and the beginning of ebb or flood currents, but in narrow channels, landlocked harbors, or on tidal creeks and rivers, the time of slack water may vary by several hours. In some places you will find that it is not unusual for the currents to continue their direction of flow long after charted predictions say they should change. Strong winds can play havoc on the navigator attempting to predict slack water. The current may often appear in places as a swift flowing river and care must be taken whenever crossing a stretch of strong current to avoid being swept out to sea or onto a bank or rocks. Some of the currents may flow from 2.5 to over 4 knots in places and in anchorages with a tidal flow two anchors is a must. Some cuts may be impassable in adverse wind conditions or in heavy swells that may exist with or without any wind. Even in moderate conditions, onshore winds against an outgoing tide can create very rough conditions. Some of the passes, cuts, and anchorages shown may be a real test of your ability. If in doubt, stay out. As with cruising anywhere, if you exercise caution you will have a safe and enjoyable cruise in The Bahamas.

VHF

The regulations pertaining to the proper use of VHF in The Bahamas are basically identical to those in the United States. Channel 16 is the designated channel for hailing and distress. Please shift all traffic to a working channel when you have made contact with your party. Please try to use channels 09-14, 17-19, and 69-72 as your working channels. By the way, if you're used to giving your radio's numbers as folks often do in the states don't do it here. It's a waste of time, it's not required, and nobody cares to hear them.

In Marsh Harbour, Abaco, you can hail a taxi on VHF ch. 06 simply by calling for "any taxi" or any particular taxi if you know their number. Please don't use ch. 06 as a working frequency, reserve it for the taxis.

Cruisers in VHF range of Marsh Harbour can take part in the daily morning Cruiser's Net on VHF ch. 68. This is a well-organized and very helpful net and will likely become a part of your morning ritual while in the Hub of Abaco. Ch. 68 is used as a hailing frequency in the Hub also and many cruisers monitor 68 throughout the day and night. More on the cruisers net in a moment.

BASRA and the medical clinic on Treasure Cay stand by on VHF ch. 83 with a powerful rig that covers most of the surrounding waters. Many of the residents on Treasure Cay stand by on ch. 66 while some of the folks on Guana Cay stand by on ch. 08.

There is an active dolphin research program in Abaco, the *Bahamas Marine Mammal Survey* (see the section on Hole in the Wall) and they urge any boater spotting marine mammals, and that includes manatees, to please call "Dolphin Research" on VHF ch. 65. You will need to give them a position report, the number of animals sighted, and especially any identifying marks such as nicks on their fins or body scars. Please reserve ch. 65 for this purpose.

When you are using your VHF assume that at least a half-dozen of your neighbors will follow your conversation to another channel. Even if you have a "secret" channel it will not take too long to find you (That's what *SCAN* buttons are for!). It is a fact of life that everybody listens in to everybody else.

The most popular radio show in Abaco is the "Cruiser's Net." The net meets every morning at 0815 on VHF ch. 68. On the net you'll find the Weather forecast, reports on conditions at Whale Cay Passage, messages from arriving and departing boats, and commercial announcements covering everything from cruiser's e-mail to happy hour specials. Centered around the Hub of Abaco, the net often reaches as far south as Cherokee and as far north as Coopers Town.

For Northern Abaco, *Fox Town Texaco* and the *Tangelo Hotel* have volunteered to broadcast the weather and announce waiting e-mail each morning on the VHF. There is an announcement on VHF ch. 16 between 0700 and 0800 and then a switch to a working channel. The exact time depends on the workload at *Fox Town Texaco* when Lillian Parker opens each morning. Just keep your radio on ch. 16, you won't miss it. You may contact either station on VHF ch. 16 during the day if you're in waters from Great Sale Cay to Angelfish Point.

WEATHER

The weather throughout the Abacos is sub-tropical with a rainy season from June through October, coinciding with hurricane season. In the winter, temperatures in the Abacos sometimes fall below 60°F but generally are above 75°F in the daytime. During the summer months the lows are around 75°-78°F while the highs seldom rise above 90°F. Seawater temperatures normally vary between 74°F in February and 84°F in August. Weather in the Abacos is much like weather in central Florida.

The humidity in the Abacos is not as bad as south Florida, which is one reason so many Florida cruisers spend their summers in the Abacos. In the summer, winds tend to be light, 10 knots or less from the southeast with more calms, especially at night. In the winter, the prevailing winds are east-southeast and stronger. It is not unusual to get a week of strong winds, 20 knots or better, during the winter months as fronts move through. These fronts tend to move through with regularity during the winter months and become more infrequent as spring approaches. The wind will usually be in the southeast or south before a front and will often be very light to calm. As the front approaches with its telltale bank of dark clouds on the western and northwestern horizon, the winds will steadily pick up and move into the southwest, west, and northwest as the front approaches. Strongest winds are usually from the west and northwest. After the front passes, the winds will move into the north and northeast for a day or two before finally settling back into an east/southeast pattern until the next front. Winds just after the front tend to be strong and the temperature a little cooler. A front passing off the central Florida coast will usually be in Marsh Harbour in about 12-24 hours.

In the summer the weather pattern is typically scattered showers with the occasional line squall. Although the main concern during June through November is hurricanes, the Abacos are more likely to be visited by a tropical wave with its strong winds and drenching rains. Tropical waves, sometimes called easterly waves, are low pressure systems that can strengthen and turn into a tropical depression or hurricane. Cruisers visiting the Abacos during hurricane season are advised to monitor weather broadcasts closely and take timely, appropriate action (see the previous section on *Hurricane Holes*).

Staying in touch with weather broadcasts presents little problem in the Northern Bahamas, even if you don't have SSB or ham radio capabilities. In the Hub of Abaco area you can pick up the weather every morning on the cruiser's net on VHF ch. 68 every morning at 8:15am You can get Silbert Mills' weather every day on *Radio Abaco* on 93.5 FM at 8:00am and about 6:20pm For Northern Abaco, *Fox Town Texaco* and the *Tangelo Hotel* have volunteered to broadcast the weather and announce waiting e-mail each morning on the VHF.

WINZ, 940 KHz from Miami, is on the air 24 hours with weather for southern Florida approximately every 10 minutes. Unfortunately this station is difficult to pick up at night. WGBS also from Miami at 710 KHz has weather four times an hour 24 hours a day.

If you have ham radio capabilities you can pick up The Bahamas Weather Net every morning at 0720 on 3.696 MHz, lower sideband. Carolyn Wardle, C6AGG begins with the local weather forecast and tides from the Nassau Met. Office. Next, hams from all over The Bahamas, and sometimes from Provo, check in with their local conditions which Carolyn later forwards to the Nassau Met. Office to assist in their forecasting. If you are interested in the approach of a front you can listen in and hear what conditions hams in the path of the front have experienced. All licensed amateur radio operators with current Bahamian and Turks and Caicos reciprocals are invited to participate. The local conditions in the weather reports follow a specific order so listen in and give your conditions in the order indicated. If requested, Carolyn will send you some information on the types of clouds and their descriptions along with a log sheet. Be sure to thank Carolyn for her tireless efforts that benefit all mariners, not only those with ham licenses. Thanks Carolyn.

At 0745 on 7.268 MHz you can pick up the Waterway Net. Organized and maintained by the *Waterway Radio and Cruising Club*, this dedicated band of amateur radio operators begin the net with a synopsis of the weather for The Bahamas (with tides), south Florida, the southwest North Atlantic, the Caribbean Sea, and the Gulf of Mexico. For a listing of marine weather frequencies, see *Appendix F: Weather Broadcast Frequencies*.

If you have marine SSB capabilities you can pick up BASRA's weather broadcasts every morning at 0700 on 4003 KHz, upper sideband. Later in the day you can pick up the guru of weather forecasters, Herb Hilgenberg, *Southbound II*, from Canada. After a short interruptions of Herb's service, he is once again operating, this time from his home in Canada. You can tune in to Herb on 12.359 MHz, upper sideband, at 2000 Zulu. On 4.426, 6.501, 8.764, 13.089, and 17.314 MHz, you can pick up the voice weather broadcasts from NMN four times a day at 0500, 1100, 1700, and 2300 EST.

Starting in the southern Bahamas and continuing on throughout the entire Caribbean, an SSB equipped vessel can pick up David Jones, *Misstine*, call sign ZHB, who operates out of Venezuelan waters. David is on the air each day at 0815-0830 AST (1215-1230 UTC) on 4.003 MHz and then moves up to 8.104 MHz from 0830-0915 AST. He begins with a 24-48 hour wind and sea summary followed by a synoptic analysis and tropical conditions during hurricane season. After this he repeats the weather for those needing fills and finally he takes check-ins reporting local conditions. During hurricane season David relays the latest tropical storm advisories at 1815 AST on 6.224 MHz.

USING THE CHARTS

The soundings for my guides have been taken by several different procedures over the years. In my earliest editions, I used the depthsounder on my boat and a portable unit in my dinghy for soundings. When the portable unit bit the dust, I turned to the old reliable lead line. The charts at this point were basically sketch charts. The outlines of the islands were taken from *Nassau Land and Surveys Department* topographical maps and scanned into my computer where I added everything else using several graphics programs. The depths were placed on the charts using a system of crossed bearings, estimates by eye, and simply dead reckoning. I now use a computer-based hydrographic system in my 16', 90hp, *Data Acquisition Vessel*, or *DAV* for short. The system consists of an off-the-shelf GPS/sonar combination that gives a GPS waypoint and depth every two seconds including the time of observation. The software records and stores this information in an onboard computer. When I begin to chart an area, I first put *DAV*'s bow on a well-marked, prominent point of land and take GPS lat/long for a period of at least 20 minutes. I use the average of all these positions to check against the lat/long shown on the topos, which are very accurate by the way. I also use cross bearings to help set up control points for my own reference. At this point I then begin to take soundings.

My next objective is to chart the inshore reefs and all visible hazards to navigation. These positions are recorded by hand on my field notes as well as being recorded electronically. The soundings taken by the system are later entered by hand, but it is the field notes that help me create the basis for the chart graphics. The computer will not tell me where a certain reef ends or begins as accurately as I can record it and show it on my field notes. Next, I chart the one-fathom line as well as the ten-fathom line (if applicable). Here is where the system does most of the work though I still stop to take field notes. Finally, I will crisscross the entire area in a grid pattern and hopefully catch hazards that are at first glance unseen. It is not unusual to spend days sounding an area of only a couple of square miles.

Due to the speed of *the DAV*, each identical lat/long may have as many as ten or twenty separate soundings. Then, with the help of *NOAA* tide tables, the computer gives me accurate depths to one decimal place for each separate lat/long pair acquired. A macro purges all but the lowest depths for each lat/long position. At this point the actual plotting is begun.

These charts are as accurate as I can make them and I believe them to be superior to any others, however, it is not possible to plot every individual rock or coral head so pilotage by eye is still essential. On many of the routes in my guides you must be able to pick out the blue, deeper water as it snakes between sandbanks, rocky bars, and coral heads. Learn to trust your eyes. Remember that on the banks, sandbars and channels can shift over time so that once what was a channel may now be a sandbar. Never approach a cut or sandbar with the sun in your eyes, it should be above and behind you. Polarized sunglasses are a big help in combating the glare of the sun on the water. With good visibility the sandbars and heads stand out and are clearly defined. As you gain experience you may even learn to read the subtle differences in the water surface as it flows over underwater obstructions.

The charts will show both deep draft vessel routes as well as some shallow draft vessel routes. Deep draft vessel routes will accommodate a draft of 6' minimum and often more with the assistance of the tide. Shallow draft vessel routes are for dinghies and small outboard powered boats with drafts of less than 3'. Shallow draft monohulls and multihulls very often use these same routes. All courses given are magnetic.

In this guide I have included GPS latitude and longitude positions for the entrances to the cuts and to give locations for the positions of shoal areas. These GPS positions are only to be used in a general sense. The positions plotted on the charts in this guide are taken with my hydrographic system with its inherent SA error of 100 meters, approximately 328'. In the worst case scenario, if you couple the inherent error of my GPS during soundings, and your GPS when you are cruising the same locale, it is theoretically possible to have a maximum error of 200 meters, 656', or a little over .1 nautical mile! That much of a possible error could be disastrous. Until the SA is turned off and I can resound these areas I repeat: use these waypoints only as a guideline, trust your eyes and your depthsounder! The best aids to navigation when near shoals and cuts are sharp eyesight and good light.

Not being a perfect world, I expect errors to occur. I would deeply appreciate any input and corrections that you may notice as you travel these waters. Please send your suggestions to Stephen J. Pavlidis, C/O Seaworthy Publications, 507 Sunrise Dr., Port Washington, WI, 53074. You can send e-mail to me through my website at http://www.islandhopping.com. Your suggestion may help improve the next edition of this guide.

CAUTION:

- The prudent navigator will not rely solely on any single aid to navigation, particularly on floating aids.

- The Approach and Index charts are designed strictly for orientation, they are not to be used for navigational purposes.

- All charts are to be used in conjunction with the text.

- All soundings are in feet at Mean Low Water.

- All courses are magnetic.

- Projection is transverse Mercator.

- Orientation all Charts-North is up.

- Datum used is WGS84.

- Differences in latitude and longitude may exist between these charts and other charts of the area; therefore the transfer of positions from one chart to another should be done by bearings and distances from common features.

- If attempting to measure distances, remember: one minute of latitude =1 nautical mile (approx.).

The author and publisher take no responsibility for errors, omissions, or the misuse of these charts. No warranties are either expressed or implied as to the usability of the information contained herein.

Note: Some official NOAA and DMA charts do not show some of the reefs and heads charted in this guide. Always keep a good lookout when piloting in these waters.

LIST OF CHARTS

#	CHART DESCRIPTION	PG.
GRAND BAHAMA		
GB-1	SANDY CAY TO INDIAN CAY, INDIAN CAY CHANNEL	43
GB-1A	WEST END, MARINA ENTRANCE	44
GB-2	FREEPORT HARBOUR	47
GB-3	DUNDEE BAY TO SILVER POINT	49
GB-4	XANADU BEACH TO MADIOCA POINT	51
GB-5	SILVER COVE, OCEAN REEF MARINA	52
GB-6	BARNETT POINT TO FORTUNE POINT, BELL CHANNEL	54
GB-7	BELL CHANNEL, PORT LUCAYA, LUCAYAN MARINA VILLAGE	55
GB-8	FORTUNE POINT TO THE GRAND LUCAYAN WATERWAY	57
GB-9	THE GRAND LUCAYAN WATERWAY, SOUTHERN ENTRANCE	58
GB-10	THE GRAND LUCAYAN WATERWAY, NORTHERN ENTRANCE	59
GB-11	PETERSON CAY	60
THE BIGHT OF ABACO		
AB-BI-1	THE NORTHERN BIGHT	63
AB-BI-2	LITTLE ABACO TO CRAB CAY, THE NORTHWEST PASSAGE	64
AB-BI-3	CRAB CAY TO SPENCE ROCK	65
AB-BI-4	LITTLE ABACO TO RANDALL'S CREEK	67
AB-BI-5	RANDALL'S CREEK TO BASIN HARBOUR CAY	68
AB-BI-6	NORMAN'S CASTLE	70
AB-BI-7	JOE DOWNER CAYS TO BIG PIGEON CAY	71
AB-BI-8	BIG PIGEON CAY TO WOOLENDEAN CAY	72
AB-BI-9	THE SOUTHERN BIGHT	73
AB-BI-10	SANDY POINT	74
AB-BI-11	CASTAWAY CAY (GORDA CAY)	75
AB-BI-12	CHANNEL CAY TO MORES ISLAND	77
AB-BI-13	MORES ISLAND	78
THE ABACOS		
AB-1	WALKERS CAY TO CARTERS CAYS	81
AB-2	GREAT SALE CAY	82
AB-3	WALKERS CAY	84
AB-4	GRAND CAYS	87
AB-5	DOUBLE BREASTED CAYS	88
AB-6	STRANGERS CAY	90
AB-7	CARTERS CAYS	91
AB-8	CARTERS CAYS TO SPANISH CAY	92
AB-9	FOX TOWN	93

INDEX CHARTS

Use these index charts to locate the chart for your area. Refer to the previous two pages to find the page number of the chart you need.

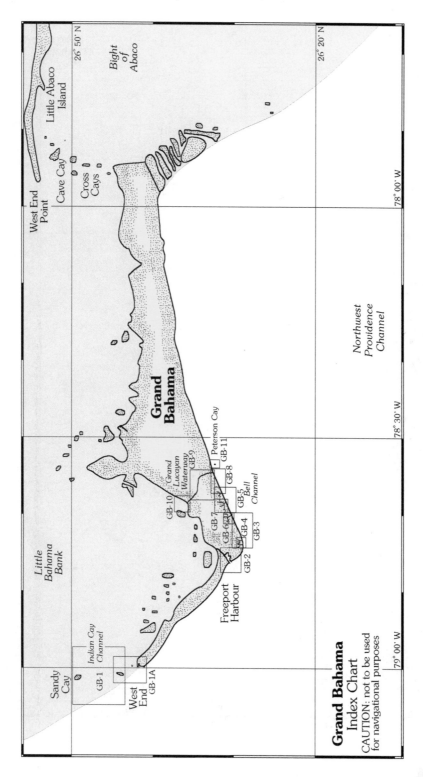

Grand Bahama
Index Chart
CAUTION: not to be used
for navigational purposes

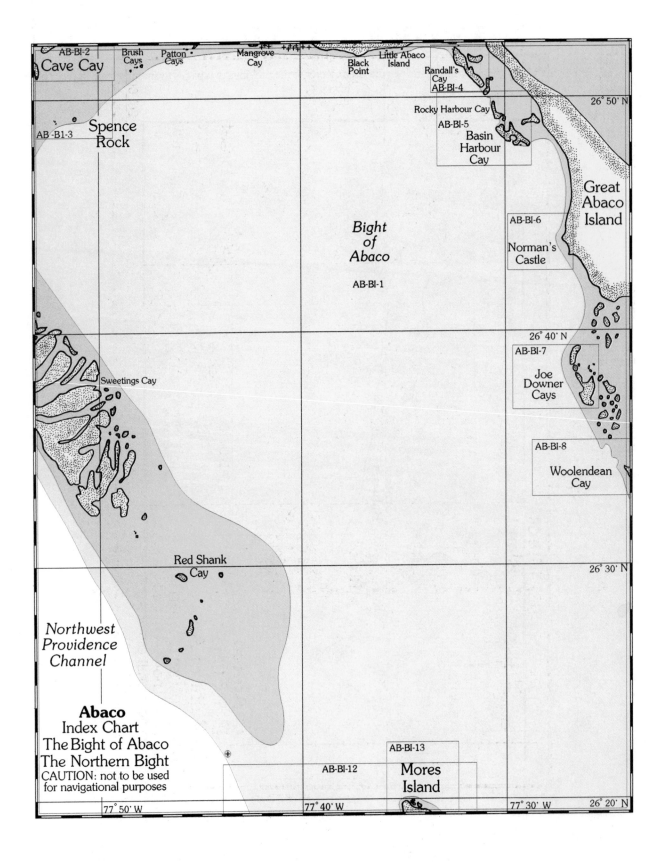

AB-BI-2
Cave Cay

Brush Cays

Patton Cays

Mangrove Cay

Black Point

Little Abaco Island

Randall's Cay
AB-BI-4

26° 50' N

AB-BI-3
Spence Rock

Rocky Harbour Cay

AB-BI-5
Basin Harbour Cay

Great Abaco Island

Bight of Abaco

AB-BI-6
Norman's Castle

AB-BI-1

26° 40' N

AB-BI-7
Joe Downer Cays

Sweetings Cay

AB-BI-8
Woolendean Cay

Red Shank Cay

26° 30' N

Northwest Providence Channel

Abaco
Index Chart
The Bight of Abaco
The Northern Bight
CAUTION: not to be used
for navigational purposes

AB-BI-13

AB-BI-12

Mores Island

77° 50' W

77° 40' W

77° 30' W

26° 20' N

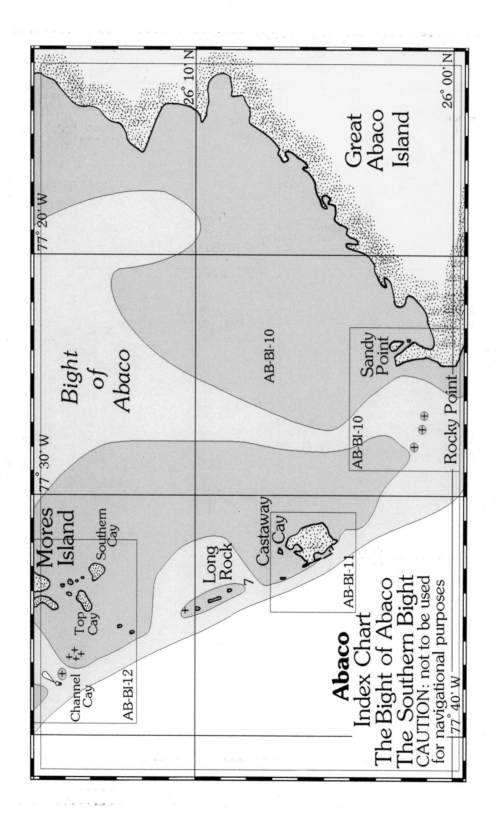

Great
Abaco
Island

26° 00' N

26° 10' N

77° 20' W

Bight
of
Abaco

AB-BI-10

Sandy
Point

77° 30' W

AB-BI-10

Rocky Point

Mores
Island

Southern
Cay

Long
Rock

Castaway
Cay

7

Top
Cay

Channel
Cay

AB-BI-12

AB-BI-11

77° 40' W

Abaco
Index Chart
The Bight of Abaco
The Southern Bight
CAUTION: not to be used
for navigational purposes

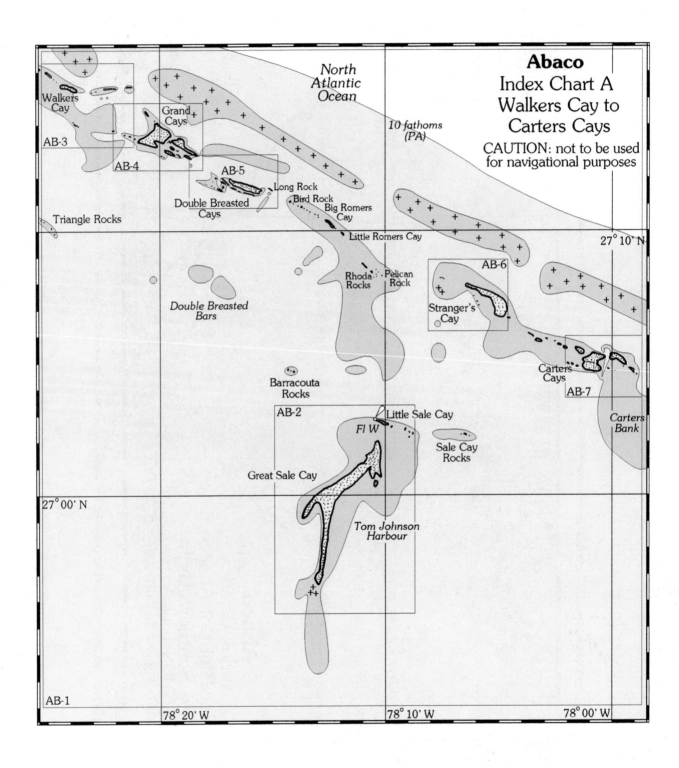

North
Atlantic
Ocean

Abaco
Index Chart A
Walkers Cay to
Carters Cays
CAUTION: not to be used
for navigational purposes

Walkers
Cay

AB-3

Grand
Cays

AB-4

AB-5

Double Breasted
Cays

Long Rock

Bird Rock

Big Romers
Cay

Triangle Rocks

Little Romers Cay

10 fathoms
(PA)

27° 10' N

Double Breasted
Bars

Rhoda
Rocks

Pelican
Rock

AB-6

Stranger's
Cay

Barracouta
Rocks

Carters
Cays

AB-7

Carters
Bank

AB-2

Little Sale Cay

Fl W

Sale Cay
Rocks

Great Sale Cay

Tom Johnson
Harbour

27° 00' N

AB-1

78° 20' W

78° 10' W

78° 00' W

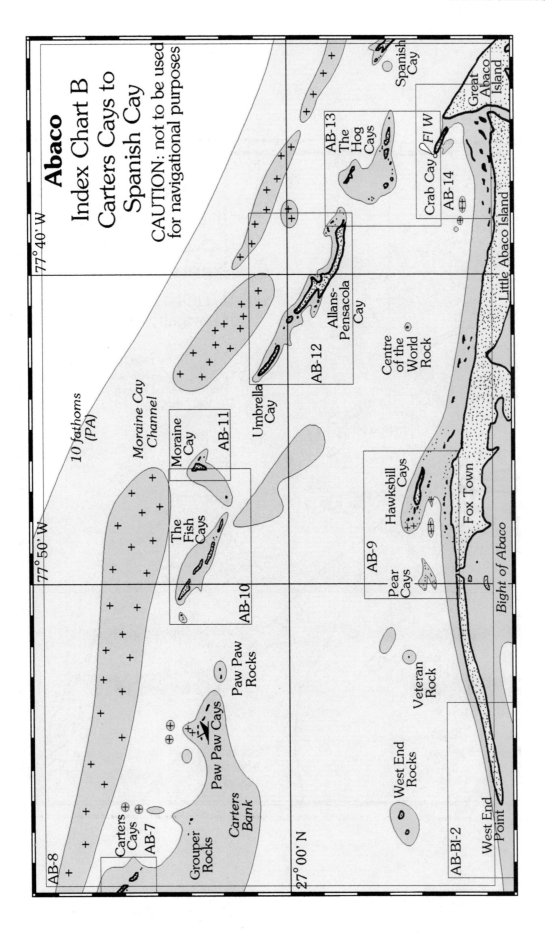

Abaco
Index Chart B
Carters Cays to
Spanish Cay

CAUTION: not to be used
for navigational purposes

77° 40′ W

77° 50′ W

10 fathoms
(PA)

Moraine Cay
Channel

Spanish Cay

AB-13
The
Hog
Cays

Crab Cay ⨍ Fl W
AB-14

Great
Abaco
Island

Allans-
Pensacola
Cay

AB-12

Centre
of the
World
Rock

Umbrella
Cay

Moraine
Cay

AB-11

The
Fish
Cays

Hawksbill
Cays

Fox Town

AB-9

Pear
Cays

AB-10

Little Abaco Island

Paw Paw
Rocks

Paw Paw Cays

Veteran
Rock

Bight of Abaco

Carters
Bank

Grouper
Rocks

West End
Rocks

AB-8

Carters
Cays
AB-7

27° 00′ N

AB-BI-2

West End
Point

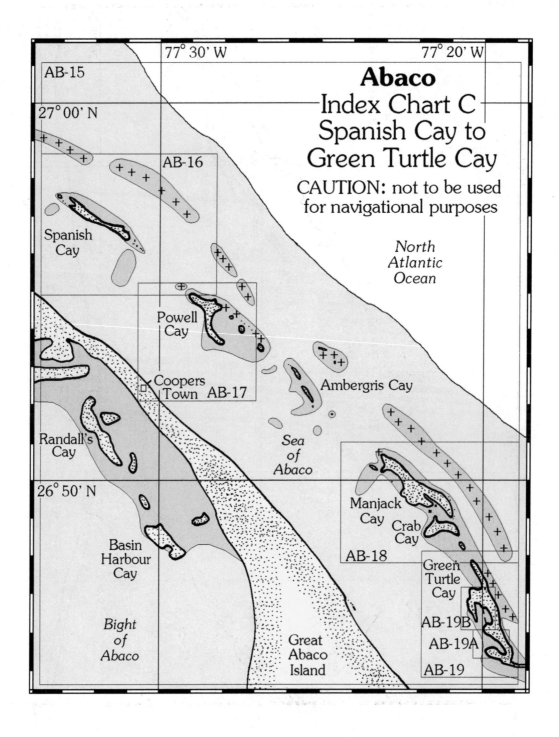

AB-15

77° 30' W

77° 20' W

Abaco
Index Chart C
Spanish Cay to
Green Turtle Cay
CAUTION: not to be used
for navigational purposes

27° 00' N

AB-16

Spanish
Cay

*North
Atlantic
Ocean*

Powell
Cay

Coopers
Town AB-17

Ambergris Cay

Randall's
Cay

*Sea
of
Abaco*

Manjack
Cay   Crab
Cay

AB-18

26° 50' N

Basin
Harbour
Cay

Green
Turtle
Cay

AB-19B

AB-19A

*Bight
of
Abaco*

*Great
Abaco
Island*

AB-19

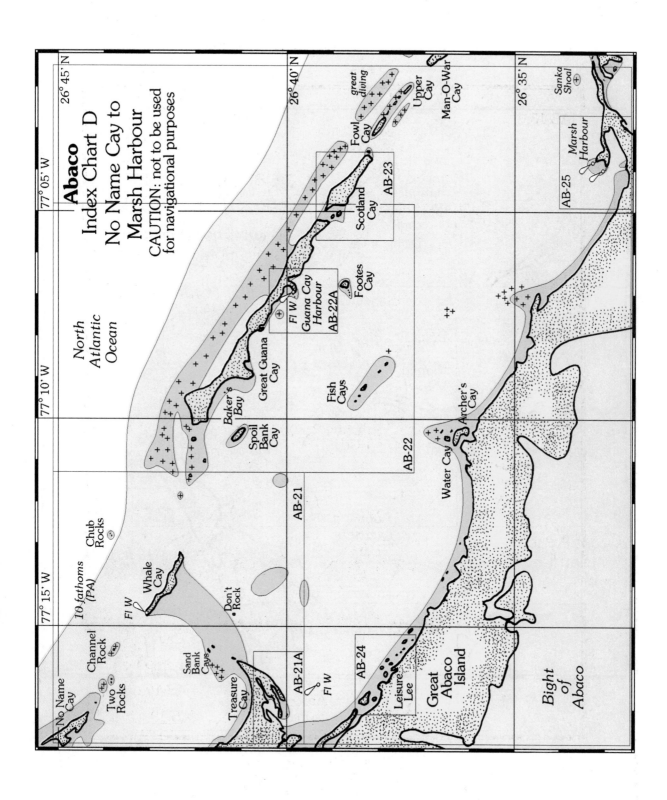

Abaco
Index Chart D
No Name Cay to
Marsh Harbour
CAUTION: not to be used
for navigational purposes

North
Atlantic
Ocean

26° 45' N

26° 40' N

26° 35' N

77° 15' W

77° 10' W

77° 05' W

No Name
Cay

Two
Rocks

Channel
Rock

Chub
Rocks

10 fathoms
(PA)

Fl W
Whale
Cay

Don't
Rock

Sand
Bank
Cays

Treasure
Cay

AB-21A

AB-21

Fl W

AB-24

Leisure
Lee

Great
Abaco
Island

Bight
of
Abaco

Baker's
Bay

Great Guana
Cay

Spoil
Bank
Cay

Fl W
Guana Cay
Harbour

AB-22A

AB-22

Fish
Cays

Footes
Cay

Scotland
Cay

AB-23

Fowl
Cay

great
diving

Upper
Cay

Man-O-War
Cay

Water Cay

Archer's
Cay

AB-25

Marsh
Harbour

Sanka
Shoal

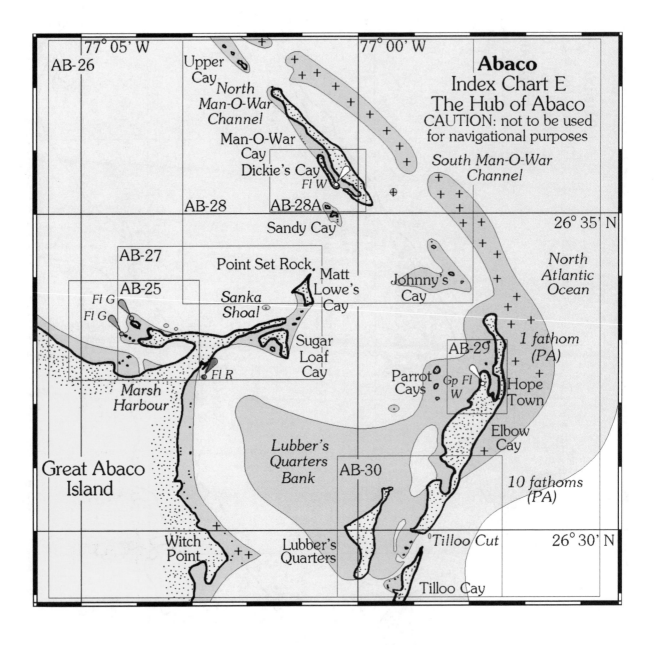

77° 05' W

AB-26

77° 00' W

Upper
Cay
North
Man-O-War
Channel

Man-O-War
Cay

Dickie's Cay
Fl W

AB-28

AB-28A

Sandy Cay

Abaco
Index Chart E
The Hub of Abaco
CAUTION: not to be used
for navigational purposes

*South Man-O-War
Channel*

26° 35' N

AB-27

Point Set Rock

AB-25

*Sanka
Shoal*

Fl G

Fl G

Matt
Lowe's
Cay

*Johnny's
Cay*

*North
Atlantic
Ocean*

Sugar
Loaf
Cay

AB-29

*1 fathom
(PA)*

Fl R

*Marsh
Harbour*

Parrot
Cays

Gp Fl
W

Hope
Town

Elbow
Cay

Great Abaco
Island

*Lubber's
Quarters
Bank*

AB-30

*10 fathoms
(PA)*

26° 30' N

Witch
Point

Lubber's
Quarters

Tilloo Cut

Tilloo Cay

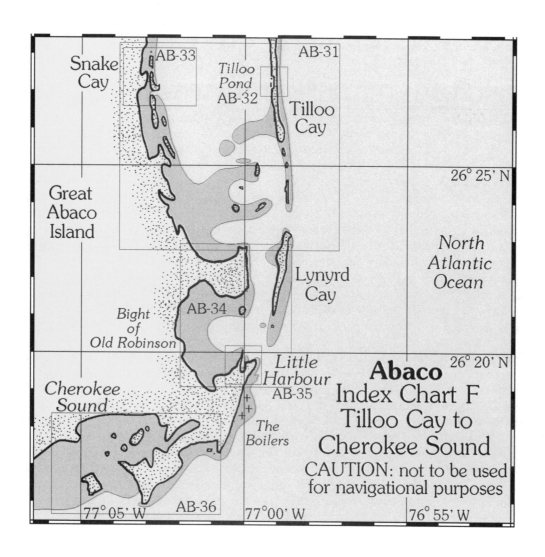

Snake Cay

AB-33

Tilloo Pond AB-32

AB-31

Tilloo Cay

Great Abaco Island

26° 25' N

North Atlantic Ocean

Lynyrd Cay

AB-34

Bight of Old Robinson

Little Harbour AB-35

Abaco 26° 20' N

Index Chart F
Tilloo Cay to
Cherokee Sound
CAUTION: not to be used
for navigational purposes

Cherokee Sound

The Boilers

77° 05' W   AB-36   77° 00' W   76° 55' W

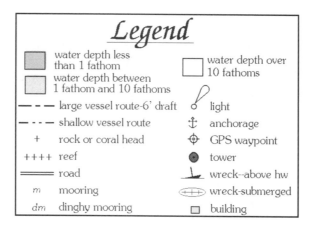

Legend

water depth less than 1 fathom

water depth between 1 fathom and 10 fathoms

water depth over 10 fathoms

– – –   large vessel route–6' draft

– · – ·   shallow vessel route

+   rock or coral head

++++   reef

road

m   mooring

dm   dinghy mooring

light

anchorage

GPS waypoint

tower

wreck--above hw

wreck-submerged

building

CROSSING THE GULF STREAM

DEALING WITH THE GULF STREAM (WHEN DO I CROSS?)

The Gulf Stream is a powerful ocean current that flows northward off the eastern shore of the United States between south Florida and The Bahamas. The Stream is comparable to a mighty river in the ocean moving a thousand times more water than the widest, longest, deepest rivers on Earth through the narrow bottleneck known as the Straits of Florida. At its narrowest point between Miami and Bimini, the Stream may be 45 miles wide and up to 2500' deep. Its waters are a beautiful deep indigo blue with a warm temperature that averages 76° even during the winter months.

Crossing the Gulf Stream provokes the most uneasiness and presents the greatest challenge, and danger, for anyone headed to The Bahamas. Not only do you have to worry about the seas created by opposing wind and current, bear in mind that if you break down, the Gulf Stream will move you northward away from your present position at 2-4 knots. However, for a well-equipped and crewed vessel, the inherent dangers in the crossing can be lessened immensely by doing only one simple thing-waiting for weather. I'm not going to tell you what type of vessel to take on your adventure and how to equip her. There are far too many naval architects and maritime experts who can do a far better job than I. Only you can testify to the seaworthiness of your vessel. Make sure you know her well and that she is sound and equipped with current charts and up to date safety devices. I have seen boats as small as 15' plywood sloops with no engines make the crossing. Whatever type of vessel you take, the most important thing to remember is to wait for the right weather window.

Since the Stream is a northward flowing current, an opposing wind (from any northerly direction-NW through NE) can cause some truly dangerous seas to build up. The Gulf Stream is no place to be in a frontal passage so unless you absolutely have to go (I can't imagine a single reason to make a skipper want to cross the Stream in a norther although some would probably thrive on the challenge), stay put and wait on the weather. Most veteran skippers will wait until the seas are down and the wind is somewhere between east and south at less than 15 knots. An east or southeast wind of 15 knots or more can build up quite a chop that will have to be bucked for the entire trip. Winds from south to west would be quite favorable for sailing vessels, but they are rare and can be the forerunners of a frontal passage during the months from October through May. When the wind seems right for you, and you have given the Stream enough time to settle down if it has been boisterous, it may be time to go. Personally I prefer to look out upon the water from a high vantage point before I leave. If I see what appears to be camel humps on the horizon I will postpone my departure for a while no matter what the wind is forecast to be. When you do get a weather window don't delay, take advantage of it and enjoy your cruise.

NAVIGATING THE GULF STREAM (HOW DO I CROSS?)

From Fort Pierce to Miami there are several jumping off spots for sailors heading to the Northern Bahamas. Some skippers prefer to leave from Angelfish Creek at Key Largo or even Marathon to make the most of the advantage that the Gulf Stream has to offer but they are usually bound for the Central Bahamas via Bimini or Gun Cay. Most boats that are headed to the Northern Bahamas choose to depart the States via Fort Pierce, St. Lucie Inlet, Jupiter Inlet, Lake Worth, Hillsboro Inlet, and Port Everglades. Although Fort Pierce is actually a bit north for a boat headed to West End, you'd be bucking the current all the way, most skippers that leave from Fort Pierce head for either Memory Rock or Walker's Cay.

The south Florida National Weather Service radio broadcasts on VHF weather ch. 1 and gives the latest Gulf Stream information 6 days a week. Mondays, Wednesdays, and Fridays from 4:00pm until 8:00pm and on Tuesdays, Thursdays, and Saturdays from 4:00am until 8:00am The broadcasts give the approximate position of the western edge of the Stream, its width, and the average northward flow in knots across the Stream. The Gulf Stream is usually slower in October and November and generally stronger in July and August with a mean difference of approximately .5 knots. The speed at the edges of the Stream may be as little as ½ knot or less while the speed at the axis, the "hump," may be as high as 4 knots or more. For the most part, strong northerly winds will slow the Stream while strong southerly winds will increase its speed. Normally though you can figure on an average speed of 2.5 knots across the Stream in a direction of 010°.

Crossing the Gulf Stream poses a nifty navigational problem in vectors that we all probably learned to solve in high school geometry. You remember high school geometry, don't you? Due to the northward flow of the Stream a certain amount of compensatory southerly heading must be employed. For example, steering the rhumb line course from Fort Lauderdale to Freeport in a sailboat making 5-6 knots will cause you to make landfall somewhere north of West End in normal conditions. By applying a certain amount of southerly heading to offset the strength of the Stream your vessel will travel the shortest, straightest path to Bimini.

The navigational problem is a classic one of finding the course to steer to make good an intended track given the set and drift of the current and your vessel's speed. For solving, you will need a plotting sheet or a current chart of the area, a pencil, a compass, and parallel rules. Let's try to work out a course from Lake Worth Inlet to West End, Grand Bahama. As in the diagram, plot point *A* as your position on the western edge of the Gulf Stream at Lake Worth Inlet on your plotting sheet or chart. Next, pencil in line *AB* of an indefinite length on the bearing that is your direct course to West End. Next plot vector *AC*, representing the Gulf Stream current, in the direction of the set of the Stream, approximately 010°, for a distance equivalent to the estimated drift, (be sure to listen to the NOAA weather broadcasts for the latest information, see above paragraph). Next take your compass with the center on *C* and swing an arc of radius equal to

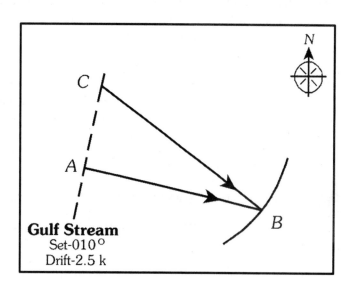

Gulf Stream
Set-010°
Drift-2.5 k

your vessel's speed, if you will be making 6 knots set it for 6 nautical miles. This will intersect line *AB* at point *B*. The line *CB* will be your course to steer allowing for the set and drift of the Gulf Stream. Use your parallel rules to measure the angle. The length of line *AB* in *nautical* miles, will be your speed of advance towards West End. In other words, you might be making 6 knots through the water but you may only be making 5.1 knots towards West End thanks to the Stream. Never forget that there are built in inaccuracies in figuring your course. Wind and wave conditions, your own ability to maintain a consistent speed, and the strength of the Stream itself all combine to give slight errors to even the best calculations but you should be "in the neighborhood" so to speak.

Even if you have a GPS aboard you must still solve the vector problem for your course. If you allow the GPS to steer to your waypoint and correct for the current you will be constantly changing course and covering more miles in a highly inefficient manner that is sometimes called a "dog curve." If you have ever seen a dog trying to swim across a body of water that is swept by a current you will understand how inefficient this type of course is. I actually witnessed this in Nassau Harbour as I followed a dog who was intent upon reaching *Club Med* on Paradise Island from the southern shore of Nassau Harbour. A dog will always keep his nose pointed to his destination even as the current pushes him downstream. As the dog I was following tried to head north towards *Club Med* the current pushed him west but he kept his nose pointed at *Club Med* even as he was getting pushed downstream. Soon he was swimming north/northeast, then northeast, and finally east towards his destination. If the pup had simply swam more northeast to begin with or moved upcurrent before crossing he would have had a far easier passage.

A final word on crossing the Gulf Stream. This narrow passage is very busy and getting busier every year. Keep a sharp lookout for other vessels and take the proper precautions to avoid collisions well ahead of time. If you don't know the "Rules of the Road," learn them.

COURSES FROM SOUTH FLORIDA ACROSS THE GULF STREAM

I will not endeavor to give the reader the proper courses to steer because all boats travel at different speeds through the water and make more or less leeway than other boats. However, I will give you the bearings and distances from different locations in south Florida to the Biminis and the reader may plot his or her own course using the aforementioned vector method. In other words, I will not do your homework for you as it won't hurt you to do it yourself, and besides, many skippers have forgotten how to plot a course across a current. So with that in mind (and I do hope that not everyone is mad at me!) the following table will give you approximate bearings and distances from south Florida to West End. All courses are magnetic, and corrections for the set and drift of the Gulf Stream must be applied to these bearings to arrive at your course to steer.

FROM	WEST END
St. Lucie Inlet	120° - 67 nm
Jupiter Inlet	110° - 60 nm
Lake Worth Inlet	99° - 56 nm
Hillsboro Inlet	70° - 65 nm
Port Everglades	65° - 69 nm

MAKING LANDFALL

As you leave south Florida in your wake you will find yourself alone on a big ocean. You will be traveling approximately 46-50 plus miles depending on your departure point and most of those miles (25-40) will be out of sight of land and any type of navigational aids. First timers will likely have feelings of apprehension. Don't panic! Even veteran skippers have those same feelings, it is quite natural when leaving port. You might be fortunate and find other cruisers going the same way and most don't mind the company. It usually increases the safety margin a little for all involved.

If you are bound for Memory Rock you will be heading for a small rock that is barely visible until you get within a few miles of it. This is no problem for GPS or LORAN but those who don't have a *boxed navigator* can still use other sources for directions. First, the high-rise buildings along the south Florida coast will stay within view for at least 10-15 miles from shore depending on their height and your own height of eye. Remember, if you have trouble or get lost you can always turn towards the west (that's where the sun sets) and sooner or later you will find Florida. Important: make sure your compass is correct and learn to trust it. Those skippers bound for Lucaya and West End will have an easier landfall. Lucaya sits along the southern shore of Grand Bahama well out of the path of the Gulf Stream while West End lies off the eastern edge of the Gulf Stream at the northwest tip of Grand Bahama. If you can sight Grand Bahama you can find both locations.

The prudent skipper uses as many navigational sources as he can muster. For confirmation of your heading keep your eyes on what is going on around you. Other boats passing you may also be headed to your destination. I once used a cruise ship's course to help me to find Bimini when my LORAN went out. I was approaching Bimini from Ft. Lauderdale and I surmised that since the ship was heading generally northeast to east that he was either going to Freeport or around Great Isaac to the Berrys. I steered just south of his course and soon found Bimini.

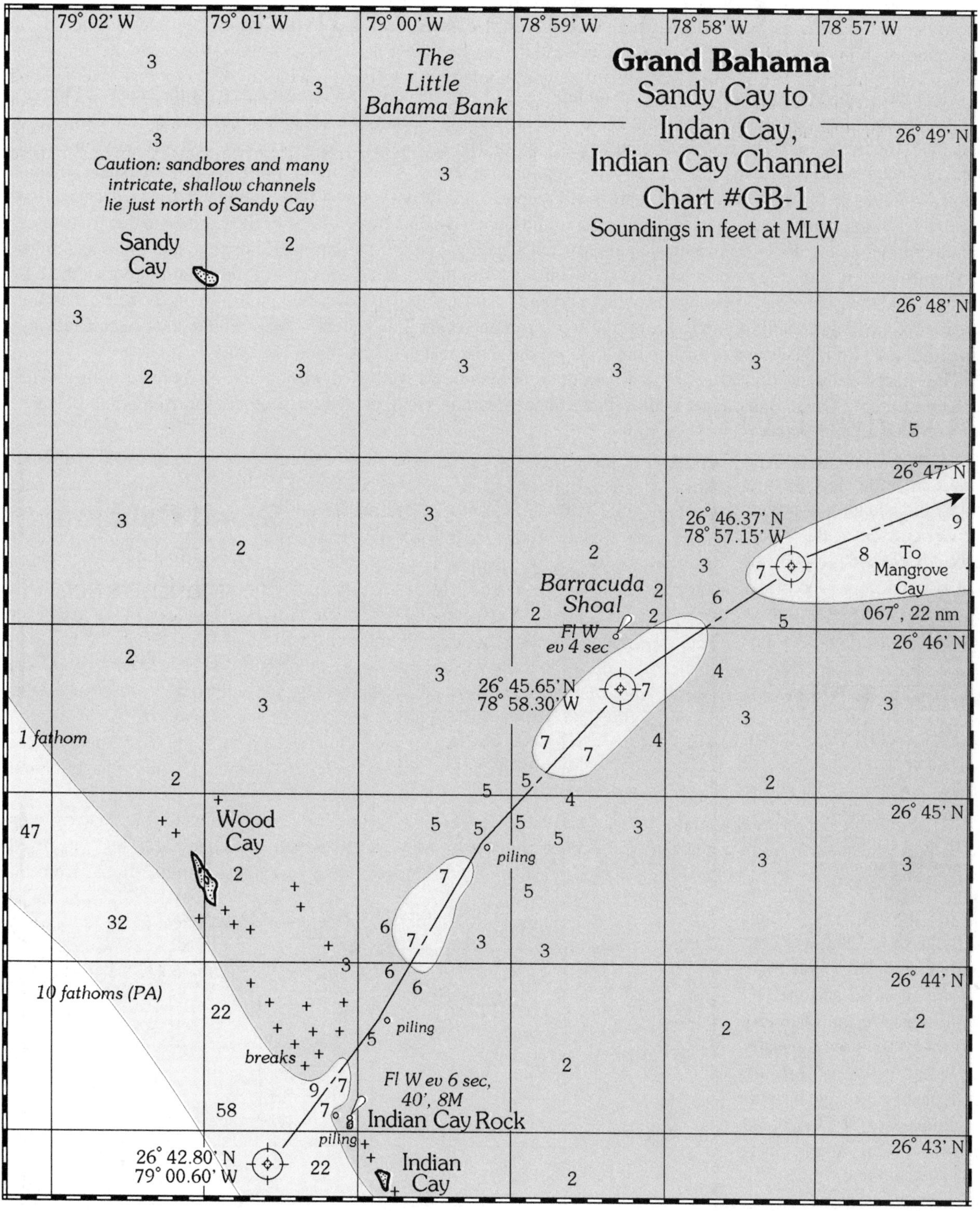

79° 02' W   79° 01' W   79° 00' W   78° 59' W   78° 58' W   78° 57' W

3

3

*The
Little
Bahama Bank*

Grand Bahama
Sandy Cay to
Indan Cay,
Indian Cay Channel
Chart #GB-1
Soundings in feet at MLW

26° 49' N

3

*Caution: sandbores and many
intricate, shallow channels
lie just north of Sandy Cay*

3

Sandy
Cay

2

26° 48' N

3

2

3

3

3

3

5

3

3

26° 47' N

2

26° 46.37' N
78° 57.15' W

9

3

3

7

8   To
Mangrove
Cay

2

*Barracuda
Shoal*

2

6

067°, 22 nm

2

2

5

26° 46' N

*Fl W
ev 4 sec*

2

3

26° 45.65' N
78° 58.30' W

7

4

1 fathom

3

7

3

5

5

5

4

2

26° 45' N

47

2

Wood
Cay

5

5

5

3

3

3

piling

2

7

5

32

6

7

3

3

10 fathoms (PA)

3

6

6

22

piling

2

2

breaks

5

58

9   7

*Fl W ev 6 sec,
40', 8M*

7

Indian Cay Rock

2

26° 42.80' N
79° 00.60' W

22

piling

26° 43' N

Indian
Cay

2

GRAND BAHAMA

The fourth largest island in the Bahamian archipelago, Grand Bahama, lies just 55 miles off the coast of Florida. The island itself has been settled for centuries; several remnants of Lucayan inhabitation have been found on Grand Bahama. Today the island boasts the second largest city in The Bahamas, Freeport/Lucaya, and it is only on Grand Bahama that you will find such a wide variety of Bahamian lifestyles. The census of 1990 reported the island's population at 40,898. In the more cosmopolitan areas of Freeport and Lucaya you will find excellent marinas, casinos, first rate hotels, championship golf courses (I've heard Grand Bahama called the Scotland of the Caribbean due to its three outstanding 18-hole golf courses), tennis courts (over 50), national parks, international shopping, and miles and miles of beautiful beaches and the associated water sports that go with them. But the Freeport/Lucaya area is not all there is to Grand Bahama. Once past the confines of Freeport and Lucaya, you'll discover Bahamians living as their out-island cousins do. Fishing, conching, and living off the sea. From the smuggling history of West End to the Conch Cracking Contest of East End, this island is much more than just the show that is Freeport and Lucaya.

The shores of Grand Bahama offer mariners good protection as well as shoreside and offshore activities. The northern shores of Grand Bahama are shallow and a bonefisherman's delight. Off the southern shore of Grand Bahama lies a wonderful reef for snorkeling or SCUBA enthusiasts. West End, at the northwestern end of the island, is routinely used by cruisers as the "door" to the Abacos and is usually the first stop on an Abaco cruise so we'll begin our tour of Grand Bahama there.

WEST END

West End Point has undergone some major changes over the last few years and if you're not aware of them you'll have a bit of a time figuring out where to go, especially if you're used to entering the marina the old way. Chart #GB-1A shows the new configuration of West End Point and the entrance into the *Old Bimini Bay Marina* (formerly *Jack Tar Marina* and usually just called *West End Marina*). A couple of years ago, the parent company of *OBB* purchased the marina and other properties. They are in the midst of a vast renovation project that will include a hotel, condos, restaurants, and several marina modifications.

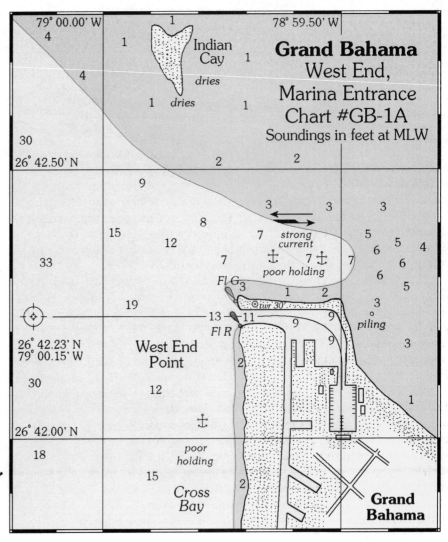

Photo by Nicolas Popov.

West End Marina, Grand Bahamas (before renovation).

If you have been here in days past, you will now notice that the new owners have sealed off the old entrance so you will now use what used to be called the "commercial" entrance. The entrance is well marked and deep and much easier to enter than the older entrance. Once inside you can go right past the fuel dock and take a slip on the western side of the marina. The entire area is under a lot of construction so be sure to call them first on VHF ch.16 for instructions.

A GPS waypoint at 26° 42.23' N, 79° 00.15' W, will place you approximately one-half mile west of the entrance channel leading into the marina. From this position head straight in between the well-marked jetties and follow the channel around toward the fuel dock and slips. You can clear *Customs* and *Immigration* here but be forewarned, the officers here have a bad reputation amongst some cruisers.

You can anchor temporarily in settled weather in Cross Bay but a wind shift could put you on the beach as it has done many other boats in the past. The seabed in Cross Bay has a lot of small rocks and coral heads scattered about and is notoriously poor holding though there are sand spots that will grab well. A better anchorage, though quite current ridden and almost as poor as far as holding goes, lies north and northeast of the northern jetty lining the entrance to the marina. You can tuck in as far as your draft allows but be prepared to ride to the current and not necessarily the wind. If a frontal passage threatens, by all means, get a slip in the marina! If you'd like a ride into Freeport, there is a daily shuttle bus to Freeport from the marina that leaves at 9:00am and returns at 3:30pm, the cost is $5.

If you vessel draws less than 3½', you can, with the help of the tide, work your way around the eastern shore of West End Point towards the settlement of West End. From the anchorage north of *OBB*, work your way around the north side of the marked piling and follow the poorly defined and even poorer marked *Goodwill Channel* (some of the local fishermen tell me that the channel will be marked soon, but if it's like everything else in the islands it will take it's own sweet time to come about). When you take the piling to starboard, basically you'll be paralleling the shore through here for a little over two miles until you come to the *Harbour Hotel Marina and Restaurant*. Because of the depth of the entrance channel, the marina is primarily used by local fishing boats. The marina has a laundromat on premises (there's also one in town). The marina is a *Texaco Star Port*, and the *Harbour Hotel* is one of the best eating spots in West End (breakfast, lunch, and dinner) with a free glass of wine with each dinner.

In West End itself you can find groceries at *Angler's*, *J&M Grocery*, *Neely's*, and at the *Seaside Bakery*. For dining a must stop is *Yvonne's Café* for true Bahamian fare, or you can visit *Ralph's Restaurant and Bar*, *The Star Restaurant and Pub*, or *Bayside Dairy and Snacks*. Despite West End's history of liquor smuggling, today the only liquor stores are *Butler and Sands* and the *T&T Liquor Store*. There is a government clinic downtown and a *Batelco* office next to the Police station. If you need propane you can make arrangements through *Old Bimini Bay Marina* to have your tanks taken to Freeport and filled. If you need a car rental or taxi, call *Seaside Bakery*.

West End has a colorful and rich history as a base for smugglers during the rum running years of Prohibition. During the years from 1920-1934, huge tin warehouses lined the shoreline and housed nothing but liquor. Bootleggers would stop here, either by boat or plane, load their wares, and then set off across the Gulf Stream to America and eager, waiting hands full of money. But it was not an easy life, there were many shootouts with the U. S. Coast Guard and many bootleggers lost their lives. For those that survived, the rewards were rich indeed. West End was a boomtown with all the trappings. Bars, money strewn about carelessly, easy party girls from Nassau, and when it was all over, the Bay Street Boys took their profits back to Nassau and left West End little more than a ghost town.

After the Prohibition years, West End's history is a tale of feast and famine periods. A huge crawfish canning factory built during WWII gave a boost to the local economy until the owner was suspected of collaborating with the Nazis. Then in the late 1940's, a British developer attempted to make West End a resort phenomenon, but that plan failed when the pound was devalued and the entire operation went bankrupt. In 1958, the *Jack Tar Village Resort* opened and was a success for two decades, but it too folded in the late 1980's. Today Old Bahama Bay is trying again to bring a cash flow into the West End area and so far they are doing that just fine. Their plans are coming together on time and the future looks bright for West End, that's why everybody's walking around with sunglasses on.

For those cruisers bound for Abaco via Indian Cay Channel or by passing north of Sandy Cay, we will study those routes in the section entitled *The Northern Abacos; Routes from West End, Grand Bahama*.

There are several small towns between West End and Freeport and since these are primarily visited by road, we will discuss them later in the *Grand Bahama by Car* section.

Photo by Nicolas Popov.

Port Lucaya Marina.

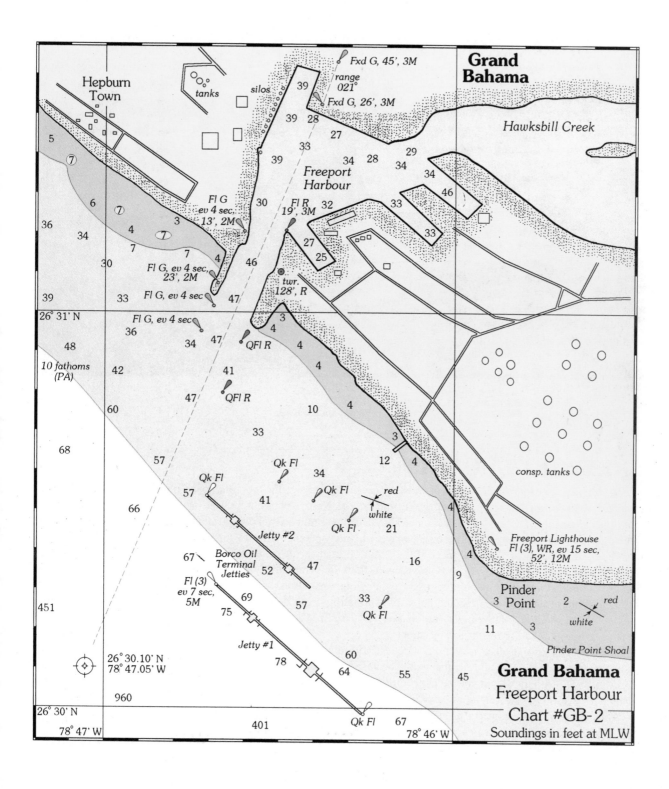

Grand
Bahama

Hepburn
Town

tanks

silos

Fxd G, 45', 3M
range
021°
Fxd G, 26', 3M

Hawksbill Creek

39

39   28

27

33

34   28   29

34

34

Freeport
Harbour

46

Fl G
ev 4 sec,
13', 2M

30

Fl R
19', 3M

32

33

33

5

7

6   7

36   34   4   7

30   7   4

Fl G, ev 4 sec,
23', 2M

39   33   Fl G, ev 4 sec

27

25

46

47

twr.
128', R

26° 31' N

Fl G, ev 4 sec

36

34   47

QFl R

3

4

4

4

48

10 fathoms
(PA)

42

41

4

QFl R

47

60

33

10

4

3

68

57

QFl R

12   4

Qk Fl

34

Qk Fl

red

white

consp. tanks

66

Qk Fl

57

57

41

Qk Fl   21

4

67

Borco Oil
Terminal
Jetties

Jetty #2

52   47

16

Freeport Lighthouse
Fl (3), WR, ev 15 sec,
52', 12M

4

9

451

Fl (3)
ev 7 sec,
5M

69

75

57

33

Qk Fl

Pinder
3   Point   2   red

white

11   3

Jetty #1

78   60

64   55

45

Pinder Point Shoal

26° 30.10' N
78° 47.05' W

Grand Bahama
Freeport Harbour
Chart #GB-2

960

26° 30' N

78° 47' W   401   Qk Fl   67   78° 46' W

Soundings in feet at MLW

Photo by Nicolas Popov.

Port Lucaya Marina fuel dock.

FREEPORT/LUCAYA

We will start our tour of the southern shore of Grand Bahama at Freeport Harbour Freeport is the second most popular tourist destination in The Bahamas, second only to Nassau but with a faster pace and a more cosmopolitan atmosphere than the old-world sophistication of The Bahamas' capital city. Freeport and Lucaya, although separate, are often referred to as one entity, as in Freeport/Lucaya, and many people will tell you that they visited Freeport when it is most likely that they actually spent most of their time in Lucaya. It's a difficult situation and I often have trouble separating the two. Both were at one time Freeport, then the community subsequently split with Lucaya becoming primarily tourism oriented. Freeport has been called by other names as well over the years; *Magic City*, for the way it was carved out of the bush in 1955 and grew to be a metropolis in one decade. Freeport has also been labeled the *Singapore of the Atlantic* for its vibrant, free-market, industrialized economy. And finally, it has also been known as the *Queen of Clean*, known for its impeccable streets.

Freeport owes its existence to Wallace Groves; you might remember him from Little Whale Cay in the Berry Islands. Groves had a dream of a city that would be an industrial and commercial giant. That dream became reality on August 4, 1955, with the signing of the *Hawksbill Creek Agreement*. That agreement gave the newly formed *Grand Bahama Port Authority* full autonomy over a large region of what was formerly Crown land with streets and bridges becoming *Port Authority* property. Under the agreement there can be no real estate or personal property taxes at least until 2015, in addition to the absence of income, sales, capital gains and death duties that the entire country enjoys. Moreover, the Port Authority, which governs the zone, can issue licenses that allow the license holder to import one car and the materials and furnishings for one house, duty-free.

Many tend to joke that the date of this agreement made Freeport a Leo, the king of the beasts. The city planners soon realized that all work and no play might not be as beneficial to their coffers as a fat slice of the tourism pie would be.

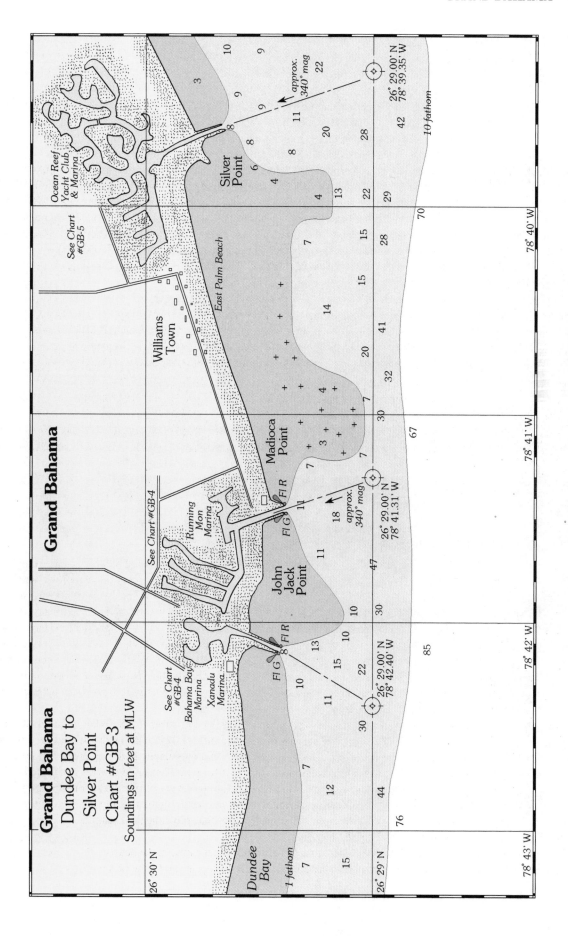

Grand Bahama

Grand Bahama
Dundee Bay to
Silver Point
Chart #GB-3
Soundings in feet at MLW

With that in mind, they struck a deal for a pair of first-class casinos and Lucaya was born. Today Freeport/Lucaya is a virtual fantasy vacationland that was little more than bush less than a half-century ago.

Today Freeport is a significant economic force in The Bahamas. Freeport Harbour has a unique and valuable position as it straddles the major trade routes between the Eastern and Gulf coasts of the United States, as well as Mexico, Panama, the Caribbean, South America and the trade lanes to Europe, the Middle East, Asia, and Australia. A new multi-million dollar harbor project may make Freeport one of the world's foremost transshipment terminals. *Hutchison Port Holdings*, a subsidiary of *Hutchison Whampoa* of Hong Kong and the worlds largest port operator, purchased 50% of the *Freeport Harbour Company* and is the midst of a $130+ million construction project. When completed, the port will have the ability to handle the largest container ships afloat and will make Freeport the transshipment hub of the Western Hemisphere. *HPH* plans to combine 2,500 acres of airport land, nearby industrial acreage, 1,630 acres of harbour (including 56 acres of container port), into a 5,000-acre complex to include a comprehensive air/sea business park. This will include new passenger terminals/facilities at the airport and secure storage areas at the container port. In addition, *HPH* plans a $150 million development of 1,600 four-star resort rooms in a huge complex comprising 50 acres of hotels (connected by walkways and plazas), waterfalls, fountains, landscaping, and exquisite beachfront. This project is scheduled for completion in 2001. The new *Plaza Hotel Resort* boasts convention facilities for 2,000 guests and a new casino.

As you can see, Freeport Harbour, Chart #GB-2, is a busy commercial port (and it will just get busier) with no yacht facilities save *Bradford Yacht and Ship* a short distance up Hawksbill Creek. A GPS waypoint at 26° 30.10' N, 78° 47.05' W, will place you approximately one nautical mile southwest of the entrance channel to Freeport Harbour. From this position take up a course of approximately 021° magnetic and you will soon see the lighted (G) range inside the harbor. You can clear *Customs* and *Immigration* at Freeport Harbour, but you must call *Harbour Control* first on VHF ch.16 for berthing directions.

Photo by Nicolas Popov.

The International Bazaar is one of the most popular stops in Lucaya.

Probably the only reason a recreational yacht would have for entering Freeport Harbour would be to make it's way to *Bradford Yacht and Ship*. If you work your way up dredged Hawksbill Creek you will quickly come to *Bradford Yacht and Ship*, the only full service yard on Grand Bahama. *Bradford* services a variety of different sized vessels and has a 150-ton travel lift, a prop shop, a full machine shop as well as fiberglass, carpentry, fiberglass, welding/fabricating, and paint shops with specialists in each one. You can reach *Bradford Yacht and Ship* by VHF on ch. 16, or by phone at 242-352-7711 or by fax at 242-352-7695.

There are several marinas where boaters can stay in the Freeport/Lucaya area and we will discuss them as we would approach them, from west to east.

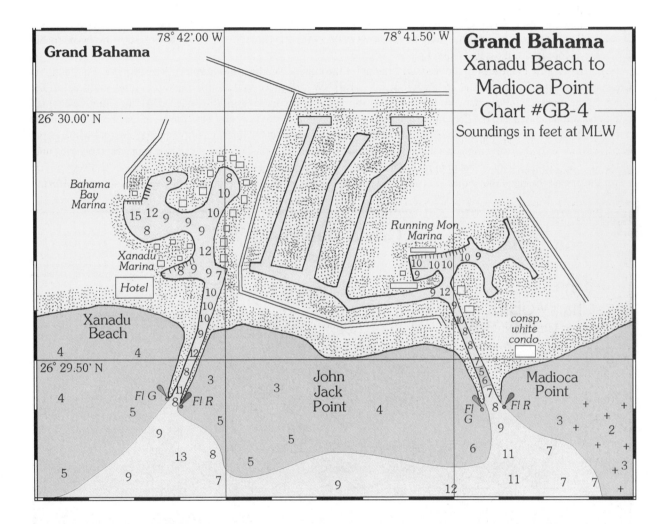

XANADU CHANNEL TO SILVER COVE

Along the southern shore of Grand Bahama is a long and shallow barrier reef. Though there are quite a few shallow spots between Xanadu Channel and Bell Channel (mostly close in to shore), the really shallow areas begin west of Bell Channel so use extreme caution and keep a good lookout. It would be prudent to stay one mile off along this shoreline.

Beginning just a few miles east of Freeport Harbour are several channels leading to marinas and private developments. The first of these is Xanadu Channel named after the famed *Xanadu Hotel*. As shown on Chart #GB-3, a GPS waypoint at 26° 29.00' N, 78° 42.40' W will place you approximately ½ mile southwest of the entrance to the channel between two marked jetties. The flashing red and green lights may not work, so bear that in mind if attempting to enter at night. From this position head towards the channel mouth between the jetties trying to remain parallel to the lie of the channel. If you stray a bit don't fret, it's fairly deep on either side of the channel with no hazards. Once inside the channel continue between the jetties as shown on Chart #GB-4 and the marina and hotel will open up to your port side very soon.

Xanadu Marina boasts 77 slips and can accommodate vessels up to 100' in length with 8' drafts. They offer fuel, ice, water, showers, cable TV, full electric and telephone hookups, a marine store and tackle shop (*Paradise Marine Supplies*), a pharmacy, and a restaurant. Room service is available to boats and a liquor store is nearby. The marina will hold your mail for you; address it to *Xanadu Marina*, PO Box F-42438, Freeport, Grand Bahama, Bahamas. The dive shop, *Xanadu Undersea Adventures,* has been taking divers to the most impressive and beautiful reefs of Grand Bahama for the past 6 years. Their professional and multi-lingual staff has more than 20 years of experience guiding and teaching all levels of divers.

If you continue past *Xanadu Marina*, and take a turn to port at the next cove, you will come to the small but friendly, *Bahama Bay Marina*. This marina offers about twenty slips with a least depth of 7' and has full electric hookups but little else except friendliness and a quiet place to tie up.

Less than a mile to the east of the Xanadu Channel is the channel leading into *Running Mon Marina*. As shown on Chart #GB-3, a GPS waypoint at 26° 29.00' N, 78° 41.31' W will place you approximately ½ mile southeast of the jetties at the entrance to the channel. From this position take up a course of approximately 340° to enter the channel mouth between the two jetties. The course here is not as important as staying parallel to the lie of the channel inside the jetties as shown on the blowup on Chart #GB-4. After you enter the channel you'll pass over a shallow spot with a depth of 5' at MLW so if you draw more, plan on using the tide to enter. The flashing red and green lights on the jetties may or may not be working so bear that in mind if you are attempting to enter at night. Once inside and past the shallow spot, forge ahead past the canal that works off to the west and the marina will open up in front of you. *Running Mon Marina*

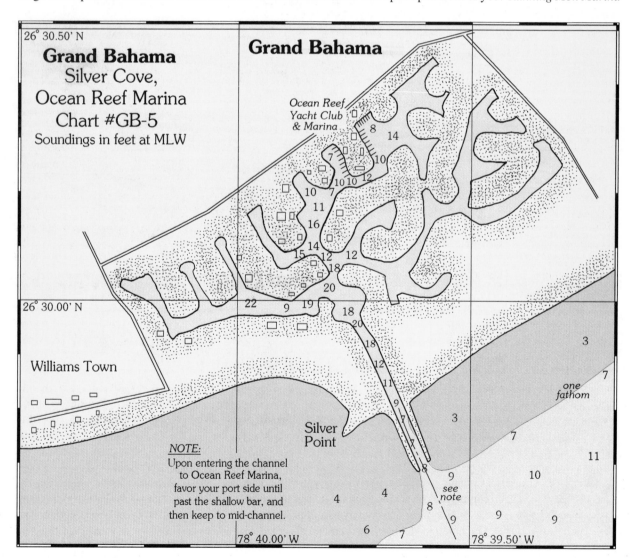

and Resort offers 60 slips with a dockside depth of nearly 9'. The also have fuel, water, ice, showers, a 40 ton Tami-lift, a tackle shop with bait, a laundry, cable TV, and a very nice hotel next door.

SILVER COVE

Silver Cove is the name of the man-made canal network that lies approximately 2 miles east of Xanadu Channel and approximately 1½ miles west of Bell Channel. Silver Cove is home to the *Ocean Reef Yacht Club and Marina* as well as a large private development.

A GPS waypoint at 26° 29.00' N, 78° 39.35' W will place you approximately ¾ nautical miles southeast of Silver Point and the jetties as shown on Chart #GB-3. Steer approximately 340° to enter the channel. The course here is not as important as staying parallel to the lie of the channel inside the jetties as shown on the blowup on Chart #GB-5. The shallower water lies to the west of the channel and to a minor degree just south and east of the eastern jetty tip as shown on the chart. As you enter the jetties keep to your port side a bit, as there is a small bar along the eastern jetty just inside the channel. You will have 7' at MLW around this bar and once past the end of the jetties the canal becomes very deep, 18'-20' in most places. To find the *Ocean Reef Yacht Club and Marina* keep in the center channel as it winds around past two curves. The marina and office will open up on your left, you can't miss it. There's even a floating dinghy dock for your convenience. If you are having any problems finding your way inside or to the marina, contact *Ocean Reef Marina* on VHF ch. 16. The *Ocean Reef Yacht Club* has 52 slips and can accommodate vessels to 80' with a 6' draft though some slips are a bit deeper. They have the usual electricity, water and ice, as well as a bait and tackle shop.

BELL CHANNEL

Bell Channel and Bell Channel Bay is by far the most popular stop on Grand Bahama for boaters of all types. Two excellent marinas with full amenities, excellent shopping, and even anchoring room can be found right here.

A GPS waypoint at 26° 29.95' N, 78° 37.30' W will place you approximately ¾ mile southeast of the jetties and the entrance to Bell Channel and just a bit northeast of the Bell Channel Sea Buoy (Fl W ev 2 sec). As shown on Chart #GB-6, if approaching from offshore keep a good lookout for the unmarked buoys to the west of this waypoint, they are for cruise ship use and constitute a hazard to the small boater. At night a flashing amber light marks their field but the individual buoys (7) are not lit. From this waypoint take up a course of approximately 340° towards the entrance between two flashing red and green markers and the lit jetties. Try not to stray to the east here as there is a shallow reef in that direction as shown on the chart. Watch out for small boat traffic and the ever-present tourist parasailing above. If you need a pilot, *Lucayan Marina Village* offers one at no charge, call them on VHF ch. 16.

Once inside Bell Channel Bay (as shown on Chart #GB-7), if you turn to port you will find the spacious and upscale *Port Lucaya Marina*, a first class marina and a Port of Entry. Here Captain Jack Chester and his staff pamper the visiting boater as well as those yachts that are left here on a long-term basis. This is a great spot to leave your boat if you need to fly back home for whatever reason. Capt. Chester and his crew will perform weekly or daily bilge checks, wash-downs, engine starting, as well as security patrols. The marina boasts 160 slips, twenty of which can handle boats of over 100' in length. The docks have first rate power, phone, and satellite TV hookups while the fuel dock sells gas and diesel, triple filtered. A pump-out facility is available. The marina offers courtesy transportation to the local grocery store and airport. Their concierge service can help you find a reliable doctor or mechanic, and even assist you in arranging air transportation. The newest amenity at Port Lucaya is their *Yacht Club* with its comfortable outdoor dining terrace. Visiting yachtsmen are given a complimentary membership in the *Yacht Club* while staying at the marina which allows them to dine on excellent cooked to order seafood dishes and sample their extensive wine list and assorted whiskies at the *Yacht Club* bar. The *Yacht Club* is open from 5:00pm to 1:00am nightly and you might wish to catch a movie at their *Mini-Cinema* or simply enjoy the *Piano Bar*. The marina itself sits across the street from a casino and fronts the *Port Lucayan Marketplace* where you can browse some 85-odd shops including restaurants, a straw market, water-sports rental facilities, a dive shop, or stay at the *Port Lucayan Resort Hotel*. If all this shopping and nightlife tires you, just walk across the street and enjoy the beach. Ask at the marina office for their evening and weekend cultural activities for children as well as adults. *Port Lucaya Marina* will hold your mail for your arrival; please address it to you, on your boat, c/o *Port Lucaya Marina*, PO Box F-43233, Freeport, Grand Bahama, Bahamas.

If, upon entering Bell Channel, you keep to starboard, you will immediately come to another first class marina, the *Lucayan Marina Village* complex, a private residential community with a private marina that offers the best in transient dockage and service. *Lucayan Marina Village*, newly rebuilt in 1995, is an official Port of Entry and can accommodate vessels up to 150'. Here Dockmaster Thomas Lockhart and his crew will pamper you in every way and even find you

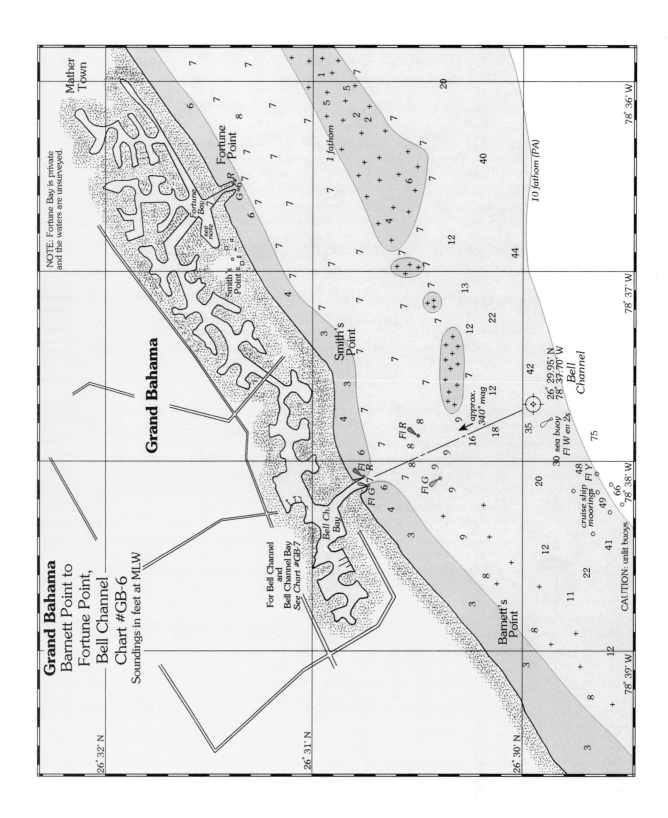

Grand Bahama
Barnett Point to
Fortune Point,
Bell Channel
Chart #GB-6
Soundings in feet at MLW

Grand Bahama

Mather Town

NOTE: Fortune Bay is private
and the waters are unsurveyed.

Fortune
Point

G°6 3/R

Fortune
Bay

see
note

Smith's
Point

Smith's
Point

For Bell Channel
and
Bell Channel Bay
See Chart #GB-7

Bell Ch.
Bay

Fl G
Fl R

Fl G

Fl R

Fl G

Barnett's
Point

1 fathom

10 fathom (PA)

26° 29.95' N
78° 37.70' W

Bell
Channel

approx.
340° mag

30 sea buoy
Fl W ev 2s

cruise ship
moorings   Fl Y

CAUTION: unlit buoys

26° 32' N

26° 31' N

26° 30' N

78° 39' W

78° 38' W

78° 37' W

78° 36' W

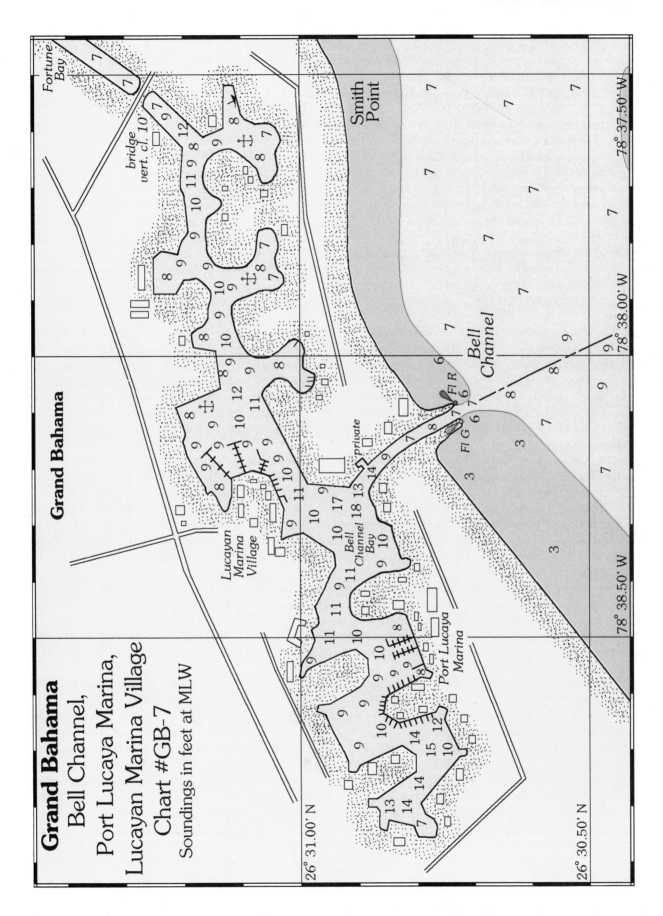

Grand Bahama
Bell Channel,
Port Lucaya Marina,
Lucayan Marina Village
Chart #GB-7
Soundings in feet at MLW

Grand Bahama

Fortune Bay

bridge vert. cl. 10'

Lucayan Marina Village

Bell Channel Bay

Lucayan Marina Village

private

Smith Point

Bell Channel

Fl R

Fl G

Port Lucaya Marina

26° 31.00' N

26° 30.50' N

78° 37.50' W

78° 38.00' W

78° 38.50' W

a mechanic or a fishing guide if you so desire and they offer a regular ferry over to the shops of Port Lucaya. The docks have first rate power, phone, and satellite TV hookups, and the fuel dock will fill you up with the highest quality diesel or gasoline. The marina's *Pelican Bay Hotel* offers first-class accommodations with a complimentary water taxi service. Here you'll find the *Ferry House Restaurant* specializing in Danish food complete with it's own bakery. If something a little more casual is to your liking, try the *Pool Bar* (yep, right by the pool!) for breakfast, lunch, or dinner and check out their afternoon munchie specials. The marina will also hold your mail for your arrival; address it to you, aboard your vessel, c/o *Lucayan Marina Village*, PO Box F-42654, Freeport, Grand Bahama, Bahamas.

If you wish to anchor here, work your way into some of the coves to the east of the marinas and pick a spot. Now that you're all secure in your berth or at anchor, let's see what's available to see and do in Lucaya. There is so much to experience in the Freeport/Lucaya area that I will only touch upon a few of the more popular sites, for a complete listing of activities, pick up any of the free booklets or small newspapers at any marina, hotel, or store in the area.

Probably the number one stop in Lucaya is the *International Bazaar* and probably the most remembered landmark is the huge oriental arch at its entrance. The *International Bazaar* is one of the oldest shopping areas in Freeport, and it truly lives up to its name. The 10 acre complex has over 80 stores that are built in the architectural style of the countries they represent. Upon entering the *Bazaar* you will notice that it has been divided into sections each representing different parts of the world such as the Mideast section, French section, Oriental section, Scandinavian and the South American section. In each of the international sections you will find shopping and dining from that region of the world.

Another one of the most popular stops is the *Garden of the Groves*, regarded as one of the most beautiful retreats in the Caribbean, opened in 1973. It is named for the one-time owners, Mr. and Mrs. Wallace Groves. In 1996, the *Garden* was taken over by Dr. Bern Levine, owner of Miami's *Parrot Jungle*. Levine implemented a five-year plan that is transforming the *Garden of the Groves* into a full-theme animal park with an amphitheater for special events, a playground for kids, and a picnic area. Levine has already added a children's petting zoo with colorful macaws and cockatoos, a potbellied pig, and pygmy goats. The retreat also has several footpaths that wind their way past cascading waterfalls, several duck-ponds, the aptly named Fern Gully, and majestic statues all set amid ornamental and native Bahamian flora.

The 100 acre *Rand Nature Center* lies just outside downtown Freeport, and is a marvelous stop for nature-minded folks. The *Rand Nature Center* is a protected Park under the jurisdiction of the Bahamas National Trust and is home to West Indian flamingos, the same kind that inhabit much wilder Inagua in the southern Bahamas. Here you can walk a beautiful 2000' long nature trail past the Flamingo Pond and its lush tropical setting complete with lily pads, reeds, wild native birds, and local (130 types including 20 types of wild orchids) and imported flora. There is also a replica of an ancient Lucayan village and a museum that documents Grand Bahama's history. The guided tours are a must. You'll learn a ton of information about the local flora and fauna, such as how certain plants are used in bush medicine and the strange courting rituals of the wild birds you'll see.

The Hydroflora Gardens are a unique showcase of flora and fauna with the centerpiece being the *Timothy Gibson Musical Cave*. The cave is actually a sunken garden named after the author of the Bahamian national anthem and even has a musical backdrop courtesy of hidden speakers. In the center of the cave is a fish pond with a huge turtle shell. A sign informs the reader that the former inhabitant of the shell traveled some 4,000 miles before being found in the Bahamas at Sandy Cay in 1974. The previous owner had been originally tagged in the Galapagos in 1971, and is thought to have traveled through the Panama Canal.

Those who love the sea will probably also want to check out *UNEXSO*, the *Underwater Explorer Society*, at Port Lucaya. *UNEXSO* has been described by *Skin Diver* magazine as the most sophisticated and best equipped diving facility in The Bahamas. Here is the opportunity for a once in a lifetime experience of swimming with dolphins. The *UNEXSO Dolphin Experience* is a place where visitors can swim with wild dolphins who are free to come and go as they please. The *Experience* was designed to study how dolphins and humans interact. Due to its immense popularity, it is necessary to make reservations at least several weeks ahead of time.

Many folks come to Grand Bahama for the casino action. As of this writing Grand Bahama has only one casino, the elegant *Bahamas Princess Casino*. Here you'll find non-stop action including slots, roulette, craps, baccarat, blackjack, spacious lounges, and cabaret shows. The *Lucayan Beach Resort* is scheduled to premier early in 2000 with its renovated hotel and casino.

As I mentioned before, Grand Bahama has been noted for its golf courses. Two fine courses await you on the grounds of the Bahamas Princess: Dick Wilson's "Emerald" and Joe Lee's "Ruby" championship courses will excite you. There's also the demanding *Lucaya Golf & Country Club* championship course nearby and the *Fortune Hills Golf*

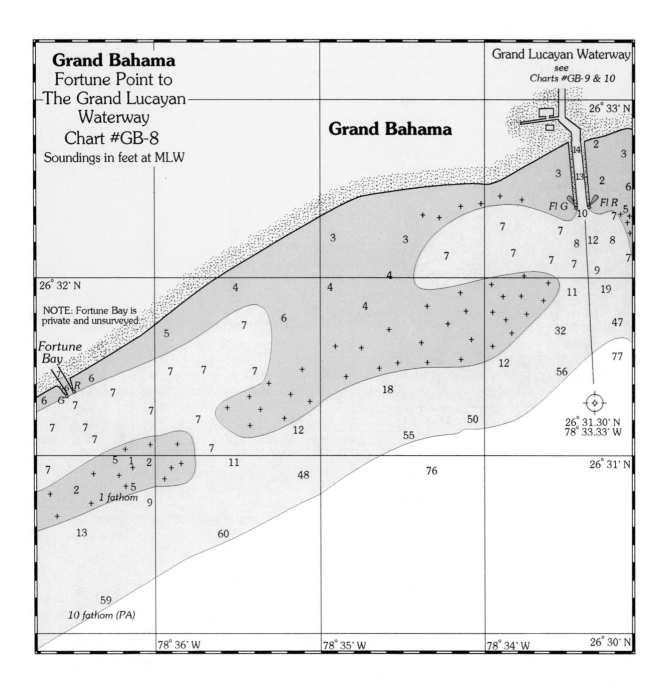

Grand Bahama
Fortune Point to
The Grand Lucayan
Waterway
Chart #GB-8
Soundings in feet at MLW

Grand Bahama

Grand Lucayan Waterway
see
Charts #GB-9 & 10

26° 33' N

NOTE: Fortune Bay is
private and unsurveyed.

Fortune Bay

1 fathom

10 fathom (PA)

26° 32' N

26° 31.30' N
78° 33.33' W

26° 31' N

26° 30' N

78° 36' W   78° 35' W   78° 34' W

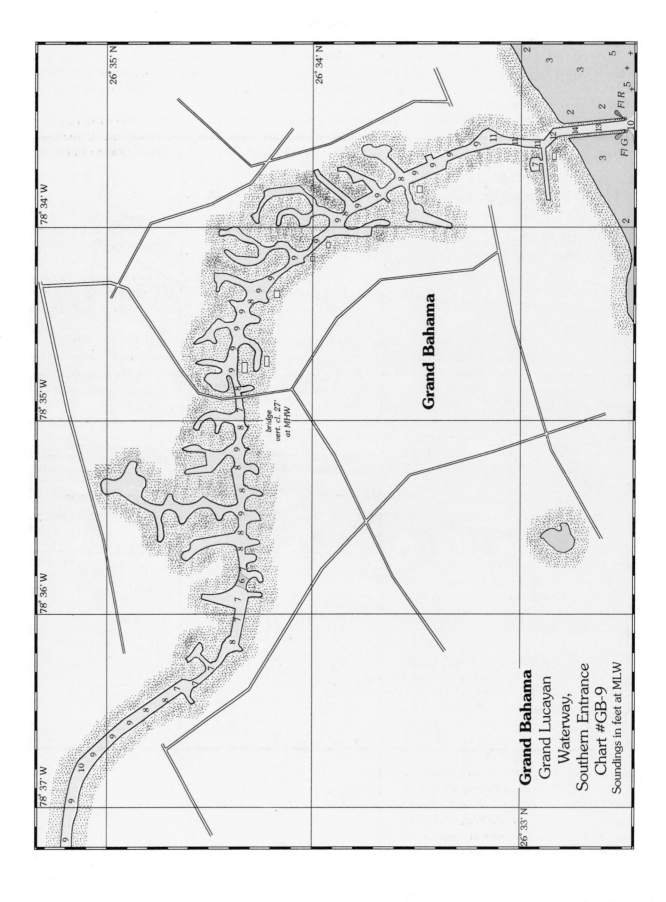

Grand Bahama

Grand Bahama
Grand Lucayan
Waterway,
Southern Entrance
Chart #GB-9
Soundings in feet at MLW

bridge
vert. cl. 27'
at MHW

& *Country Club.* When the *Lucayan Beach Resort* reopens, the golf course that was formerly known as the *Bahama Reef* will reopen with it. The course has been redesigned by Arnold Palmer.

The world's first semi-submersible is now available in Freeport – "a submarine experience at a fraction of the price" is how it's advertised. This unique craft allows you to relax in an air-conditioned viewing area suspended beneath the vessel, then submerge 5' below the surface where you can stay dry and gaze at colorful coral reefs teaming with marine life that a diver hand feeds.

If you need groceries, you'll find them at *Winn Dixie*, *Food World*, *Grand Union* and at the *World Food Market*. For hardware try *Lucayan Hardware* next to *Winn Dixie* or *World of Products* on the Queen's Highway. If you need propane, consult with your dockmaster, or take your tank to *Freeport Oil* on the Queen's Highway near the harbour.

THE GRAND LUCAYAN WATERWAY

Just to the east of Bell Channel lies the entrance to the Fortune Cove private canal complex. There are no facilities here, only homes and private docks. The entrance is gained by paralleling the shore inside the reef. From Bell Channel simply parallel the shore outside of the one fathom line until you can line up the entrance to Fortune Bay. You will have 7' through here at MLW but keep a sharp eye out.

A little less than three miles east of Fortune Cove lies the Grand Lucayan Waterway, a manmade canal that effectively splits Grand Bahama in two and offers some of the best residential opportunities on the island; you will see some of the finest homes on Grand Bahama lining these banks. For the most part, the entire system is concrete walled with many small coves leading off the main canal.

If you need shelter the Grand Lucayan Waterway offers excellent protection from seas for vessels with drafts of over 7', but of course, if you draw that much you can only enter the waterway from the south. As shown on Chart #GB-8, a GPS waypoint at 26° 31.30' N, 78° 33.33' W will place you approximately one mile south of the entrance to the Waterway between two lit jetties. From this waypoint head north and enter the between the jetties and continue up the canal in good water.

If you are seeking shelter a nice protected cove lies just north of the first canal that leads off to the west after entering the waterway from the south (as shown on Chart #GB-9). As with most of the canals in this area, the bottom is dredged and holding can range from poor to good so use extreme caution when setting your anchor if you expect a blow. Some of the canals offer excellent protection in narrow, protected dead-ends. You'll have to explore with your dinghy first and probably want to secure yourself with some lines ashore. Never tie up to someone's private dock without permission please.

A few miles up the Grand Lucayan Waterway is a fixed bridge with a 27' vertical clearance at high water. This is the controlling height for the waterway and bars sailboats and tall powerboats from utilizing the shortcut through to the Little Bahama Bank.

If you're approaching the Grand Lucayan Waterway from the north, from Mangrove Cay, you must first clear the point of a sandbank that lies south/southwest of Mangrove Cay and is marked by a lit, though not working, piling and light (FL W). A heading of 200° from Mangrove Cay for ten miles will take you to this position. From here, head to a GPS waypoint at 26° 38.40' N, 78° 39.70' W, which sits in 7' of water in Dover Sound as shown on Chart #GB-10. From this point take up an approximate course of 152° to the first set of lit markers that will lead you in to the Waterway proper via a dredged channel. The water shallows to 3' here at MLW and the tide must be used if you draw more (note that the tide here is 2 hours behind the tide at Freeport or Lucaya). Once

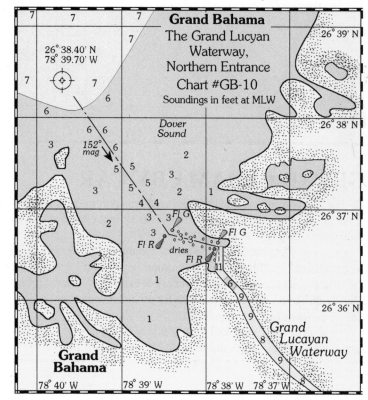

between the two markers, split the rest of the pilings and you will come to a lit pair at the end of the channel at the entrance to the Waterway. Turn to starboard here keeping the two single pilings to starboard. The depths in the Waterway itself run from 6'-12' and there is a bit of current that you will really notice at the bridge.

PETERSON CAY

Tiny Peterson Cay lies some two miles east of the southern entrance to the Grand Lucayan Waterway. The cay is protected by The Bahamas National Trust and the anchorage here should be considered a day anchorage only, or a night anchorage if one can expect only settled weather. If the wind should pipe up and/or shift during the night, you may not be able to find your way out so plan your stay here accordingly.

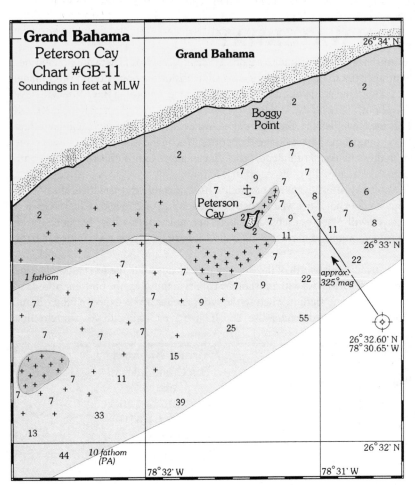

Peterson Cay is rarely used by cruisers, it is however, very popular with the local boating crowd as well as some commercial operations that like to stop and serve their customers lunch on the small beach. Be prepared to share the cay during daylight hours, especially on weekends and holidays.

As shown on Chart #GB-11, a GPS waypoint at 26° 32.60' N, 78° 30.65' W, will place you approximately ½ mile southeast of the entrance to the anchorage in the lee of Peterson Cay. From this position take up a course of approximately 325°. The course is not that important, what is important is that you clear the tip of the reef that lies northeast off Peterson Cay. After you round the tip of the reef, turn to port to anchor where your draft allows. There's good snorkeling on the reefs south and southwest of the cay and relaxing on the beach itself may be all you really need if you're seeking to escape the more cosmopolitan Freeport/Lucaya community.

GRAND BAHAMA BY CAR

The best way to explore Grand Bahama is by renting a car and taking the time to venture from one end of the island to the other. There are several car rentals listed in the back of this book and almost all will equip you with maps and even pick you up at your marina.

Once you clear out of the downtown and traffic of Freeport along the Queen's Highway, West End and the northwestern tip of Grand Bahama is just a short jaunt. You'll pass by Freeport Harbour and soon enter Eight Mile Rock. This community seems more like a suburb of Freeport than a separate establishment though I'm sure the residents would heartily disagree with me. Here you'll find a *Batelco* office, a *Winn Dixie*, a combo ice cream parlour/deli, and the *Above the Rim Sports Bar and Grill*.

Heading towards West End from here you'll find several small communities, all with welcoming signs that boast of each town's virtues. Just outside Eight Mile Rock is Jones Town, "The Home of Friendly People," Sea Grape, "The

Home of Contentment," Holmes Rock, "The Home of Togetherness," and Deadman's Reef, "The Home of the Enchanting Reef."

Deadman's Reef is actually the home of the *Paradise Cove Resort*, well hidden off the road and only marked by one small sign. Here you can find some of the best snorkeling on Grand Bahama just 50 yards offshore, while 200 yards inland is the Duck Pond where you'll see a variety of native bird life such as herons, wild ducks, and egrets.

Just before you reach West End, "The Home of Hospitality," you'll pass through Bootle Bay where you can grab a bite to eat at *Bernie's Place,* or you can venture further to Smith's Point and eat at *Mama Flo's*. We've already discussed what is in store for you in West End, so now let's turn our attention to the road east of Lucaya.

Heading east from Lucaya you'll first cross the bridge over the Grand Lucayan Waterway, and from then on tall pines will surround you all the way to the eastern end of the island. Your first stop will likely be at the *Lucayan National Park* whose 40 acres showcases a 1,000 foot beach with a backdrop of high sand dunes. A truly fine adventure is to take the tour of the *Lucayan National Park* where you set off from Gold Rock Creek in kayaks through a canopy of mangrove roots to a wooden boardwalk. Here you'll set off on foot and discover a beautiful beach and explore Ben's Cave. The cave has a vast network of underwater tunnel systems that lead to the ocean, one of the largest charted systems in the world.

Seven miles east of the *Lucayan National Park* is High Rock. High Rock's aptly named highest point is a 30' tall jagged rock overlooking the Northwest Providence Channel. You'll want to check out *Bishop's Beach Club* and their Saturday Fish Fry.

East of High Rock you'll come to Free Town and Gambier Point where you can get gas at *Smith's Gas and Convenience*. Just east of here is the Riding Rock oil terminal. You'll pass by an old cruise ship that sits at the docks there, quite out of place. At Pelican Point you'll want to check out *Breezer's Bar & Grill* situated right on the beach.

At the far eastern end of the highway lies McClean's Town, the Conch Cracking Capital of the World. Here you'll find a huge new fish house, the *Sunrise Restaurant & Disco*, *VB Convenience Store*, *Zelma's Take Out*, as well as a clinic and *Batelco* office. Once a year the folks from here and nearby Sweetings Cay gather together for a Conch Cracking Contest. The reigning champ cracked and cleaned 42 conch in two minutes. Now that is a lot of conch in a very short time! The creeks surrounding these areas are dotted with blue holes awaiting adventurous explorers.

Deep Water Cay and the *Deep Water Cay Club* lies just west of McClean's Town and is one of the premier bonefishing destinations on Grand Bahama with access to over 250 square miles of bonefishing flats. The club was established in 1958 by Gilbert Drake, a gentleman sportsman and avid fisherman who created this sanctuary for folks that shared his passion for the elusive bonefish. Club tradition has everyone (up to 22 guests) dining together in celebration of the day's adventures and triumphs in an intimate and relaxed atmosphere. The club also has a marina with two slips that will accommodate boats with drafts of less than 5'. Call the club on VHF ch. 16 for the intricate entry instructions or a pilot. The club also has a website at http://www.deepwatercay.com.

THE BIGHT OF ABACO

The Bight of Abaco is so rarely visited by cruising yachts and that's a shame. In good weather it's a fantastic cruising ground with several lee-shore anchorages and two cays that offer protection from the shifting winds of a frontal passage (even more safe havens if yours is a shallow draft vessel, say 3' or less).

The shorelines of the cays in the Bight tend to be a bit rocky, with less sandy beaches than on the Abaco cays that line the Sea of Abaco while tall pines grace the western shoreline of Great Abaco in so many places. To the west of Great Abaco and in close to her shoreline there are several areas of shallow water where bonefish abound and anchoring is impossible for all but the shallowest draft vessels. You'll see few other boats on your cruise through here, but some folks enjoy that, and the boats you do see are escaping the masses the same as you. You'll notice a never ending supply of local fishermen from Abaco out for a day's sport, and here and there a bonefishing boat silently poles along through the shallows in search of their elusive, skittish prey.

As you travel the western shore of Abaco you can still stay in touch by VHF with your friends at Green Turtle Cay, Manjack Cay, Powell Cay, Spanish Cay, Coopers Town, Treasure Cay, and sometimes even Marsh Harbour. You'll only be a few miles west of them although you're a long way away by boat.

Although many of the boats that cruise here enter the Bight from the south, we'll explore the Bight of Abaco from the north. As I've mentioned elsewhere in this book, I'm going to show you a good route into the Bight of Abaco from the north for boats with drafts over 6'. So let's begin our Bight of Abaco cruise with West End Point and the "Northwest Passage" and work our way southward along the western shore of Great Abaco to Sandy Point. Here we'll turn our bow northward and visit Castaway Cay and Mores Island.

WEST END POINT AND THE NORTHWEST PASSAGE

Whether northbound or southbound in the Bight, until now the biggest obstacle to a Bight of Abaco cruise has been negotiating the West End Bars just off West End Point at the western tip of Little Abaco Island. By the way, please do not confuse West End Point on Little Abaco with West End, Grand Bahama. Most skippers who contemplate a Bight cruise are aware of the route around the tip of West End Point that only carries 3' at MLW. This has been a huge deterrent for many cruisers with a 6' draft. There is no reason that a vessel of 6' (and with the help of the tide 6½' and more) cannot enjoy the Bight of Abaco. The passage around West End Point is no longer the controlling depth for a Bight of Abaco cruise, the shallows north of Spence Rock now hold that honor, but we will deal with that route in just a moment.

West End Bar is a long shallow area made up of rocks, corals, and sand that stretches west/southwest from West End Point. In dealing with the West End Bars some publications suggest passing the eight miles to the west of West End Point to avoid them while other publications suggest only 4½ miles to clear the same area. As I promised in the *Introduction*, there is a viable alternative to this madness, a sort of "Northwest Passage" if you will, that carries 6'-7' in most places at MLW with only a small spot that shows 5½'. The amazing thing about this route is that it lies only ¾ mile west of West End Point and saves cruisers time and fuel if headed to the east from the Bight of Abaco or if headed into the Bight from Fox Town, Great Sale Cay, or points east and north. I am shocked that nobody has shown this passage before; I came by it quite by accident. I was sounding the route close-in around West End Point and I looked to the west and saw that the rocky brown bar eventually ended. I headed west in my 16' boat and found plenty of water. Before long *IV Play* had made this passage some thirty times as we ventured into the Bight at will to explore and sound the areas.

If approaching from Fox Town, Great Sale Cay, Mangrove Cay, or anywhere in the northern Abacos, head for a waypoint at 26° 53.90' N, 77° 58.15' W as shown on Chart #AB-BI-2. This will put you in deep water just north of the West End Bar. From this position the "Northwest Passage" is a breeze. Simply head dead south, straight down 77° 58.15' W, until you're in deeper water. This route takes 5½' at MLW and will take over 7' with a good high tide. Note that the tides here are 3-4 hours later than Nassau tides so plan accordingly, less or more according to wind and sea conditions. For instance, strong southerly winds will produce a longer ebb while strong northerly winds will produce a longer flood tide. As you run down your longitude you will enter depths of 7', then 6', then a small area where the depth is 5½' before getting progressively deeper. Once you're back in water of 7' and more you can head east towards Cave Cay or shelter from northerly winds behind Little Abaco Island. If you're leaving Cave Cay and heading north, make

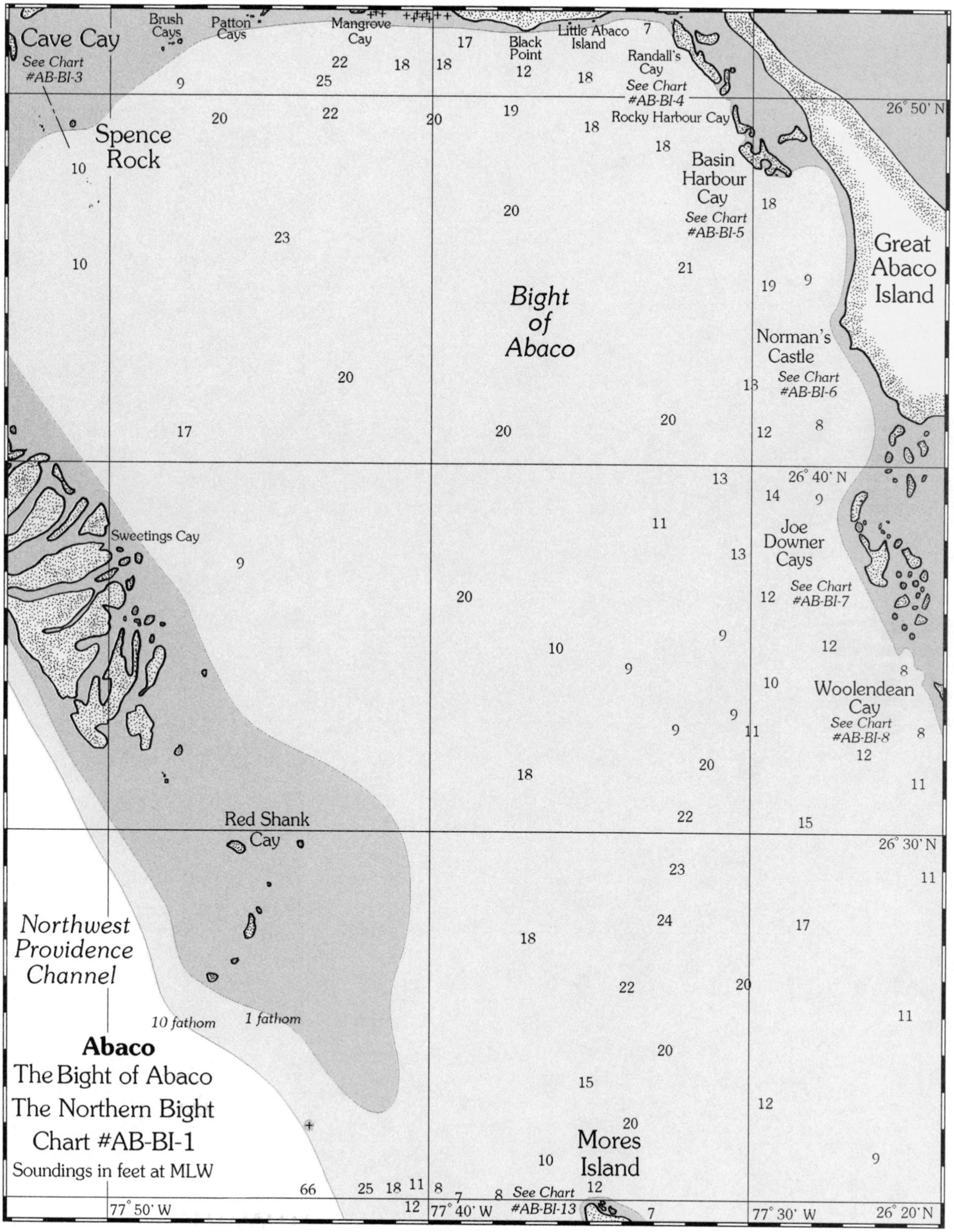

Cave Cay
*See Chart
#AB-BI-3*

Brush
Cays

Patton
Cays

Mangrove
Cay

Black
Point

Little Abaco
Island

Randall's
Cay
*See Chart
#AB-BI-4*

Rocky Harbour Cay

Spence
Rock

Basin
Harbour
Cay
*See Chart
#AB-BI-5*

*Bight
of
Abaco*

Great
Abaco
Island

Norman's
Castle
*See Chart
#AB-BI-6*

26° 50' N

26° 40' N

Sweetings Cay

Joe
Downer
Cays
*See Chart
#AB-BI-7*

Woolendean
Cay
*See Chart
#AB-BI-8*

Red Shank
Cay

26° 30' N

*Northwest
Providence
Channel*

10 fathom   1 fathom

Abaco
The Bight of Abaco
The Northern Bight
Chart #AB-BI-1
Soundings in feet at MLW

Mores
Island

*See Chart
#AB-BI-13*

77° 50' W   77° 40' W   77° 30' W   26° 20' N

9 10 10 20 23 17 20 22 25 17 18 18 7 12 18 18 19 18 18 21 19 9 18 20 12 8 13 14 9 11 13 12 9 12 10 9 9 11 20 8 8 12 11 18 22 15 11 23 24 17 11 22 20 11 20 20 12 15 20 9 10 66 25 18 11 8 7 8 12 12 7

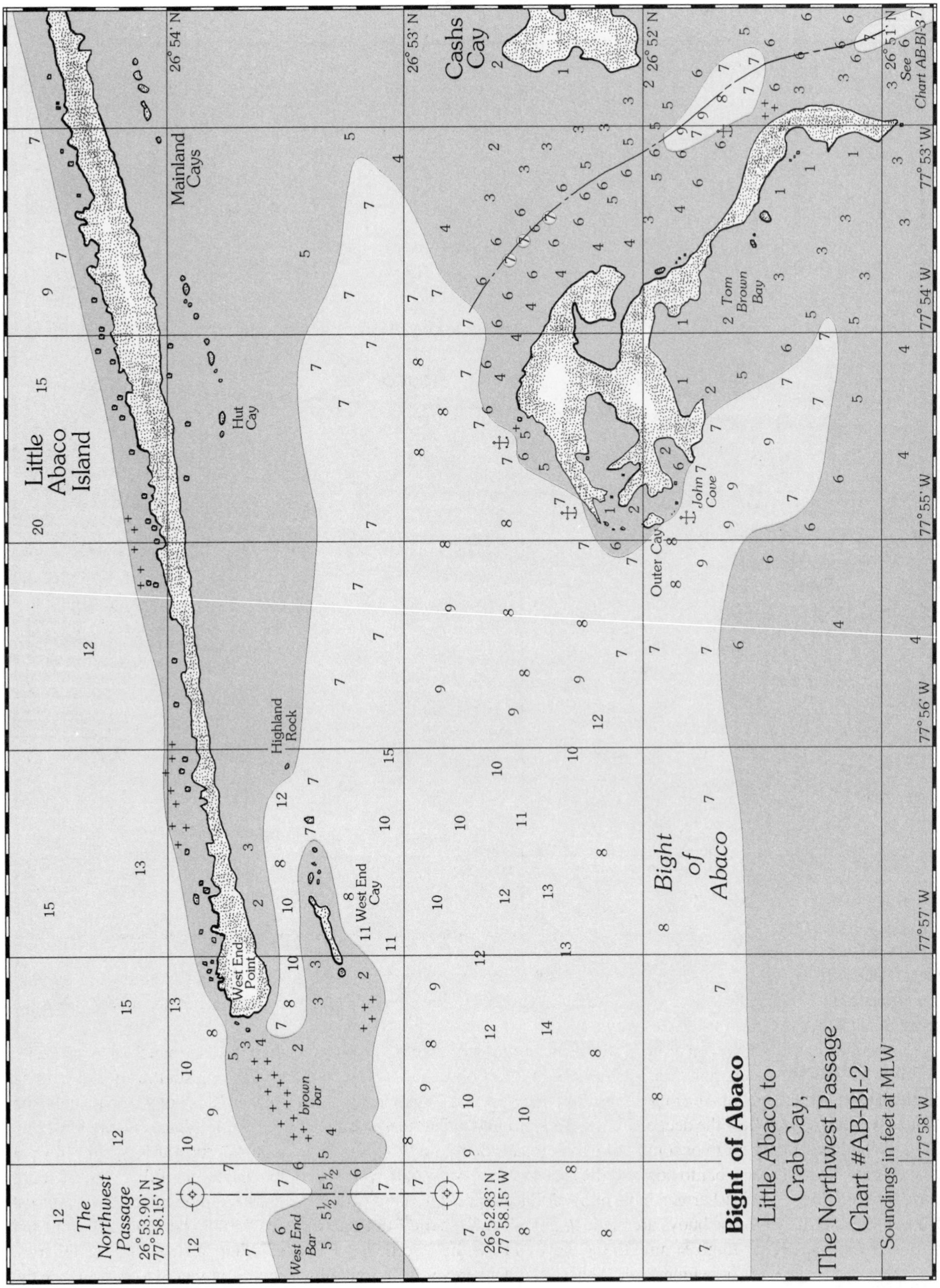

The Northwest Passage

12
The
Northwest
Passage
26°53.90' N.
77°58.15' W

Little
Abaco
Island

West End
Point

Highland
Rock

Hut
Cay

Mainland
Cays

West End
Cay

West End
Bar

brown
bar

26°54' N

26°52.83' N.
77°58.15' W

Cashs
Cay

Tom
Brown
Bay

Outer Cay

John
Cove

26°53' N

26°52' N

26°51' N

See
Chart AB-BI-37

Bight of Abaco

Bight
of
Abaco

Little Abaco to
Crab Cay,
The Northwest Passage
Chart #AB-BI-2

Soundings in feet at MLW

77°58' W   77°57' W   77°56' W   77°55' W   77°54' W   77°53' W

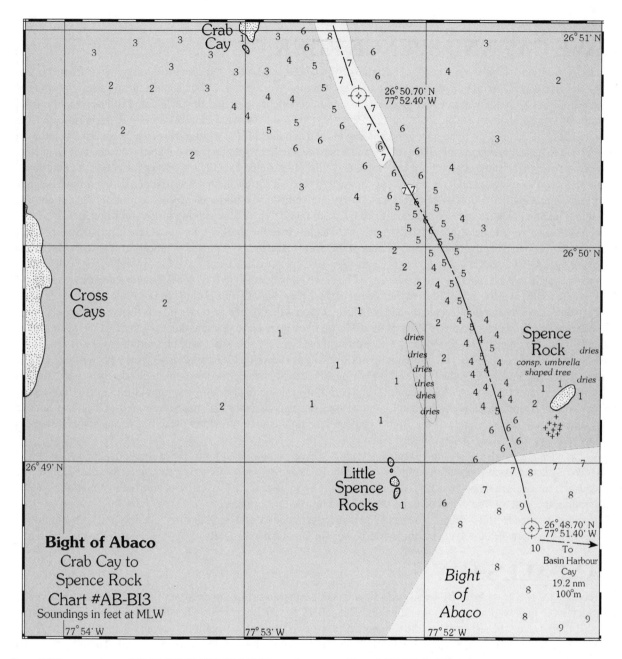

Bight of Abaco
Crab Cay to
Spence Rock
Chart #AB-BI3
Soundings in feet at MLW

for a GPS waypoint at 26° 52.83' N, 77° 58.15' W, as shown on Chart #AB-BI-2. From here, run northward up your longitude, until over the bar where you can take up a course for Great Sale Cay, points north and east, or head along the shore of Little Abaco eastward to Fox Town.

The shallow passage close in around West End Point is still usable by boats with drafts of less than 5'. It is far easier to follow it from the south, northward around West End Point, than it is to pick it up heading southward. If heading northward from the Bight of Abaco pass between the West End Cays and Highland Rock in 7'-12' of water as shown on Chart #AB-BI-2 and follow the deeper, darker water around to the west passing between Little Abaco and the West End Cays. Whether heading north or south through here, as you round West End Point about 50-100 yards off, you'll want to keep between the brown bar to port and the rocks to the east just off West End Point, and be careful…there's a lot of current here. Some local fishermen have buoyed this channel but don't expect the markers to be there and don't trust them if they are there. These buoys are made to guide small, shallow draft powerboats through here, not a 5' draft sail or power cruiser. Better to go ¾ mile to the west and use the "Northwest Passage." Skippers seeking shelter from northerly winds can duck in behind Little Abaco Island wherever their draft allows, but be prepared to move when the wind moves into the east.

CAVE CAY AND SPENCE ROCK

Congratulations! You're now inside the Bight of Abaco! Once past the "Northwest Passage" your first stop will likely be Cave Cay. Once you hit deeper water after crossing the West End Bar you can take up an easterly heading to approach Cave Cay as shown on Chart #AB-BI-2. Good anchorages surround this island and offer protection from virtually all wind directions. If you are facing the prevailing east/southeast winds, any anchorage on the northwestern or western shore of Cave Cay will be fine, good holding in sand abounds. If the wind moves into the southwest and west you'll need to be on the eastern side of Cave Cay and when the wind bears down from the north you can tuck up in John Cove or move behind Little Abaco for a lee. Cave Cay also offers some excellent shallows for bonefish enthusiasts. Many years ago there was a small community on the eastern shore of Cave Cay that was founded by freed slaves shortly after their emancipation. As is so often the case in Bahamian history, a hurricane decimated the settlement and the remaining inhabitants were moved to Little Abaco Island to found Crown Haven lying just west of Fox Town.

If heading deeper into the Bight of Abaco you'll need to pass over the shallows between Cave Cay and Spence Rock (Chart #AB-BI-3) to enter the much deeper waters of the Bight. And unless yours is a shallow draft vessel you'll want to pass to the east of Cave Cay. As shown on Chart #AB-BI-2, pass to the east of Cave Cay, rounding the northeastern tip and passing between Cave Cay and Cashs Cay. The controlling depth here is 6' at MLW with a deeper area of 7'-9' between the southern tip of Cashs Cay and the "knee" of Cave Cay. I give no waypoints for this route; you must develop a feel for the deeper water and be able to read the channel (you will also need a rising tide as the controlling depth for this passage as you approach Spence Rock is 4' at MLW). You'll be passing a couple of hundred yards to the east of Cave Cay and if you begin to get too far westward towards Cave Cay the water will thin rapidly as it does eastward towards Cashs Cay. As you pass the southern tip of Cave Cay as shown on Chart #AB-BI-3, you'll be in a large area of 7' deep water that will shoal gradually the closer you get towards Spence Rock. From this area take up a course to pass a few hundred yards to the west of Spence Rock and east of the sandbar that dries at low to mid-tide well to the west of Spence Rock. Spence Rock is easily identifiable by the conspicuous umbrella shaped tree on it. Once past Spence Rock and into the deeper waters of the Bight, you can take up a course for Mores Island or perhaps you'll want to explore the cays to the west of Great Abaco Island.

Vessels heading north and wishing to run this route in reverse should head for a GPS waypoint at 26° 48.70' N, 77° 51.40' W. This will place you south/southwest of Spence Rock and a good a spot as any to wait on the tide to follow the above route in reverse. The Cross Cays that lay well to the southwest of Cave Cay is an excellent area for dinghy exploration, the waters close in can be quite shallow and few people go there.

If you're headed to Mores Island, go ahead and take up your course and we'll discuss that destination in a moment, but first let's explore the cays lying off the western shore of Great Abaco Island.

RANDALL'S CAY

Randall's Cay, Charts #AB-BI-1 and #AB-BI-4, is the northernmost of the cays that lie west of Great Abaco and offers a fair lee in prevailing east/southeast winds. Randall's Cay is actually quite a beautiful little island where cactus covered bluffs face the west while shallow bonefish flats lie to the east between the cay and the mainland of Great Abaco. Both Randall's Cay and nearby Rocky Harbour Cay were once farmed and worked for sisal. There are the ruins of an old house still standing on Randall's Cay.

A GPS waypoint at 26° 51.60' N, 77° 32.90' W, will place you just west of the northernmost lee anchorage. When approaching Randall's Cay from the west (Spence Rock), as shown on Chart #AB-BI-1, you'll pass tiny Mangrove Cay where you can find shelter from northerly winds in its lee or maneuver your way eastward to Black Point to lie in its lee in 10'-12'. Beware of the long reef that lies east of Mangrove Cay.

As you approach Randall's Cay, a good landmark is the *Batelco* tower in Cooperstown. As shown on Chart #AB-BI-4, one can anchor off the northwest tip in prevailing winds. About midway down the western shore is Cooling Temper Bay where, in a small bight between some off-lying rocks and Randall's Cay, you'll find good protection from north through east winds.

A shallow draft vessel of 4' or less can work it's way up into Randall's Creek at the south end of Randall's Cay for protection from a frontal passage, but this anchorage has a lot of current and a rocky/marl bottom in many places. If seeking shelter from a front, you would be better off two miles further south at Basin Harbour Cay. A GPS waypoint at 26° 50.00' N, 77° 31.50' W, will place you approximately ¼ mile west of the mouth of Randall's Creek.

Just south of Randall's Cay, as shown on Chart #AB-BI-5, is Rocky Harbour Cay and Bamboo Cay. Once separate,

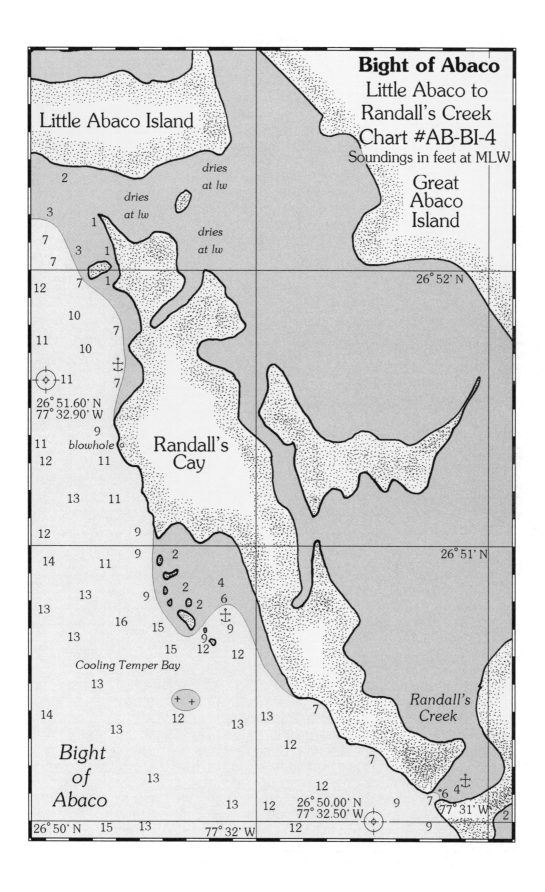

Bight of Abaco
Little Abaco to
Randall's Creek
Chart #AB-BI-4
Soundings in feet at MLW

Little Abaco Island

Great
Abaco
Island

dries
at lw

dries
at lw

dries
at lw

2

3

7

7

1

3   1

7   1

12

10

7

11

10

10

11

26° 52' N

26° 51.60' N
77° 32.90' W

9
blowhole

Randall's
Cay

11

12   11

13   11

12   9

9

9   2

14   11

13   9

13

16   15

13

15

15   12   12

Cooling Temper Bay

13

14

13

Bight
of
Abaco

2

2   4

2   6

9

9

12

26° 51' N

13

12   13

7

13

12

7

Randall's
Creek

12

26° 50.00' N
77° 32.50' W

9

7   6   4
77° 31' W

2

12

9

26° 50' N   15   13   77° 32' W   12

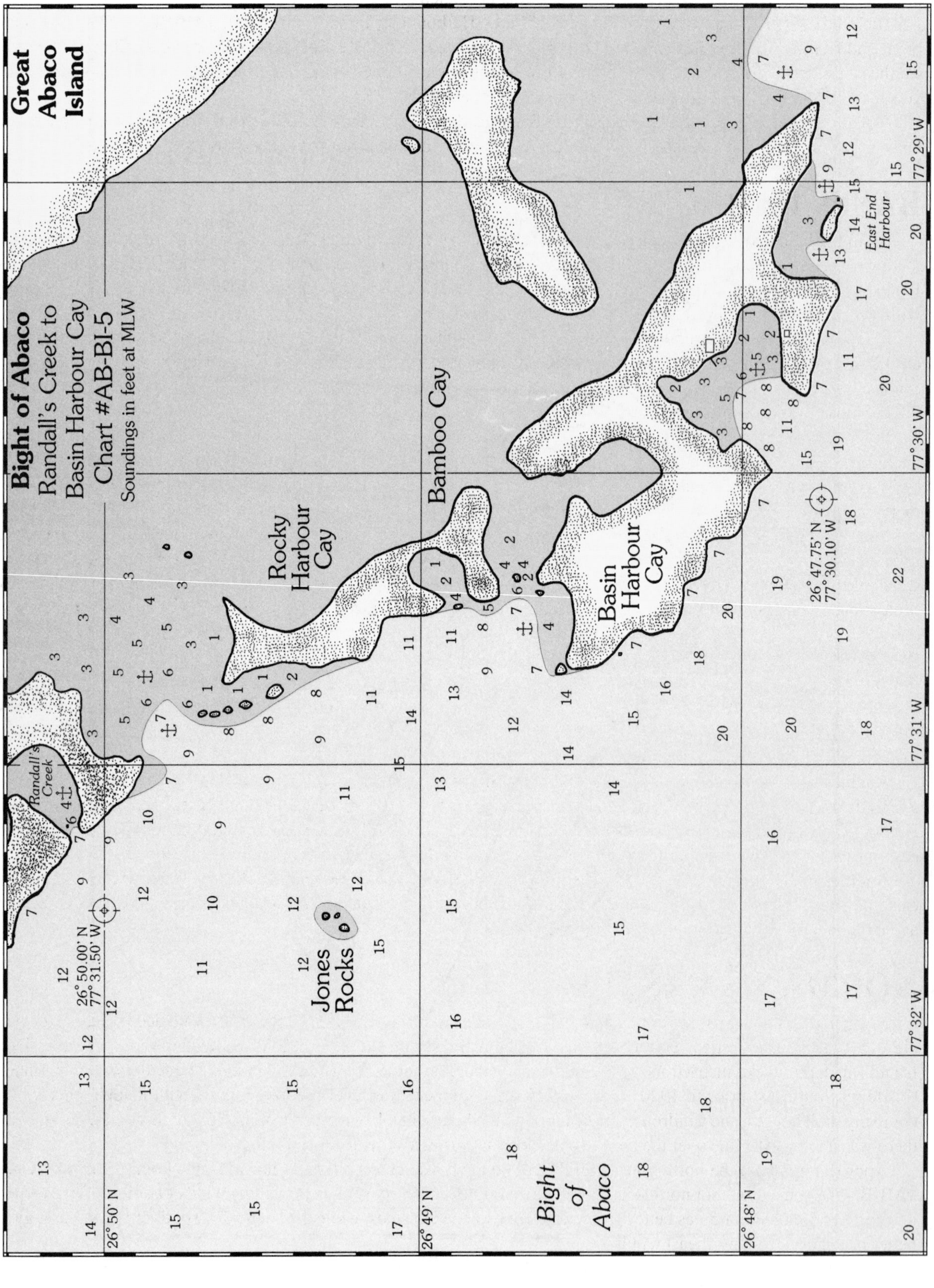

Great Abaco Island

Bight of Abaco
Randall's Creek to
Basin Harbour Cay
Chart #AB-BI-5
Soundings in feet at MLW

Rocky Harbour Cay

Bamboo Cay

Basin Harbour Cay

East End Harbour

Randall's Creek

Jones Rocks

Bight of Abaco

26°50.00' N
77°31.50' W

26°47.75' N
77°30.10' W

26°50' N

26°49' N

26°48' N

77°32' W

77°31' W

77°30' W

77°29' W

they are now joined and the creek that separated them is now just a shallow basin that will allow only the shallowest draft vessels inside. Both cays are home to magnificent tropicbirds.

There is a wonderful anchorage just north of Rocky Harbour Cay as shown on Chart #AB-BI-5. It lies in a small bight and shallows out the further east and northeast you steer. This is even a good spot in winds from northeast to southeast as the waters to the east are very shallow and little chop builds up. If you head east/northeast in your dinghy you'll come to a small landing that will lead you to Coopers Town.

A shallow creek divides Bamboo Cay from Basin Harbour Cay and offers good protection from frontal passages, but only for shallow draft vessels. Take care setting your anchor as the bottom is rocky in here.

BASIN HARBOUR CAY

Basin Harbour Cay, besides being one of the prettiest cays in the Bight of Abaco, offers some of the best protection in all weather conditions. If you wish to make one place your base of operations for your Bight of Abaco explorations, Basin Harbour Cay should be the spot. The shoreline is lovely, high rocky bluffs covered in cactus lead to an opening with an excellent anchorage that is only open to the southwest.

If approaching Basin Harbour Cay from the north, a fair anchorage can be found in the bight between its northwestern tip and the mouth of the creek that separates Basin Harbour Cay and Bamboo Cay as shown on Chart #AB-BI-5. Some charts inaccurately portray this anchorage as having much more water than what I show, but don't expect to tuck in very close; it is indeed as shallow as I have marked.

For all around protection it is best to head for the center of Basin Harbour Cay and its wonderful though shallow anchorage. A GPS waypoint at 26° 47.75' N, 77° 30.10' W will place you approximately ¼ mile southwest of the entrance to this anchorage and a bit over 19 nautical miles east/southeast from Spence Rock. From this position enter the harbour and anchor where your draft allows. You will find that the harbour rapidly shallows to a fairly uniform 5' or so and gradually shallows as you approach the shore. There is house on the eastern shore of the harbour that is often used and another, smaller house on the southern shore of the harbour. The anchorage itself is open to the southwest and west so if southwest winds are forecast it is best to anchor in the southwestern corner of the anchorage for the best protection. After the winds moves into the west, it would be better to move to the northern side of the anchorage where the water is a little deeper. In strong southeasterly through southwesterly winds, this anchorage develops a surge as swells work their way into the harbour around the southern tip of the harbour mouth. This surge is not dangerous, only uncomfortable; a bridle arrangement that allows you to pivot your bow into the swell will take care of the problem and give you a pleasant night's sleep. As the wind swings into the southwest your bow will automatically come more into the wind and sea easing the motion. The bottom in this harbour is marly, and the holding here is tricky at times, make sure your anchor is set well.

Another possible anchorage is either east or west of the unnamed rock in East End Harbour (also shown on Chart #AB-BI-5). This entire harbour was once deep but has now filled in between the unnamed rock and the shore of Basin Harbour Cay. If you anchor to the west of the unnamed rock, you will find shelter from west through northeast, almost east, winds, while if you anchor to the east of the rock you will have shelter from northwest to northeast winds.

Another anchorage that will give you shelter from west winds is off the eastern tip of Basin Harbour Cay. Round the eastern tip and venture in as far as your draft allows. This is not a good anchorage in winds from southeast through south and a bit choppy in winds from northeast through east.

NORMAN'S CASTLE

Norman's Castle lies a bit over five nautical miles south/southeast of Basin Harbour Cay with deep water all the way (12'-15'). Norman's Castle is the name of an old logging transshipment settlement on the western shore of Great Abaco Island which provides a nice lee anchorage with plenty of opportunities for land exploration. The settlement of Norman's Castle was built just prior to 1920, and by 1925 the settlement was a certified boomtown with its own doctor, 250 company built houses, and a railroad. From a production highpoint of over twelve million board feet of lumber in 1925, there was a steady decline over the next two decades as Norman's Castle passed into history.

Approaching from the north your landfall will be the conspicuous hill and bluff at Davis Point (shown on Chart #AB-BI-6). You can anchor north or south of Davis Point in 6'-7' of water in prevailing wind conditions. The anchorage north of Davis Point gives better protection from southeast winds, while the anchorage south of Davis Point gives better protection from northeast winds.

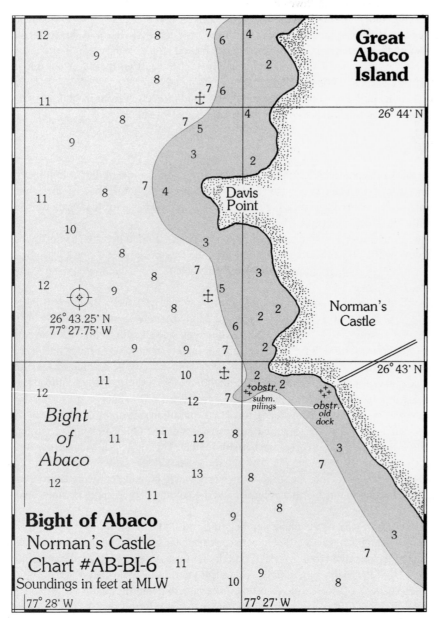

Bight of Abaco
Norman's Castle
Chart #AB-BI-6
Soundings in feet at MLW

A GPS waypoint at 26° 47.75' N, 77° 30.10' W will place you approximately ¾ mile west of the point and ruins of Norman's Castle and equally as far southwest of Davis Point. Don't venture too close in to shore as shown on the chart, there are numerous submerged hazards such as concrete and steel pilings. There is an old dock and some ruins at the end of the road just south of the point. You might get lucky and see some folks that have driven here from the Great Abaco Highway, and it might be possible to hitch a ride into Treasure Cay or Marsh Harbour from here.

THE JOE DOWNER CAYS

About three miles south of Norman's Castle lies a small string of cays known as the Joe Downer Cays as shown on Charts #AB-BI-7 and AB-BI-8. This area was once called Point of Bank and was used by spongers as a repository for their sponges. You might find the remains of old wells as you walk these cays. At the northern end of the chain lies Little Joe Downer Cay where a hard bar stretches north/northwest. The cay has several small beaches that invite dinghy exploration. At the southern end of the cay, in Little Creek, is a small pool of deep water but only small shallow draft vessels can work their way in as the shallows to the west of the creek dry in places at low water.

Just south of Little Joe Downer Cay lies Big Joe Downer Cay, sometimes shown as South Joe Downer Cay, where the best anchorage is in Amos Bight. A GPS waypoint at 26° 36.90' N, 77° 26.90' W places you ¾ mile west of Amos Bight and the anchorage area. Amos Bight is good for winds from northeast to southeast with good holding in sand. Here you'll find several more beaches just waiting for you to land and explore.

South of Big Joe Downer Cay lies a rocky bar that extends south/southwest as shown on Chart #AB-BI-8. The southern end of this bar is sometimes marked with a stake or small buoy but these are not likely to be there, and if they are, give them a wide berth, the bar is easily seen. Skippers can work their way inside the bar to the northeast where you can tuck up behind it for shelter from westerly winds. This shallow (1'-2') bar offers a good lee with little sea working its way over it. It's actually pretty amazing how much this bar breaks the seas! From this position you can head over to anchor in the lee of Big Pigeon Cay and Pigeon Cay Rock or in the small bight north of Woolendean Cay. From here a channel heads to Great Abaco Island that many fishermen use. The channel used to take 6' at MLW but today has filled in to about half that.

Another good lee anchorage is off the beach on the northwestern edge of Woolendean Cay. On the beach you'll see some small fishermen's shacks that are still used. The small cays stretch southward for about ten miles from Woolendean Cay, but they only offer fair lee protection at best. Mastic Point lies farther south and offers a good lee anchorage in sand but you must anchor over ½ mile off as closer in the bottom is extremely rocky.

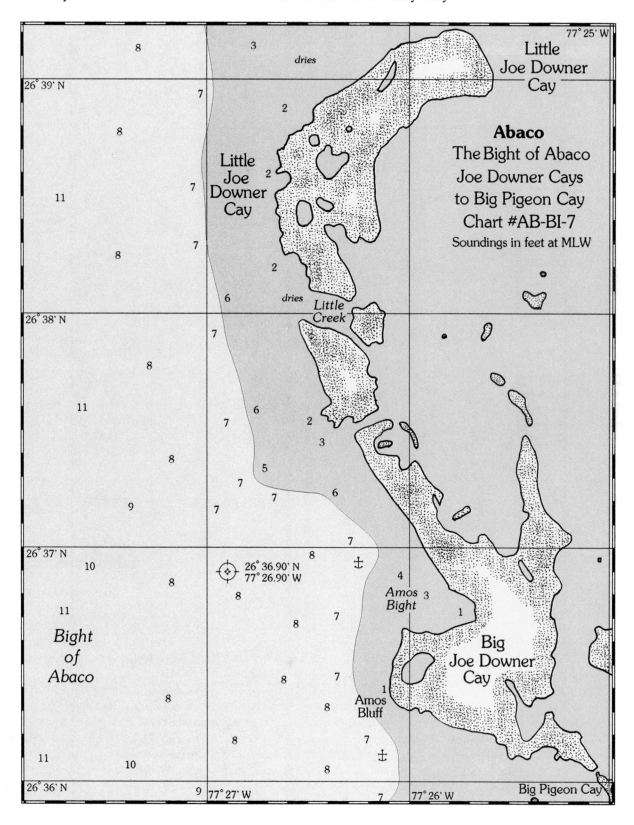

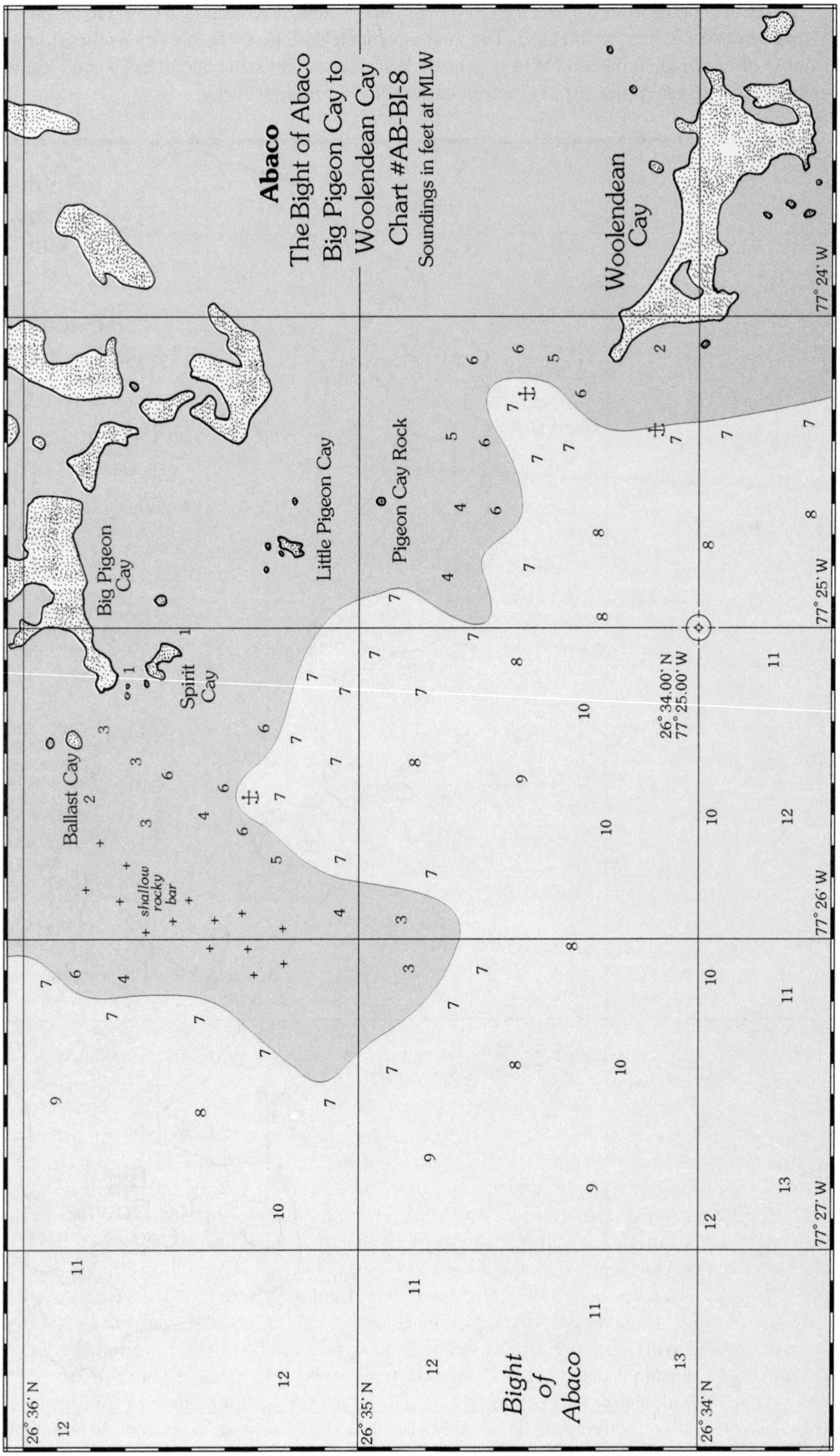

Abaco
The Bight of Abaco
Big Pigeon Cay to
Woolendean Cay
Chart #AB-BI-8
Soundings in feet at MLW

Woolendean
Cay

Big Pigeon
Cay

Little Pigeon Cay

Pigeon Cay Rock

Spirit
Cay

Ballast Cay

shallow
rocky
bar

26° 36' N

26° 35' N

26° 34' N

26° 34.00' N
77° 25.00' W

Bight
of
Abaco

77° 27' W

77° 26' W

77° 25' W

77° 24' W

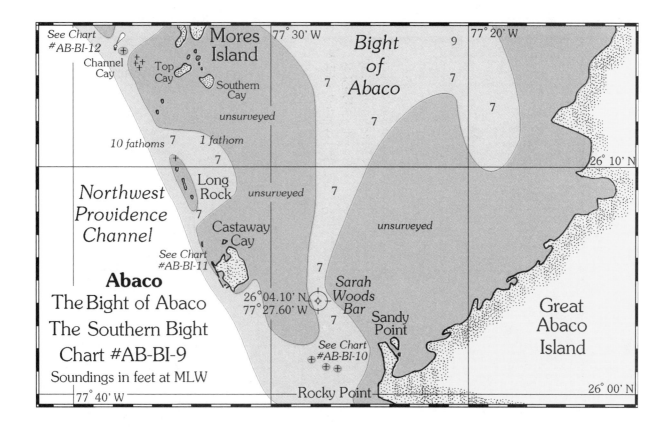

SANDY POINT

Sandy Point lies at the southwestern tip of Great Abaco Island and is a favorite stopover for cruisers bound north or south through the Bight of Abaco as well as those bound east and west using the Northwest or Northeast Providence Channels. If you are approaching Sandy Point from the north you must negotiate rocky Sarah Woods Bar. From inside the Bight of Abaco make your way to a GPS waypoint at 26° 04.10' N, 77° 27.60' W as shown on Chart #AB-BI-9. Use caution to avoid the shallows lying east of Mores Island and Castaway Cay and the shallow areas lying west of Great Abaco Island. From here you can head approximately 150° to pass south and west of the Sarah Woods Bar. A flooding tide will tend to push you northeastward onto the bar which is easily seen and just as easily skirted.

If approaching Sandy Point from the south, from the Northwest or Northeast Providence Channel, you must clear the vast shoals that lie southwest of Rocky Point as shown on Chart #AB-BI-10. Head for a GPS waypoint at 25° 59.60' N, 77° 25.80' W which will place you in deep water well to the southwest of the southwestern tip of the shoals. From this position head north/northeast towards Sandy Point keeping clear of the shallows lying west of the mainland. Watch out for a few small patch reefs to the west of this route also.

A GPS waypoint at 26° 01.10' N, 77° 24.70' W will place you just off the community in a bight between shallow water to the north and south as shown on Chart #AB-BI-10. If a front threatens, and if your draft is 5' or less, you can work your way northward around the point to anchor to the east of Sandy Point in a narrow, but deep channel. The route is fairly easy to see, you'll notice the deeper water curving eastward around the northern tip, picking up the beginning of the route is the tricky part. At the time of this writing a small buoy marked the shallowest area, but like all privately maintained navigational aids in The Bahamas, it cannot be trusted to be there. If you're good at eyeball navigation you'll be able to pick out the channel as the water is very, very shallow on either side of it, 1' in places. The best time to attempt this passage is on a rising tide, just before high so that if you run aground, you'll have a bit of high tide still to come to help you float off. From the previously mentioned anchorage, head almost due north and try to pick out the channel as it curves around to the east. If you need a pilot, simply place a call on VHF ch. 16 for *Pete and Gay's Guest House*. Pete Dean runs a fine inn with excellent accommodations where the focus is on bonefishing.

Sandy Point is a delightful, picturesque community of colorful houses set amid a stand of coconut palms. Besides *Pete and Gay's Guest House* you'll have *Oeisha's Resort* a bit closer to the airstrip. Ask about their Sunday barbecues

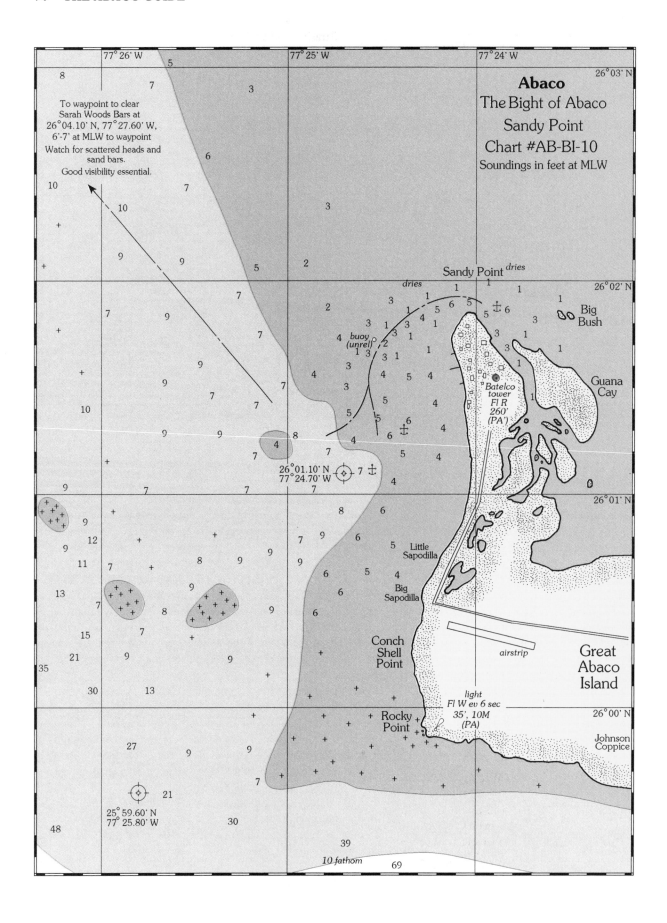

77° 26' W 77° 25' W 77° 24' W

8 5 26° 03' N

7 3

To waypoint to clear
Sarah Woods Bars at
26°04.10' N, 77°27.60' W,
6'-7' at MLW to waypoint
Watch for scattered heads and
sand bars.
Good visibility essential.

6

Abaco
The Bight of Abaco
Sandy Point
Chart #AB-BI-10
Soundings in feet at MLW

10 7

10

9 9 3

5 2 26° 02' N

7 Sandy Point *dries*

7 *dries* 1 1 1

7 9 2 3 1 5 5 5 6 Big Bush

4 *buoy (unrel)* 2 3 3 1 1 3 5 1

7 1 3 1 3 1 1 3

9 4 3 3 1 1 Guana Cay

5 4 Batelco tower Fl R 260' (PA') 1

10 7 5 5 6 1

9 9 8 4 6 1

7 4 5 4

26°01.10' N 7 4 26° 01' N
77°24.70' W

8 6

9 9 7 6

12 9 5 Little Sapodilla

11 7 8 9 6 5 4 Big Sapodilla

13 9 6

15 7 8 9

21 9 Conch Shell Point Great Abaco Island

35 13 *airstrip*

30 *light Fl W ev 6 sec 35', 10M (PA)* 26° 00' N

27 9 9 Rocky Point Johnson Coppice

7

25° 59.60' N
77° 25.80' W 21 30

48

39

10 fathom 69

at the beach. You can find water at the government dock and trash receptacles also. For dining you can chose from *Pete Gay's*, *Nancy's Seaside Inn*, *Oeisha's*, *Big J's*, and *Marion's Takeaway* while the *E&E Department Store* and *Florence's Grocery* can handle all your pantry needs. For gasoline head straight for *Thompson's*. There is a shuttle bus to Marsh Harbour three times a week and it's possible to get your propane filled by using this convenient service. Phone and fax service is available at the local *Batelco* office and there is a medical clinic in town.

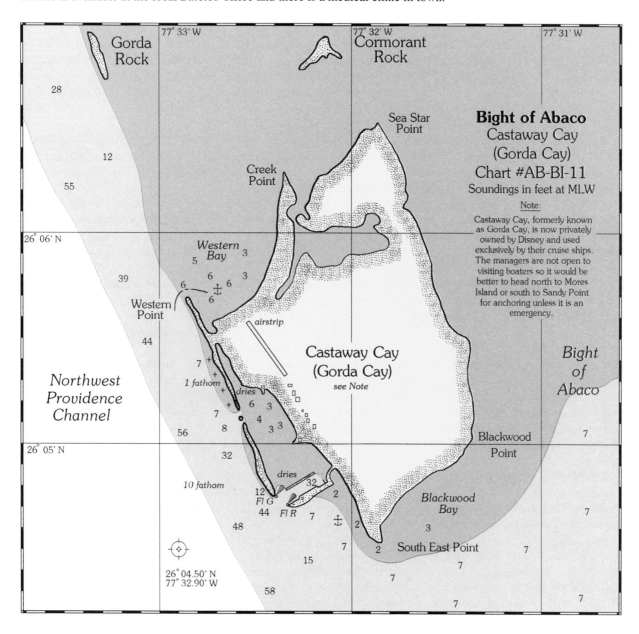

CASTAWAY CAY (GORDA CAY)

Castaway Cay, once called Gorda Cay, lies about nine miles northwest of Sandy Point on the edge of the bank bordering the Northwest Providence Channel and can be seen from Sandy Point. The cay is home to a major Disney cruise ship stopover and visits ashore are by invitation only. The best way to access Castaway Cay is via the Northwest Providence Channel as shown on Chart #AB-BI-9. It is possible to head to Castaway Cay from Sandy Point by skirting the Sarah Woods Bars, but that area is filled with heads, small patch reefs, and shallow bars which must all be negotiated with good light and visibility. The inner harbour at Castaway Cay can be used by yachts in emergencies, but visiting yachtsmen are not encouraged to visit the cay, this is strictly for the paying guests.

A GPS waypoint at 26° 04.50' N, 77° 32.90' W will place you approximately ½ mile southwest of the newly dredged harbour and cruise ship docks. It is still possible to work your way up between the small off-lying cay and the new breakwater, but only in emergency situations. If yours is an emergency situation try calling the cay first on VHF ch. 16. You can also anchor south of the cruise ship dock in northerly to easterly winds and north of the cay in Western Bay.

Not too long ago, when Castaway Cay was still Gorda Cay, the island was the hub of smuggling operations in the Abacos between 1979 and 1983. The island's operations went through four phases, each run in turn by either Frank Barber, Luis Garcia, Abner Pinder of Spanish Wells, and Barry Thompson. Frank Barber fist bought Gorda Cay in 1979. At one point during his career on the cay Barber wanted to kill two young men from Sandy Point. In October of 1979 the two young men stumbled onto the airstrip and Barry Thompson, the caretaker of Gorda Cay, brought them to Barber at gun point. Barber then told Thompson to take them to Gorda Rock, a small rock nearby, and maroon them. Thompson, after having served three years and eight months in prison, was hired as the caretaker at Gorda Cay for $500 a week. Soon he realized that the cay was being used as a smuggling operation and he immediately demanded more money which he finally received after several arguments and threats.

Barber and his men established a security system and using armed guards and dogs kept intruders off the cay, which did nothing but create animosity with the population of Sandy Point. When asked about these allegations Barbers said that the people of Sandy Point had been using Gorda Cay for years as a smugglers base, but that since he arrived all smuggling activity has ceased and he intended to keep it that way.

Barber was arrested in the Spring of 1982, and later that year sold the island to Abner Pinder, a Spanish Wells fisherman. Luis Garcia began his operations on the Cay just after Barber's arrest and lasted until the end of 1982. Pinder also started operations in October of 1982, overlapping Garcia by a few months during which time Garcia paid Pinder for the use of the island. Actually, the first night of Pinder's new ownership, Barry Thompson and some of his cronies, all of them armed with automatic weapons, confronted Pinder. They told Pinder that they worked for Garcia and that if Pinder did not allow them to use the cay, Thompson would make sure that Pinder would never be able to make use of it. Pinder agreed and Garcia eventually paid Pinder $1,000 per kilo of coke and $20 per pound of pot that he moved through Gorda Cay. By this time Garcia had virtually retired from the drug smuggling business and moved to a quieter life in sunny South Florida. Pinder, in a meeting with Garcia in Miami where he had gone to pick up a payment, told Garcia that he did not trust Barry Thompson and wanted him off the cay. Word of this filtered down to Thompson, who once again confronted Pinder at gunpoint, stealing a large quantity of marijuana and a boat from him. In January of 1983, through Garcia's intervention, Pinder settled his differences with Thompson. By mutual agreement, Pinder left the workings of Gorda Cay to Thompson, and Garcia guaranteed Pinder would continue to receive his payments. Although Pinder received no further payments form either Garcia or Thompson, he did receive $120,000 from two Cuban Americans for using his cay. The Cubans should have paid him more but they complained that Barry Thompson had stolen part of their load. In April of 1983, Pinder claimed to have given up involvement with drugs of any kind and boasted to have cleared over a million dollars from Gorda Cay.

Disillusioned, Abner Pinder agreed to sell Gorda Cay to Barry Thompson for three million dollars. Thompson gave him a down payment of $400,000 and a subsequent payment of $300,000 and then, true to form, the payments stopped. Thompson continued to run drugs through Gorda Cay until September of 1983 when a permanent police presence was established on the island and the illegal activities came to an end.

Now when Frank Barber boasted of cleaning up Gorda Cay, the DEA didn't believe him and their *Operation Grouper* focused on the drug smuggling activities going on at Gorda Cay. Then Prime Minister Sir Lynden Pindling contends that the operation was illegal and was executed without the knowledge and cooperation of the Bahamian Government. The Bahamas insists that the DEA even helped set up the operation on Gorda Cay to catch smugglers and that they actually caught some of their own people. The Government of The Bahamas insists that when Frank Barber was caught, he was offered a chance to help the DEA nab more suspects in return for reducing his charges to a minor offense. Barber allegedly agreed and the DEA netted some 90 persons in the U.S. and Bahamas in connection with Barber's activities on Gorda Cay. The Government insisted that Jeffery Scharlatt, whom the DEA called an "investor in Gorda Cay" and who was sentenced to five years and fined $15,000, was actually a former DEA agent.

And while we're discussing the wealth passing through this area, let me remind you that there have been several wrecks of Spanish treasure ships in the waters between Mores Island, Gorda Cay, and Sandy Point. In 1719, between Gorda Cay and Sandy Point, the *San Pedro* sank with over half a million in gold and silver aboard. In 1595, a Spanish treasure vessel sank off Mores Island, and in 1717, the *El Capitan* sank off Southern Cay with over $2 million in treasure aboard.

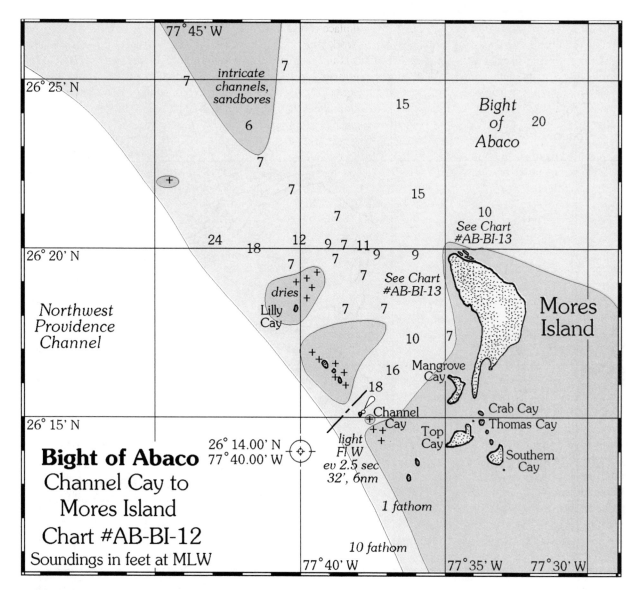

77°45' W

intricate
channels,
sandbores

26° 25' N

7

15

*Bight
of   20
Abaco*

6

7

7

15

7

10
*See Chart
#AB-BI-13*

24   18   12   9 7 11
9   9

26° 20' N

7   7

7

*See Chart
#AB-BI-13*

*Northwest
Providence
Channel*

dries
Lilly
Cay

7

7   7

10   7

Mores
Island

16   Mangrove
Cay

18

Crab Cay
Thomas Cay

26° 15' N

Channel
Cay

Top
Cay

Southern
Cay

26° 14.00' N
77° 40.00' W

light
Fl W
ev 2.5 sec
32', 6nm

Bight of Abaco

Channel Cay to
Mores Island
Chart #AB-BI-12
Soundings in feet at MLW

1 fathom

10 fathom

77° 40' W   77° 35' W   77° 30' W

MORES ISLAND

Mores Island lies northwest of Castaway Cay and southeast of the shallow banks area that is the southeastern tail of Grand Bahama. There are two small settlements on Mores Island, Hard Bargain and The Bight, both of which were established by freed slaves. Landfall can be fairly easy as the 200' *Batelco* tower (Fxd R at night) at Hard Bargain can be seen for miles.

If you are approaching Mores Island from the northern Bight of Abaco, from Spence Rock to Norman's Castle or even Woolendean Cay, head for a GPS waypoint at 26° 20.55' N, 77° 35.20' W (as shown on Chart #AB-BI-13) which will place you about ¾ mile northwest of the northern tip of Mores Island. From here simply head south keeping at least a quarter mile offshore to reach Hard Bargain.

If approaching Mores Island from the deep water of the Northwest Providence Channel you can head to a GPS waypoint at 26° 14.00' N, 77° 40.00' W which will place you approximately two miles southwest of Channel Cay and the entrance channel to Mores Island as shown on Chart #AB-BI-12. From this position head northeast passing Channel Cay to starboard (north of the cay). Tiny Channel Cay is easily picked out by its conspicuous 32' tall light (flashing white every 2½ seconds). You can pass south of Channel Cay, but this is not recommended as there are submerged rocks in that area that are a hazard to navigation. Never attempt to enter by Channel Cay at night; it would be prudent to heave to offshore and wait for daylight. As you pass Channel Cay keep heading in a general northeasterly direction heading for the northern tip of Mores Island and the *Batelco* tower at Hard Bargain some five miles away.

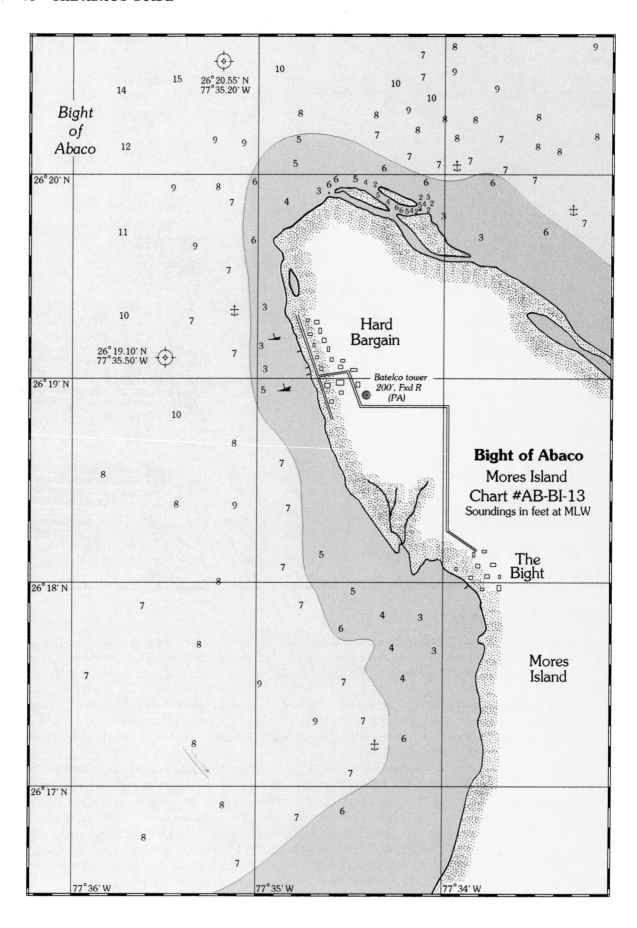

Bight
of
Abaco

26° 20.55' N
77° 35.20' W

26° 20' N

26° 19.10' N
77° 35.50' W

26° 19' N

26° 18' N

26° 17' N

Hard
Bargain

Batelco tower
200', Fxd R
(PA)

Bight of Abaco
Mores Island
Chart #AB-BI-13
Soundings in feet at MLW

The
Bight

Mores
Island

77° 36' W   77° 35' W   77° 34' W

As you approach the lee anchorages at Mores Island as shown on Chart #AB-BI-13, you can head for a GPS waypoint at 26° 04.50' N, 77° 32.90' W which lies about ½ mile west of Hard Bargain. In prevailing wind directions, northeast to southeast, the anchorages along the western shore of Mores Island are great…tuck up as close as your draft allows but watch out for a few submerged and easily seen wrecks just off the main street at Hard Bargain. You'll find few conveniences in Hard Bargain, there are a couple of small stores and a tiny gas station right on the shoreline where you can pick up some gasoline or diesel.

Off the northeast shore of Mores Island you can gain shelter from winds from southwest to northwest. Round the northern point of Mores Island staying about ¼ mile off and proceed around the northern and northeastern tip in 6'-9' of water. Anchor wherever your draft allows. The deeper water, 6'-7', lies about 200 yards or so offshore, and as far south as the beach that sits under the conspicuous casaurinas about ¾ mile southeast of the northern tip of the island. As you round the northern point of Mores Island you will come upon two small creeks, the first is far too shallow for anything of any real draft, perhaps a *Gemini* catamaran but that's about all. The second creek that you come to as you head eastward around the northern tip is quite a bit deeper, 5'-7' at MLW in spots. Of course there are a few places where it's 2'-3' in spots also, but this is a good spot to ride out a front if you're caught in one while in the area. The bar at the mouth of the creek will take drafts of less than 5' at high tide, and 5' on a very high tide. This is one of those places you're going to check out with the dinghy first. Needless to say good visibility is needed here. The entrance channel is straightforward. Steer for the middle of the opening parallel with the lie of the creek itself, and squiggle around any shallow spots that you come upon. Once over the bar, about 3'-4' at MLW, you will be in 5'-6' at MLW. You can venture farther up the creek, but the channel shifts around some shallow, grassy bars of about 2' at MLW. Five feet can be carried all the way to the end of the creek, and you can even pass between the small mangrove islets and the large cay to the northeast, but that channel will end in a 2' grassy bar as shown on the chart. It should go without saying that you'll need two anchors set in a Bahamian moor here as there is a lot of tidal current. The creek is open to the northwest, but even a strong northwest wind will send very little sea into the creek; the bar breaks most of it.

Tiny Black Rock, lying just northwest of Mores Island, was a focal point for smugglers back in the late 70's and early 80's. The Government of The Bahamas claims that their officers found a cache of marijuana on the cay that, if stacked 6' high, would stretch for two miles.

If I am headed out into the Northwest Providence Channel and Grand Bahama from Mores Island, I will head west from the northern tip of the island to pass north of the shallows lying northeast of Lilly Cay as shown on Chart #AB-BI-12. Keep an eye peeled for shallow bars and heads on this route, but rest assured it is a safe shortcut to the deep water if you have good light and maintain a lookout.

To the northwest of Mores Island lies the tail of Grand Bahama Island where you'll find numerous cays separated by narrow channels, some deep, some shallow. You'll find a couple of lee anchorages here and several places to explore such as Burrow's Cay, Water Cay, and Red Shank Cay. You'll need good visibility to maneuver around the heads and shallow bars that abound hereabouts, but it will be worth it if you just want to get off the beaten path.

THE ABACOS

The Northern Abacos

ROUTES FROM WEST END, GRAND BAHAMA

As I mentioned in the section on Grand Bahama, West End is often used as the "door" to the Abacos; more Abaco-bound cruisers stop here to clear in than any other Port of Entry. From West End, Grand Bahama there are two places where you can enter the Little Bahama Bank for your trip to the Abacos, Indian Cay Channel, or the route that lies north of Sandy Cay; your draft will likely decide for you which one you choose. There is another route via Memory Rock, but that is primarily used by vessels that ordinarily bypass West End, Grand Bahama.

If you intend to use Indian Cay Channel as shown on Chart #GB-1, head to a GPS waypoint at 26° 42.80' N, 79° 00.60' W. This position lies approximately ½ mile north/northwest of West End, Grand Bahama and just a bit west of Indian Cay, about ½ mile southwest of the entrance to Indian Cay Channel. Indian Cay Channel can be a pain during a really low tide and there are a few spots that show only 4½' at MLW. This route is not recommended for vessels with drafts of more than 6'-6½' and only a rising, almost high tide.

From the waypoint, take Indian Cay light (Fl W ev 6 sec, 40', 8M) and the piling to the west of the cay to starboard and proceed northeastward towards the next two pilings keeping them both on your starboard side. Once past the second piling you can work your way to a GPS waypoint south of Barracuda Shoal at 26° 45.65' N, 78° 58.30' W. A light that flashes white every four seconds and should be considered unreliable, marks the southern edge of Barracuda Shoal. From the Barracuda Shoal waypoint head to your next waypoint at 26° 46.37' N, 78° 57.15' W where you'll find deep water all the way to Mangrove Cay or Great Sale Cay.

If you're heading across the banks and wish to exit the banks via Indian Cay Channel, make your way to the waypoint at 26° 46.37' N, 78° 57.15' W and then follow the above directions in reverse. If you're unsure about using the Indian Cay Channel, or if your draft is simply too deep, you can always enter the banks a few miles north of Sandy Cay. From West End, Grand Bahama, head northwestward, paralleling the edge of the bank as it curves in that general direction. Try to stay in 10 fathoms or so of water as the edge of the bank has numerous shallow banks and rocks along through here (Never attempt any entrance onto the bank hereabouts at night.). When you reach latitude 26° 52.50 N, you can turn east and head onto the banks. Use extreme caution here at all times. If you head east between Sandy Cay and 26° 52.50' N you might find yourself in a maze of sandbores and rocks, I've been there and that is exactly what's there. I once managed to pass off the banks less than two miles north of Sandy Cay, but only because I had a high tide, excellent visibility, and a huge amount of luck. The locals that were fishing and diving around me as I worked my way through the sandbores looked at me as if I was quite out of my mind. Anyway, once you pass abeam of Sandy Cay on latitude 26° 52.50 N you can take up your course for Great Sale or other destinations.

The Memory Rock route is a popular passage for boaters with deeper drafts or those crossing from Lake Worth or Jupiter Inlet. The best route lies about 2 miles south of the light on Memory Rock and is just a bit north of the route that I mentioned above that lies 4 miles north of Sandy Cay. A GPS waypoint at 26° 54.75' N, 79° 05.75' W will place you approximately 2¼ miles south of Memory Rock. From here, head east onto the banks and take up your course for Great Sale Cay or Walkers Cay, if you desire. Be careful if you're heading to Walkers Cay from this waypoint as there are some shallows about 2½ miles east/southeast of Memory Rock that must be avoided.

Another popular entrance on the Little Bahama Bank is at a spot called White Sand Ridge. White Sand Ridge is popular for dolphin enthusiasts who flock there in great numbers in May of every year when the bottlenose dolphins return to frolic and mate in the clear water. A GPS waypoint at 27° 08.00' N, 79° 11.00' W, will place you about ½ mile west of the entrance to the bank. Simply head east from this waypoint and you're on the Little Bahama Bank at White Sand Ridge. Once you're on the bank you can take up your course to Walkers Cay or Great Sale as you choose. Watch out for commercial traffic through here as some larger boats use this route at times.

Some cruisers heading east from Memory Rock or West End, Grand Bahama still stop at Mangrove Cay, but most today opt to head on towards Great Sale Cay. Mangrove Cay offers shelter from east through southeast winds and has a non-operational (as far back as many can remember) light atop a pole off the cay's northwestern tip. Use caution if

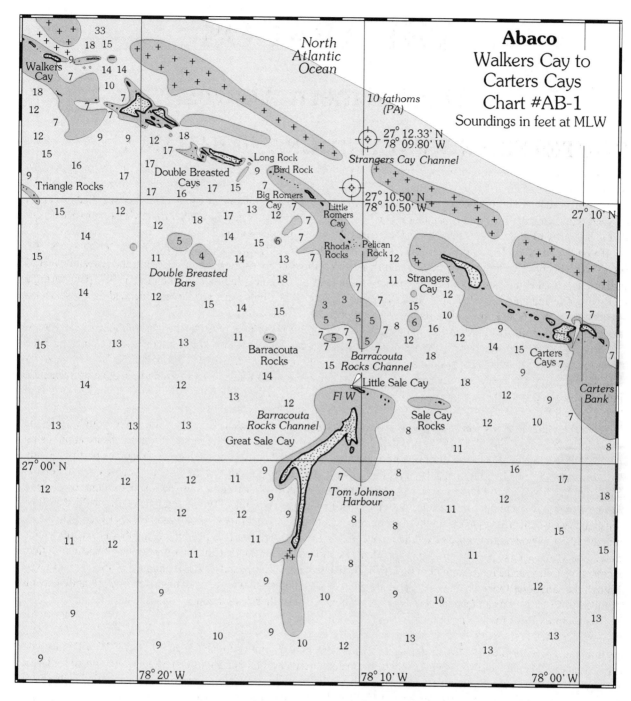

heading south of Mangrove Cay as the waters there shoal steadily the closer you get to Grand Bahama. A GPS waypoint at 26° 55.50' N, 78° 37.50' W, will place you approximately ½ mile northwest of Mangrove Cay.

A common sight on the Little Bahama Bank are fish muds. These are large areas that appear sandy white/yellow and seem to be shoal water. At first you'll probably steer around them, but as you grow accustomed to their presence you'll build up the nerve to pass right through them. You'll find your hands tightly clenched to your wheel or tiller, your eyes fast on your depth sounder while your vessel slowly inches ahead. Suddenly you will feel a growing sense of relief that you are still in 16' of water even though it appears like less than a quarter of that depth.

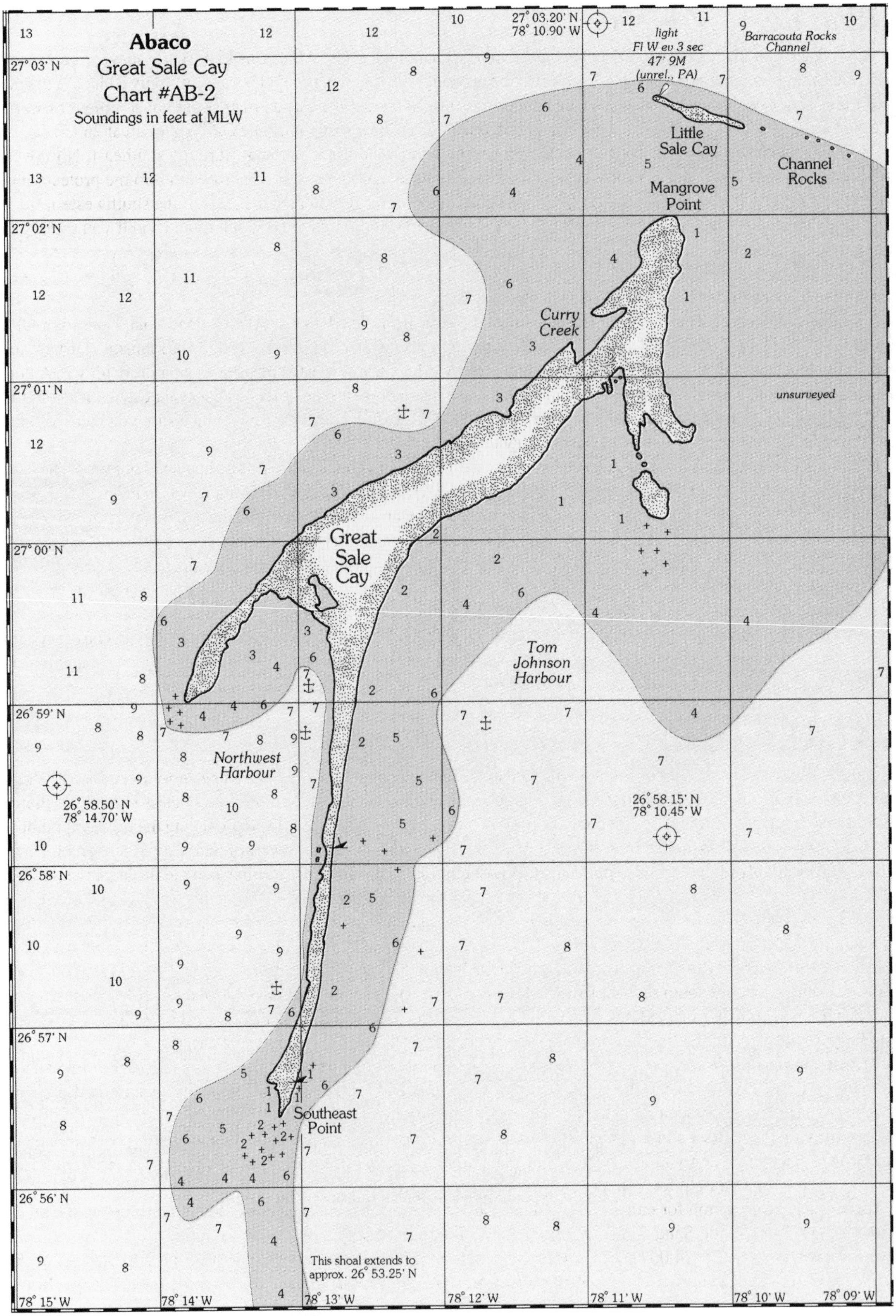

Abaco
Great Sale Cay
Chart #AB-2
Soundings in feet at MLW

Little Sale Cay

Mangrove Point

Barracouta Rocks Channel

Channel Rocks

light
Fl W ev 3 sec
47' 9M
(unrel., PA)

27° 03.20' N
78° 10.90' W

Curry Creek

unsurveyed

Great Sale Cay

Tom Johnson Harbour

Northwest Harbour

26° 58.50' N
78° 14.70' W

26° 58.15' N
78° 10.45' W

Southeast Point

This shoal extends to approx. 26° 53.25' N

27° 03' N

27° 02' N

27° 01' N

27° 00' N

26° 59' N

26° 58' N

26° 57' N

26° 56' N

78° 15' W   78° 14' W   78° 13' W   78° 12' W   78° 11' W   78° 10' W   78° 09' W

GREAT SALE CAY

Most Abaco bound cruisers usually make the wonderful anchorage at Great Sale Cay their first stop when eastbound across the Little Bahama Bank. Some folks like to stop at Mangrove Cay for the night because it's only a bit over twenty miles from West End, but most push on to the better protection at Great Sale Cay another twenty or so miles eastward.

If you are approaching from West End, Grand Bahama you can steer straight for the GPS waypoint at 26° 58.50' N, 78° 14.70' W as shown on Chart #AB-2. In the prevailing wind conditions, northeast through southeast, Northwest Harbour will be your anchorage. From the waypoint simply head east and round up northward into the protection of Northwest Harbour. If you're a bit north of the waypoint, make sure that you give the reefs of the southwestern tip of Great Sale Cay a wide berth upon entering Northwest Harbour. The holding here is good in sand and if you tuck up as far as you can in the northern part of the harbour you can get some shelter from westerly seas. Northwest Harbour is great for winds from north through east to southeast, but if you need shelter from southwest or west winds you'll need be in the lee of Great Sale Cay in Tom Johnson Harbour.

If you're approaching Tom Johnson Harbour from the east, from Fox Town or Allan's-Pensacola, head for a GPS waypoint at 26° 58.15' N, 78° 10.45' W. This will put you in deep water just southeast of Tom Johnson Harbour and south of the shallow bank as shown on the chart. From here work your way westward as far as your draft allows. A note on approaching Tom Johnson Harbour; using caution when heading west from Allan's-Pensacola Cay, you'll want to avoid the large shoal south of Moraine Cay. If you're bound westward from Fox Town, make sure you clear Veteran Rock and West End Rocks. These hazards are shown on Chart #AB-8.

If you wish to enter Tom Johnson Harbour from the western side of Great Sale Cay you have two options. The long way or the short way, your draft will likely decide for you which route you'll take. The long way is to head north around Great Sale Cay and Little Sale Cay and then turn eastward in the Barracouta Rocks Channel to pass the large shoal area to port passing between the Channel Cays and the Sale Cay Rocks (see Chart #AB-1). Once past Sale Cay Rocks you'll head south to finally round back westward into Tom Johnson Harbour. This route is good for deeper draft vessels, 7' or more. The short route is to head south of Great Sale Cay. Vessels with drafts of 6' or less can cross right over the shoal that extends south of Great Sale Cay. From Northwest Harbour clear the shallows off the southern tip of Great Sale Cay and you will come to an area where the shoal is between 4'-6' at MLW (as shown on the chart) where you can cross with the tide. Once over the shallows head north/northeast to Tom Johnson Harbour. In settled weather a nice anchorage is of the northwestern shore of Great Sale Cay where you can tuck in fairly close to shore.

WALKERS CAY

Walkers Cay is the northernmost inhabited island in the entire Bahamas archipelago and is most noted for its fishing (tuna, dolphin, marlin, kingfish and more) and diving opportunities and is a favorite stop for boaters leaving Ft. Pierce and St. Lucie Inlet in Florida. If you're coming from offshore, an easy entrance is by approaching the GPS waypoint at 27° 16.20' N, 78° 21.55' W, which places you approximately ½ mile north/northwest of Seal Cay as shown on Chart #AB-3. Do not simply plug in this waypoint and head straight for it. You must use caution to avoid the large reef system that lies just north/northwest of Walkers Cay that is partially shown on Chart #AB-1. From this waypoint you have two choices for entrance. The easiest lies just a bit west of south from the waypoint as you pass between Tom Browns Cay and Seal Cay. Once clear of Tom Browns Cay you can head westward paralleling the shoreline of Tom Browns Cay as shown on Chart #AB-3. Pass Gully Rocks and head for the marked entrance to the marina in 7'-9'. Watch out for a couple of shallow patches south of Tom Browns Cay as shown on the chart. The second route, 9' at MLW, takes you from the GPS waypoint as you pass between Gully Rocks and the submerged rocks that lie west of Walkers Cay. Once past Gully Rocks just parallel the shoreline of Walkers in good water until the entrance opens up.

Vessels approaching Walker's Cay from Grand Cays or Double Breasted Cays should pass south of the Grand Cays as shown on Chart #AB-4. Keep the small string of rocks that end with Burying Piece Rock to starboard, passing between them and the easily seen shoal to port. Once clear of Burying Piece Rock, turn to starboard and head northward between Burying Piece Rock and Elephant Rock as shown on Charts #AB-3 and AB-4. Head towards the eastern tip of Tom Browns Cay and when you are clear of the shoal area to your west, turn to port and pass between it and Tom Browns Cay and head straight for Walkers and the marina entrance.

There is one more option for entrance to Walkers Cay from the bank, and that is the marked channel as shown on Chart #AB-3. From White Sand Ridge, Memory Rock, West End, Mangrove Cay, or even Great Sale Cay, you can make for a waypoint at 27° 14.00' N, 78° 24.20' W, which places you approximately ¼ mile south/southwest of the entrance to the marked channel leading to *Walkers Cay Marina*. The primary hazard on this route is the Triangle Rocks

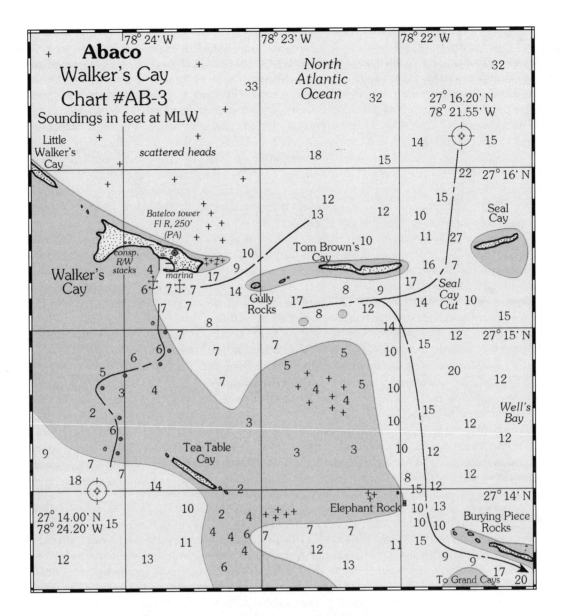

Abaco
Walker's Cay
Chart #AB-3
Soundings in feet at MLW

Little Walker's Cay

scattered heads

North Atlantic Ocean

27° 16.20' N
78° 21.55' W

Batelco tower
Fl R, 250'
(PA)

consp.
R/W
stacks

Walker's Cay

marina

Seal Cay

Tom Brown's Cay

Gully Rocks

Seal Cay Cut

Tea Table Cay

Well's Bay

Elephant Rock

Burying Piece Rocks

27° 14.00' N
78° 24.20' W

To Grand Cays

as partially shown on Chart #AB-1. You must use caution when approaching this crescent shaped string of small rocks. Also, do not attempt to pass from Burying Piece Rock to the above waypoint using a route passing south of Tea Table Cay. The area there has shoaled considerable and there is a stretch where the depth is about 2' at MLW.

From the waypoint you'll see a string of marked pilings leading off across the very visible bank marking a difficult-to-see channel that carries about 5' at MLW. Pass between the first two pilings, they will be marked red and green (red, right, returning), and will have small arrows that point to which side to take pass them on. You'll actually split the first and last pair, and unless they've added some new pilings since this writing, the rest can be taken to starboard when approaching Walkers from the south. Once past the last pair, head straight for the marina entrance.

Walker's Cay Hotel and Marina is the only show in town. They offer 75 slips with a minimum depth in some slips of only 4½', but most slips average 6' and a little more. The marina monitors VHF chs. 16 and 68 and will talk you in if you need assistance. If you need to clear in let them know, and they'll notify *Customs* and *Immigration* for you. The marina has full electric hookups (included in your dockage rate), diesel and gas, water, ice, showers, a laundry, and satellite TV. They can be reached in the states at 1-800-WALKERS. *The Lobster Trap*, right next to the marina, serves seafood specialties and sumptuous desserts with lunch in the winter and lunch and dinner in the summer. Nearby, the *Conch Pearl* also serves up first-rate seafood for dinner and is also open for breakfast. *The Treasure Chest*, located at the hotel, features a distinctive line of resort wear.

For dive trips, *Sea Below* boasts hand-fed tame groupers and exciting shark encounters such as the Shark Rodeo where you may enjoy being around a hundred or more sharks. Divers will also marvel at the gorgeous shallow reefs, wrecks, caverns, and an underwater cathedral filled with fish.

Photo by Nicolas Popov.

Crawfisherman, Grand Cays, Abaco.

As I mentioned earlier, Walkers Cay is noted for two things, their fishing and their diving. Highlighted in *Skin Diver* magazine and on the *Today Show*, Walkers Cay offers some of the best diving in The Bahamas. The *Sea Below Dive and Gift Shop* offers scuba instruction, equipment rentals, (including 35mm cameras), and daily dive trips (they recommend that divers bring their own BC and regulator). If you're coming to Walkers Cay during the winter bring a wet suit as the temperatures hover in the low to mid-70's. Professionally edited videos of your dive trips are set to music for you to purchase. *Sea Below* also rents snorkeling gear and small boats.

GRAND CAYS

The Grand Cays are a wonderful destination; a lot of things to do ashore, as well as a protected anchorage in case a front should approach. There is a sizable population on these cays, most of whom work at Walkers Cay or fish for a living. Trivia lovers might wish to know that the Grand Cays were one of former President Nixon's favorite haunts.

There are several ways to access the Grand Cays. From Walkers Cay or offshore of Walkers, head to the waypoint north of Seal Cay as described in the last section on Walkers Cay. From the waypoint pass between Tom Browns Cay and Seal Cay (see Chart #AB-3) and continue southward to pass between Elephant Rock and Burying Piece Rock. Once clear of Burying Piece Rock turn to port and parallel the shoreline of the Grand Cays as shown on Chart #AB-4. Vessels in this area can also take advantage of a very nice anchorage off the western shore of Grand Cay in Wells Bay as shown on Chart #AB-4. As you'll see on the chart there is a deep-water passage between Grand Cay and the first small rock to its west. This cut is a shortcut to the route along the southern shore of Grand Cay, but is only mentioned for those skippers who are experienced in piloting such passageways since there is a lot of current there.

As you parallel the southern shore of The Grand Cays you will pass south of Sandy Cay and head for a GPS waypoint at 27° 12.60' N, 78° 18.80' W. At this point you will be approximately ½ mile south of the entrance channel to the protected anchorage off Little Grand Cay as shown on Chart #AB-4. From the waypoint head north and then northwestward as you pass south of Felix Cay and the light on its western tip. The channel here carries about 6' at MLW and winds its way west/northwest to the anchorage area off Little Grand Cay. The deepest water is just as you enter and it shallows the further in you go to the west and north. This is a nice anchorage in all conditions short of a hurricane, but make sure your anchor is set well, the bottom tends to be marl in places.

If approaching from Double Breasted Cays follow the long string of cays that lie northwest of the Double Breasted Cays as shown on Chart #AB-5. Head for the waypoint and as you approach the Grand Cays you'll see some more small rocks, some awash, that you need to keep to starboard. Enter the channel as described above. If approaching from Great Sale Cay you can steer for the waypoint mentioned above but you must make sure you avoid the Double Breasted Bars as shown on Chart #AB-1.

On shore you'll find nice walkways to carry you around the small island. *Rosie's Place* offers dockage (15 slips), but use caution, the bottom is only 5' or so in spots here at MLW. At Rosie's you can get water, ice, bait, fuel, and rooms at the *Island Bay Motel*. The restaurant serves up good food and cold drinks as well. *Rosie's* answers to *Love Train* on VHF ch. 68. In town you'll have your choice of several small stores for groceries, but don't expect a large assortment. Try *Ida Cooper's Bakery and Dry Goods* and *Ena's Bakery* for fresh baked breads. There is also a small *Batelco* office and a new clinic in town. If you wish to dine out you can of course eat at *Rosie's* or you can try *The Hilltop Bar and Restaurant*, the *Runway 87 Snack Bar,* or the *New Palms Restaurant and Bar.*

DOUBLE BREASTED CAYS

The uninhabited Double Breasted Cays are arguably the most beautiful cays in the Abacos; they certainly are one of my favorite spots. This area offers a great beach, good snorkeling and diving, conch, fishing and a well-protected, tricky to access anchorage that is excellent for riding out those tough winter fronts.

A GPS waypoint at 27° 10.85' N, 78° 16.40' W will place you approximately ½ mile south of the cays as shown on Chart #AB-5. If you're approaching Double Breasted Cays from Great Sale Cay as shown on Chart #AB-1, you can set your course directly for this waypoint once you clear the anchorage at Great Sale Cay. The only dangers on this route are the easily seen and avoided Barracouta Rocks. The only other possible hazard is the Double Breasted Bars, but these usually lie well to the west of the courseline from Great Sale Cay to Double Breasted. This does not mean you should not keep a lookout, the tide may push you off your course so keep an alert watch at all times.

If you're approaching Double Breasted Cays from Grand Cays, simply keep west of the long string of rocks (see Chart #AB-5) that lie northwest of the Double Breasted Cays toward the Grand Cays. From the waypoint at Double Breasted Cays, as shown on Chart #AB-5, you have several options for anchoring. In north to northeast winds you can anchor directly off the southern shore of the Double Breasted Cays in 9'-15' of water at MLW. The holding is good, but

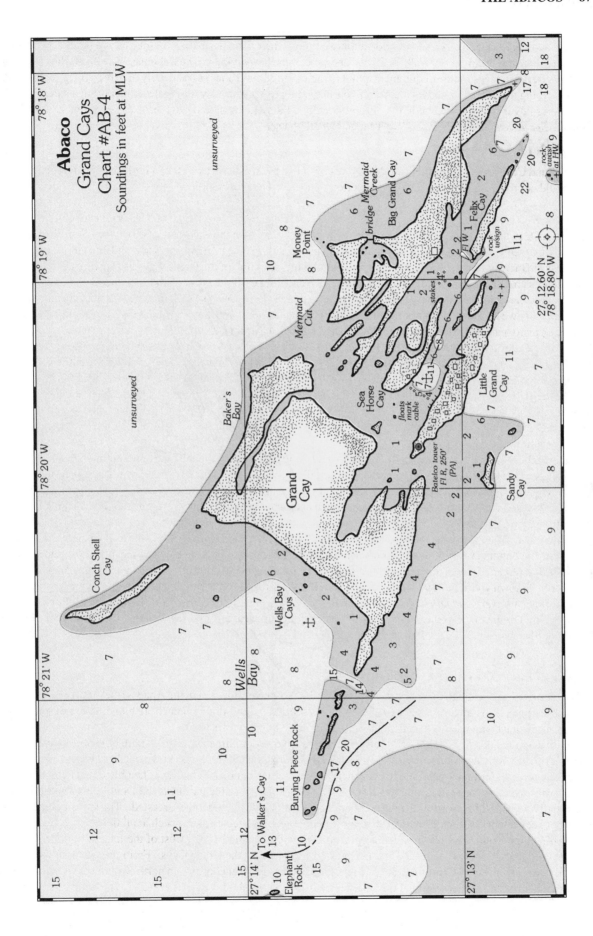

Abaco
Grand Cays
Chart #AB-4
Soundings in feet at MLW

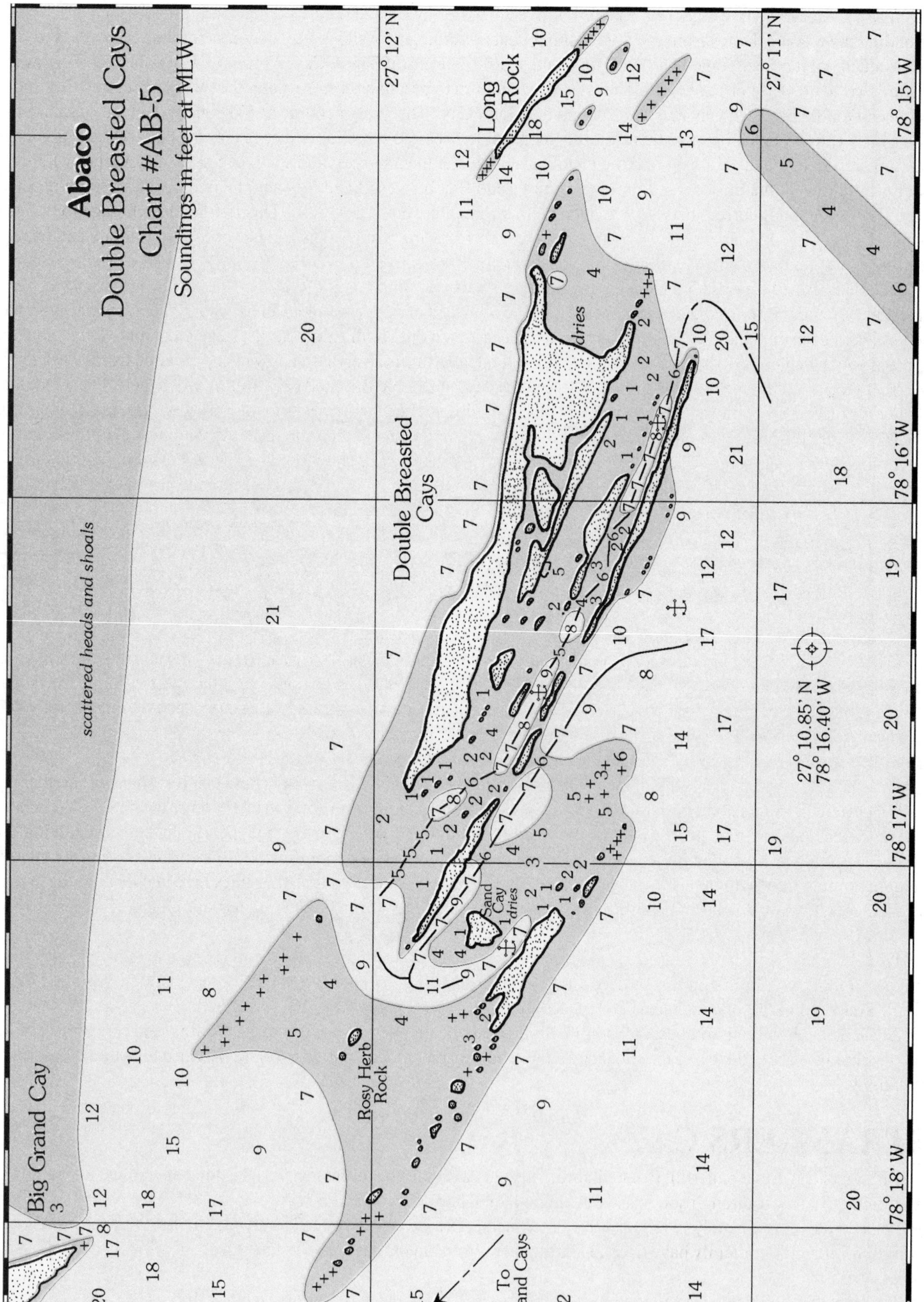

Abaco
Double Breasted Cays
Chart #AB-5

Soundings in feet at MLW

27° 12' N

Long
Rock

Double Breasted
Cays

scattered heads and shoals

Big Grand Cay

Rosy Herb
Rock

Sand
Cay

dries

To
Grand Cays

27° 11' N

78° 15' W

78° 16' W

78° 17' W

78° 18' W

27° 10.85' N
78° 16.40' W

it is not the place to be in winds from east through south to northwest. Another note, cruisers anchoring here will have to endure the passing wakes from the Sportfishing boats returning to Walkers Cay that pass through here at speed.

A much quieter anchorage lies to the west and south of beautiful Sandy Cay. From the waypoint head northward towards the southern shore of Double Breasted Cay and turn to port to pass close along the Double Breasted Cay shore between Double Breasted Cay and the aptly named Sand Cay. There are a couple of 6' spots through here, so use the tide a bit if your draft is more than that. Parallel the Double Breasted shoreline and once past the northwestern tip of the cay turn to port to make your way into the visible deeper water that lies west and south of Sand Cay. Anchor wherever your draft allows. The most serene spot is south of Sand Cay between Sand Cay and the unnamed cay south of Sand Cay. There is a lot of current here so two anchors in a Bahamian moor is a must. This is a good anchorage for a front as the shallows break almost all the seas that can find their way in. Sand Cay is a great spot for swimming and lazing, but cruisers will have to share it with the Sportfishing boats from Walker's Cay at times.

Double Breasted Cays is noted for shark sightings; usually seen in the waters between the cays, they can also be seen off Sand Cay at times, not always, but sometimes. I've seen a lot of fishermen clean their catch right off the back of their boats at the beach on Sand Cay. This practice should cease as it does nothing but attract large predators. I urge you not to clean your catch here, do it before arriving or after you leave, this is a very popular spot and children use these waters!

My favorite anchorage lies in the creek between the cays at Double Breasted Cay. Buggy when there's no wind, this anchorage offers great holding and an excellent place to ride out even the fiercest frontal passages. You must be careful when entering this creek and once in it, the farther you go up the creek, the more hazards you must avoid. From the waypoint, steer towards the southeastern tip of Double Breasted Cay as shown on the chart. Pass around this tip and immediately turn to port, and head up the creek paralleling the lie of the channel. The entrance has a shallow bar of 6' at MLW with an even shallower spot just north of the channel, so be careful when entering and leaving. You might wish to check it out by dinghy first. Once over the first shallow spot you'll find yourself in water from 7'-9' deep. Anchor here if you like or you can work your way up the creek even farther if you'd like. If you desire to proceed up the channel you must first make sure the sun is not in your eyes or you'll never see the bars that you must steer around. Conversely, you cannot leave too early in the morning as the sun will also be in your eyes and you'll have a devil of a time trying to trace your entrance route. It might be best to have someone on the bow through here.

Okay, as you proceed up the creek from the entrance you'll notice that I've tried to mark on the charts the locations of the shoals you'll come upon. For the most part these are easily seen as you approach them if the sun is overhead. They are mostly sand and grass but they are very shallow, 1'-2' in places, but if you dare to, weave your way around them and you'll be rewarded with an anchorage all your own. You can actually work your way through the entire creek with the tide, but it's far safer to enter and leave via the southeastern tip of Double Breasted Cay.

One final note about anchoring in the creek at Double Breasted Cay: Use two anchors in a Bahamian moor, there is a lot of current here, and don't be careless with your scope, don't have a lot of slack in it. If you're anchored NW/SE and a SW/NE wind should pipe up, it might push you to the side of the channel even though your anchors are holding. If you're expecting to ride out a blow here, you might consider anchors in those directions also (don't worry about seas though, nothing builds up in this narrow channel). If you have to weave your anchor lines here and there in the creek, rig them to allow small boats to pass through. A lot of the local folks from Grand Cay use this channel on their way to and from their fishing grounds.

Double Breasted Cays are a birder's paradise, at night the sounds created by the avian residents of the cays may make you think you're in a jungle in deepest darkest Africa. If you explore the creeks of the Double Breasted Cays you'll find the remains of conch pens and turtle kraals in the backwaters.

The Romer Cays lying southeast of Double Breasted Cays offer very good fishing, snorkeling, and conching, but the only anchorages are in the lee of the shoal and should be considered for daytime use only. It's best to explore these cays by dinghy.

STRANGERS CAY

Strangers Cay is a wonderful, isolated, rarely visited cay with a beautiful beach and a good anchorage in prevailing conditions (northeast through southeast). As shown on Chart #AB-6, a GPS waypoint at 27° 07.10' N, 78° 06.70' W will place you approximately ½ mile southwest of the anchorage area. Do not simply plug in this waypoint and steer straight for it, you'll certainly have trouble getting there from almost anywhere in the nearby vicinity as you can see on Chart #AB-1.

If you're approaching from the southeast, from Carters Cays, head west/northwest along the edge of the very visible bank and follow it around right up to the anchorage. From Great Sale Cay you must leave Great Sale Cay and Little Sale

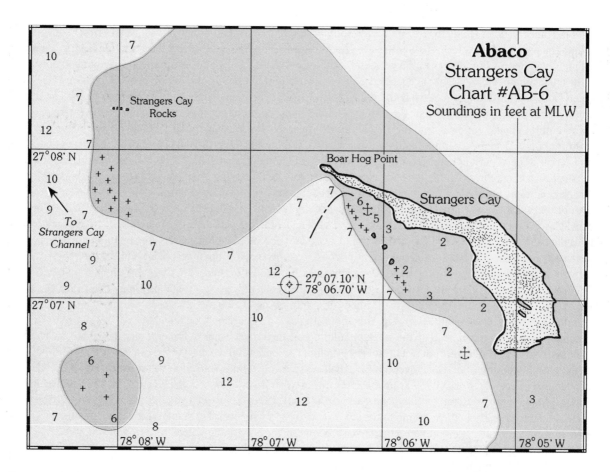

Cay to starboard heading eastward just north of Little Sale Cay in Barracouta Rocks Channel. Once abeam of Little Sale Cay you can alter course to the waypoint at Strangers Cay, but there are dangers that you must avoid. You must be careful to avoid the huge shallow bank that lies north of Little Sale Cay and a couple of shoals between Little Sale Cay and Stranger's Cay, all are easily seen in good visibility…never try this at night.

If approaching from the north, from Walkers Cay or Double Breasted Cay, you must also avoid the large bank area north of Little Sale Cay as well as the Double Breasted Bars and Barracouta Rocks as shown on Chart #AB-1. Once in Barracouta Rocks Channel and clear of the large shoal area north of Little Sale Cay alter course to Strangers Cay and keep an eye out for the smaller shoals that I mentioned are on this route.

From the waypoint at Strangers Cay as shown on Chart #AB-6, head roughly north/northeast towards a point a bit east of Boar Hog Point. The anchorage lies between Strangers Cay and the reef that lies northwest of the small offlying cays southwest of Strangers Cay. As you approach the northern tip of Strangers Cay keep an eye out for the reef to starboard. Round this reef in 6'-7' at MLW and proceed southeastward and anchor where your draft allows (4'-6' at MLW); please note that the water shallows the closer you get to the small offlying cays.

Strangers Cay Channel, as shown on Chart #AB-1, is a wide and deep passage between the reefs and an excellent passage onto and off of the banks. Approaching from the ocean, a GPS waypoint at 27° 12.33' N, 78° 09.80' W will place you approximately ¼ mile north of the channel. From this waypoint steer just west of south, approximately 190°-200°. The course is not as important here as using your eyes and staying between the reefs. Strangers Cay Channel is almost a mile wide and from 18'-30' deep and the reefs are easily seen in good light. Never attempt this cut or any cut at night using just waypoints, that is asking for disaster! Once inside the reef steer approximately 155°-160° until the tiny Strangers Cay Rocks come into view (see Chart #AB-6). Once again, the course is not as important as avoiding the reefs to the north and the large shoal area the borders the Romers Cays. Take Strangers Cay Rocks to port and turn southward avoiding the reef south of Strangers Cay Rocks and the shoals between these rocks and Barracouta Rocks Channel.

Vessels wishing to exit the banks via Strangers Cay Channel should make their way to the area between the outer reefs and the shoal area that borders the Romers Cays. If you're leaving the anchorage at Strangers Cay, head generally west/southwest following the edge of the bank that lies west of Strangers Cay. Once past the reefs south of Strangers

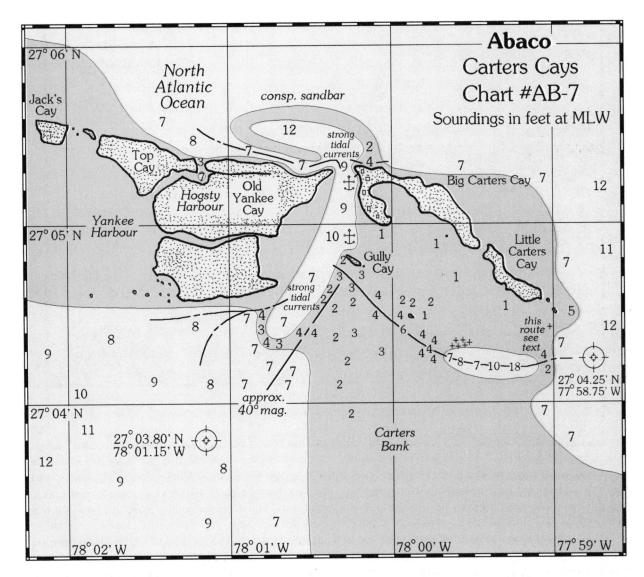

Cay Rocks, head for a GPS waypoint at 27° 10.50' N, 78° 10.50' W, but use caution and avoid the Romers Cays shoal area. From the waypoint head just east of north, approximately 10°-20°, passing between the reefs in Strangers Cay Channel. As I mentioned earlier, the course is not that important as staying between the reefs here. If you find you must head 000° then by all means do just that, anything to stay between the reefs. Remember that there may be a difference as large as .1 nautical mile between the GPS system that recorded these soundings and yours. I cannot repeat this enough...TRUST YOUR EYES AND YOUR DEPTH SOUNDER!

CARTERS CAYS

The Carters Cays, though a bit tricky to access, offer a good anchorage in the event of a frontal passage as well as a small hurricane hole. You'll find that although Big Carters Cay is inhabited there are no real amenities ashore. Entry to the anchorages must be made with the tide and I'll show you a new one that is far easier than the traditional approach which has shallowed over the years. So let's begin.

As shown on Chart #AB-7, a GPS waypoint will place you about a mile southwest of Gully Cay in water from 7'-9' in depth. From here, the closer you get to the Carters Cays the shallower the water becomes. If you're approaching from Great Sale Cay, once you clear Little Sale Cay in Barracouta Rocks Channel you can head directly for the waypoint at Carters Cays. If you're approaching from the southeast, from Angelfish Point, Fox Town, or perhaps Allan's-Pensacola, you must avoid the large sandbank south of Moraine Cay and the Carters Bank as you approach the waypoint (as shown on Chart #AB-8). We'll discuss the route north of the Carters Bank in a few minutes.

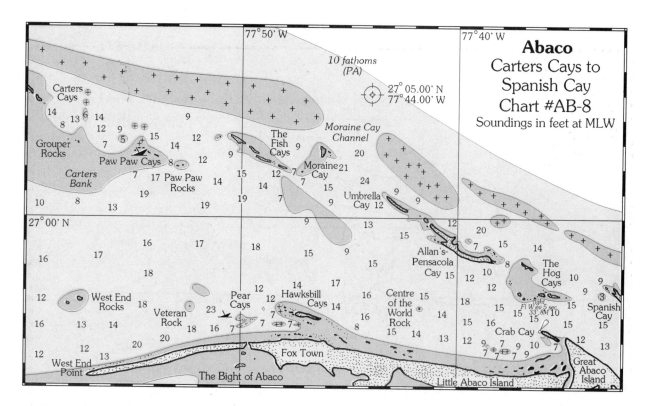

From the waypoint southwest of Carters Cays you have two options to access the anchorages. The traditional route is to put the diamond shaped range on Gully Cay on your bow and approach it on a course of approximately 40°. When you're only about 50' off Gully Cay turn to port, roughly to the northwest, and cross over a shallow bar into the conspicuous deeper water. This route used to work fine, but over the last few years this area has filled in and the controlling depth now is about 2'-2½' at MLW here. As you approach Gully Cay you'll notice lots of long marks in the bottom where people have drug keels and damaged props. This is no longer a very boater friendly route for deeper draft vessels (over 4'). I use a different approach. From the waypoint you'll notice the deeper blue water that lies southwest of Gully Cay and you should be able to discern the shallow bank that lies between you and that deeper water as shown on Chart #AB-7. I'll head up towards the shore of the large unnamed cay south of Old Yankee Cay and head generally eastward to cross the visible bar in about 4' at MLW. When used with the tide, this route saves a lot of wear and tear on your boat as well as your nerves. You can also cross the same bar at the extreme southwestern tip of the deeper water.

Whichever route you take, once you're in the deeper water you can anchor north of Gully Cay between Gully Cay and Big Carters Cay. This spot is a bit out of the strong currents here and is a favorite. The other spot is near the northwestern tip of Big Carters Cay just off the houses. By all means use two anchors in a Bahamian moor, there is a LOT of current here.

Now let's discuss the route north of the Carters Bank. This route is primarily for those who wish to access this anchorage when approaching from Moraine Cay Channel or the Fish Cays. If approaching from Moraine Cay Channel, pass between the outer reef and Moraine Cay passing north of the Fish Cays heading for the Carters Cays as shown on Chart #AB-8. When approaching from the Fish Cays, pass north of the Paw Paw Cays and watch out for some scattered heads along through here. Head to a GPS waypoint at 27° 04.25' N, 77° 58.75' W, which will place you southeast of Little Carters Cay and just north of the Carters Cay Bank as shown on Chart #AB-7. The next part of this route is very tricky and demands that you have the ability to read the water (at least) and nerves of steel (it helps). Only run this route on a rising tide!

From the waypoint look to the west and you'll see a very shallow bank with a patch of deeper water to the west of it. As you leave the deeper water at the waypoint you'll be heading for a small slot where two shallow banks come together, this will lead you to the deeper water. (CAUTION: The configuration of these two shallow banks may change by the time this is written, check it first with your dinghy if in doubt.) Cross over the shallows into the deeper water and proceed westward aiming for a point just a bit north of west at the far end of the deeper water where you'll see some

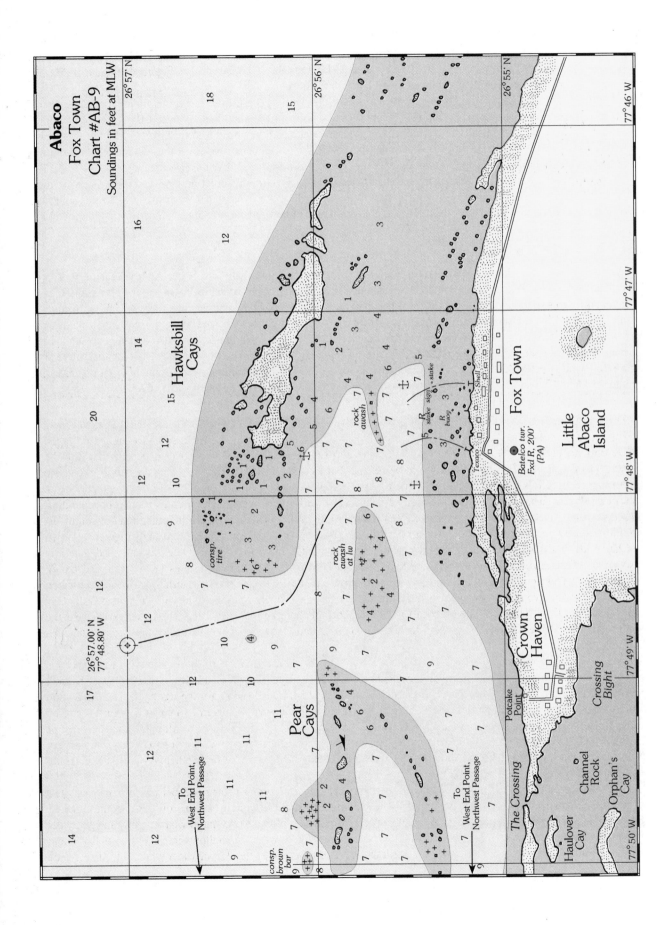

Abaco
Fox Town
Chart #AB-9
Soundings in feet at MLW

Hawksbill Cays

Pear Cays

To West End Point, Northwest Passage

To West End Point, Northwest Passage

26°57.00' N
77°48.80' W

consp. tire

rock awash at lw

rock awash

consp. brown bar

R. stake sign. stake

R. buoy

Shell

Texaco

Fox Town

Little Abaco Island

Batelco twr. Fxd R. 200' (PA)

Crown Haven

Potcake Point

The Crossing

Crossing Bight

Channel Rock

Haulover Cay

Orphan's Cay

submerged rocks. You'll want to keep these rocks to starboard as you head north of west as shown on Chart #AB-7. Just as you pass abeam of the rocks you'll want to adjust your course towards Gully Cay taking Gully Cay and the lone rock halfway to Gully Cay to starboard. You'll have 4' and a bit more through here at MLW but it will shoal to 3' MLW at Gully Cay. Pass close to Gully Cay and cross the bar into the deeper water.

If you don't like the above route, you can always pass to the north of Big Carters Cay giving it a wide berth. Pass westward around the conspicuous curving sandbank that lies north of the anchorage between Big Carters Cay and Yankee Cay. Take the western arc of the sandbank on your port side and then head eastward, paralleling the shoreline of Old Yankee Cay to enter the harbour as shown on Chart #AB-7. You can also cross over the southeastern end of the curving sandbank just north of Big Carters Cay with the tide; it's almost 4' at MLW through here.

Between Top Cay and Old Yankee Cay is the entrance to Hogsty Harbour, sometimes called Safety Harbour, the local hurricane hole. The entrance is straightforward from the north over a 3' bar at MLW. Inside you'll find room for two good sized boats in water 7'-10' deep. Please note that these routes may have changed since Hurricane Floyd.

FOX TOWN

What a great little anchorage awaits you at Fox Town. Though there really aren't any beaches to speak of, you can avail yourself of some fine dining in town as well as fuel. The anchorages between Fox Town and the Hawksbill Cays are wonderful in prevailing winds, but no place to be in the event of a frontal passage when the winds blow from the southwest to northwest. Explorers will want to check out The Crossing west of Crown Haven. Here is a man-made cut that was designed to be a shortcut to the Bight of Abaco, but in reality is a small break in the land with a heck of a lot of current. About three miles west of Fox Town, and northwest of the Pear Cays is a very visible sunken barge, ideal for snorkeling while the Hawksbill Cays offer excellent dinghy exploration opportunities. Ask around town for a guide to Saunder's Hole, a wonderful blue hole lying just south of Little Abaco and southwest of Moses Cay.

Photo by Nicolas Popov.

A fishing boat, Abaco Cays.

There are several ways to access the anchorage at Fox Town. If you're approaching from West End Point on Little Abaco as shown on Chart #AB-8, you can simply parallel the shoreline of Little Abaco, staying about ¼ mile or more offshore to avoid the shallows and small rocks that line the shore. As you approach Fox Town you can pass between the Pear Cays and The Crossing as shown on Charts #AB-8 and #AB-9.

If you're approaching from Great Sale Cay, you can head either north of south of Great Sale Cay, and when in deeper water (once you've cleared the bar south of Great Sale Cay or once you've cleared Sale Cay Rocks to the north), you can make a beeline for the GPS waypoint at 26° 57.00 N, 77° 48.80' W as shown on Chart #AB-9. Your only hazards on this route are the West End Rocks and the shoal north of Veteran Rock as shown on Chart #AB-8.

If you're approaching from Angelfish Point you can head directly to the waypoint keeping an eye out for tiny Centre of the World Rock. From the anchorage at Crab Cay you can also parallel the shoreline of Little Abaco westward, but if you choose this route you must keep an eye out for the reefs shown on Chart #AB-8.

From the waypoint the entrance to the anchorages is not difficult. Pass to the west of the Hawksbill Cays, giving them a wide berth as the shallows stretch a bit more westward than shown on some other charts of the area. The northwestern-most of the Hawksbill Cays is a small rock that is easily spotted, it has a very conspicuous tire sitting atop a piling. As you pass south of the string of cays leading westward from the Hawksbill Cays you'll want to bring your bow around a bit more to port to avoid the huge shoal area that dries at low water (as shown on Chart #AB-9). From here you can anchor to the south of the largest of the Hawksbill Cays, which offers great protection in north through east winds. Or if you prefer you can work your way closer to town to anchor just outside the string of rocks that lay north of Fox Town and mark the edge of the deeper water; this spot is good in winds from east through south.

Getting the big boats into the dock at *Fox Town Shell* (to the east) or *Fox Town Texaco* (to the west) takes some doing (3'-4' at MLW along these routes). The best advice I can give is to call ashore on VHF and request a pilot while still outside the string of four small cays, unless you are content to dinghy in with jerry jugs. The routes I show on Chart #AB-9, although somewhat marked (privately maintained), may seem quite intimidating to someone unused to piloting in shallow water, if in doubt ask for a pilot.

Fox Town Shell sits right on the water's edge next to the *Valley Bar and Restaurant* (with a pool table!) and offers fuel, water, ice, and groceries and boasts 5½'-7' at high water. The entrance here is not too difficult; leave the four conspicuous small cays to starboard when entering the channel to the dock, keeping the easternmost rock close to starboard. From here simply head straight for the *Fox Town Shell* dock. Just west of the *Shell* station is the *Texaco Star Port* (*Fox Town Texaco* on VHF ch. 16) dock where you can fuel up and purchase oil. Entrance is gained by passing the westernmost of the four cays to starboard and heading in towards the dock. If you plan to stay overnight, check out *Mimi's Guest Cottages* or the *Tangelo Hotel*. You can order dinner by VHF at the *Valley Bar and Restaurant* by calling *Fox Town Shell* on VHF. Fox Town is in the middle of a bit of a construction boom, they are currently erecting a huge new government *Clinic*.

For cruisers interested in their e-mail, *Fox Town Texaco* and the *Tangelo Hotel* have volunteered to broadcast the weather and announce waiting e-mail each morning on the VHF. Usually there will be an announcement on VHF ch. 16 between 0700 and 0800 with a switch to a working channel. The exact time depends on the workload at *Fox Town Texaco* when Lillian Parker opens each morning. Just keep your radio on ch. 16 and you'll hear her call. You can contact either station on ch. 16 at any time of day to check on e-mail if you're in the area, roughly from Great Sale Cay to Angelfish Point. *Fox Town Texaco* even offers an "arrival report" e-mail service that will send an e-mail message for you announcing your safe arrival.

To the west of Fox Town is the tiny community of Crown Haven. Crown Haven, little more than a good walk west of Fox Town, offers a telephone, the *Black Room Bar and Restaurant*, and *E&J's Ice Cream Parlour and Video Tape Rental*. If you're hungry and have forgotten to call ahead for a meal, simply stop by and see Bookie Butler at the *Chili Bar Restaurant*, he's pretty handy in emergencies. Crown Haven, like so many communities in The Bahamas, has an interesting past. Many of the residents remember when they lived on nearby Cave Cay in the Bight of Abaco. A hurricane in the 1930's destroyed their homes and the Government moved them to the island of Little Abaco at the end of the road and today we have Crown Haven – a haven courtesy of the Crown.

THE FISH CAYS

The Fish Cays, as shown on Chart #AB-10, is a small sting of low-lying cays that offer a pair of decent anchorages, though no place to ride out a frontal passage. Located just west of popular Moraine Cay, you'll find some nice snorkel-

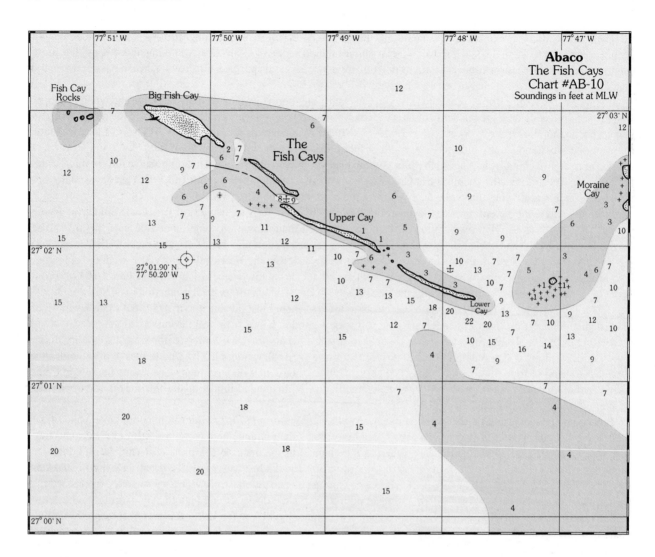

ing and diving on the reefs just to the north of these cays as well as in between the cays themselves. Don't confuse these Fish Cays with the Fish Cays that lie south of Great Guana Cay between Guana and the mainland of Great Abaco.

Lower Cay offers a great lee in south through west winds. I ducked in behind this cay once when it was blowing about twenty from the southwest and found a great, flat, anchorage. Though the island is low and I still had the wind, the water was flat calm as I tucked in close.

If you're at Fox Town, you can head generally west of north to arrive at the Fish Cays as shown on Chart #AB-8. A GPS waypoint at 27° 01.90' N, 77° 50.20' W will place you approximately ½ mile southwest of the Fish Cays in 15' of water. If you're approaching the Fish Cays from Great Sale Cay or Carters Cays, you must first clear the southern tip of Carters Cay Bank before working your way towards the Fish Cays as shown on Chart #AB-8. A good stop on this route is at the Paw Paw Cays to dive on the wrecks there. You can pass between the Paw Paw Cays and Paw Paw Rocks in 8' though other charts and publications do not show this. In east through southeast winds, pass north of the Paw Paw Rocks to anchor in their lee off their western shore. Watch out for a couple of scattered heads and shoals on this route. If you are approaching the Fish Cays from Carters Cays and you have crossed or passed Carters Cay Bank to the north, simply head straight for the Fish Cays as shown on Chart #AB-8 keeping a sharp eye out for the shoals and heads along this route.

If you're at Moraine Cay and want to access the Fish Cays, leave the anchorage at Moraine and head southwest keeping the very visible shallow sand bank to starboard as shown on Chart #AB-10. Once you clear the offlying rock and its surrounding reefs, you can pass between it and Lower Cay to anchor in the lee of Lower Cay. If you want to head to the anchorage between Upper Cay and Fish Cay, pass south of the lay of the Fish Cays (watch out for the shallow bank to the south of Lower Cay) and then follow their lie. Make sure to give a wide berth to the large shoal that lies west of Upper Fish Cay. In prevailing wind conditions you can anchor in the bight of the southwestern tip of Big Fish Cay or, by playing the tide, you can work your way into the anchorage between Fish Cay and Upper Cay. This is a deep anchorage, 8' and more in places, but there is a lot of current here so two anchors are a must. The anchorage is a good spot in winds from north through east to southwest.

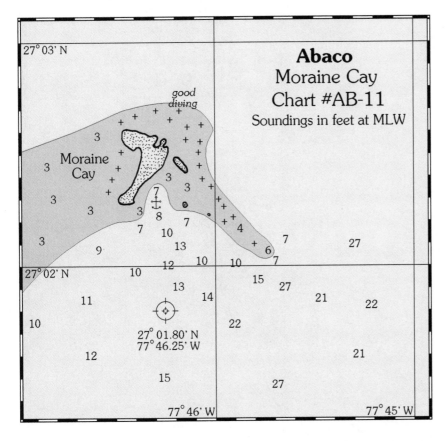

MORAINE CAY

A surveyor described Moraine Cay in the 1920's as "...the most attractive cay in the (Abaco) range. It would suit a person who desires to be monarch of all he surveys." The island was once farmed for sisal but today its primary attraction is its anchorage and its reefs and flats.

As shown on Chart #AB-11, a GPS waypoint at 27° 01.80' N, 77° 46.25' W, will place you approximately ½ mile south of the anchorage. The entrance to the small anchorage is straightforward and the small bight is open to the southeast through south to west. Moraine Cay is good in winds from northwest through north to east but it can get lumpy in southeasterlies. There is a lovely beach by the anchorage and the island itself is criss-crossed with trails to ease exploring.

If you're approaching Moraine Cay from Allan's-Pensacola or Angel Fish Point it is virtually a straight shot as shown on Chart #AB-8 with the only hazards being the shallows off Umbrella Cay. If you're approaching from Fox Town you'll need to avoid the large shoal area lying south of Moraine Cay, also shown on Chart #AB-8. If you're approaching Moraine Cay from the Fish Cays you just need to follow the southern edge of the very visible bank around to the anchorage as shown on Charts #AB-8 and #AB-10.

Just to the north/northeast of Moraine Cay is Moraine Cay Channel (Chart #AB-8), wide and deep it is an excellent spot to head out into the ocean if you so desire. If you're approaching Moraine Cay Channel from the ocean, you can make your way to a GPS waypoint at 27° 05.00' N, 77° 14.00' W. From this waypoint simply put Moraine Cay on your bow and head towards it, turning southeastward to avoid the reefs that lie to the northeast of Moraine Cay of course.

ALLAN'S-PENSACOLA CAY

Allan's-Pensacola Cay is a bit of a paradox. On the northwestern end is a fair harbor with notoriously poor holding, while on the eastern end is one of the best hurricane holes in this section of the Abacos. Once two cays, Allan's Cay and Pensacola Cay, they were united during a hurricane in the not too distant past and remain as one today. Onshore there are the remains of a missile tracking station and along the northern shore are several areas where cruisers have hung up flotsam and jetsam and decorated a nice little niche in the shoreline.

A GPS waypoint at 26° 59.20' N, 77° 42.20' W will place you approximately ¾ mile west/southwest of the entrance to the harbour on the northwestern shore of Allan's-Pensacola Cay as shown on Chart #AB-12. If you're approaching from Great Sale Cay, actually Barracouta Rocks Channel, you must be sure to avoid the shallow sandbank lying south of Moraine Cay as shown on Chart #AB-8. From Fox Town, once you clear the Hawksbill Cays you have a straight shot to the harbour at Allan's-Pensacola. If you're approaching from the south, from Spanish Cay or other spots in the Sea

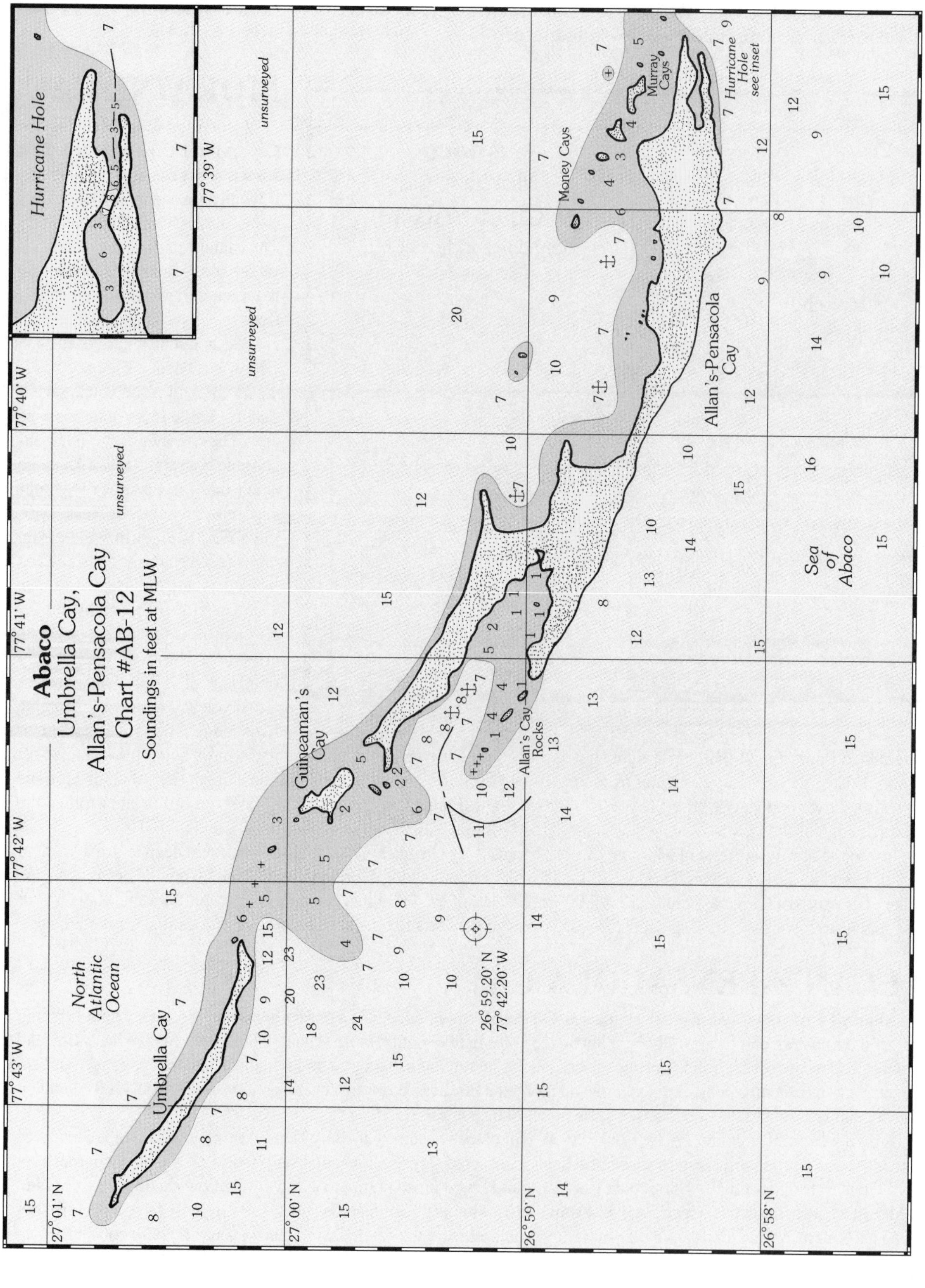

Hurricane Hole

7
7
7
5 3
8 6 5
3 6
3

77° 39' W

unsurveyed

unsurveyed

unsurveyed

77° 40' W

7

9
7 *Hurricane Hole see inset*

5
Murray Cays
4
3 4
4
3
6
7
7

7

9
12
12
12
9
8
15
10
10
9
10

Money Cays

15

20

10
9
7

7

7

7
10

Allan's-Pensacola Cay

12

14

Abaco
Umbrella Cay,
Allan's-Pensacola Cay
Chart #AB-12
Soundings in feet at MLW

77° 41' W

77° 42' W

12

15

15

10

13

12
13
14

8

16
15

15

12

14
10

*Sea
of
Abaco*

15

*Guineaman's
Cay*

12

5

2
2
2
5

7
7

7
8
7

7 8
7

5 2
1 1
1 0 1
1
8

10

13
14

15

15

*North
Atlantic
Ocean*

77° 43' W

15

7
Umbrella Cay
7
15
6 + 5
5 + +
15
12 15
9
12 23
20 23
18 23
24

3

5

4
7 7
7 7
9
8

10 9
10

26° 59.20' N
77° 42.20' W

9

14

8

15

15

10 + + + +
11 10 1 4
12 10

*Allan's Cay
Rocks*
13

14

15

15

27° 01' N
7
8
10
15

7
8 7
11

14
12
15
13

27° 00' N

15

26° 59' N
14

26° 58' N
15

of Abaco south of Angel Fish Point, make sure you clear the shoals at the Hog Cays (passing between the Hog Cays and Angelfish Point) before turning towards Allan's-Pensacola.

From the waypoint outside the harbour at Allan's-Pensacola you can head a bit north of east and pass north of the submerged rocks lying northwest of Allan's Cay Rocks. Once past the submerged rocks, turn to starboard and anchor where your draft allows. The water thins gradually the further in you go, and the holding is poor at times. You must make sure your anchor is set well here. I was anchored here one night and we had a succession of three very violent squalls pass through between 0200-0500 with 40+ knot westerly winds. Six out of 15 boats wound up on the beach and I myself wound up 100' short of the beach after a dragging trawler fouled my starboard anchor. For some reason every time I anchor at Allan's-Pensacola Cay we have bad weather from the west. So if you see me anchored at Allan's-Pensacola you'd better check your anchors, it's a sure sign of bad weather!

In southwesterly and westerly winds I have anchored off the northern shore of Allan's-Pensacola and the water was flat calm. But bear in mind that westerly winds usually mean a shift to the north, especially in the winter months, and the northern side of Allan's-Pensacola is no place to be when that happens. There are two ways that you can access these anchorages as shown on Chart #AB-12. First, you can head east around the eastern tip of Allan's-Pensacola and the Murray Cays and then double back to the west once you clear the Murray Cays and the Money Cays. The Money Cays are called that because a squatter named Murray is said to have found a treasure trove there. Your other option is to round the northwestern tip of Umbrella Cay and parallel the lie of Umbrella Cay, Guineaman's Cay, and Allan's-Pensacola Cay staying ½ mile offshore until you find the spot that you like.

At the eastern end of Allan's-Pensacola Cay is the aptly named Hurricane Hole. As shown on Chart #AB-12, the entrance is between two spits of land with your course favoring the southern spit. Don't stray north here as the water shallows quickly and the bottom is rocky. It's best to sound this route by dinghy first. This route will take 5' at high water and the shallowest spot is just inside the end of the southern spit with about 3' at MLW. From here the water gets progressively deeper, 7'-9' in spots in the narrow creek that leads back to the small, shallow pond. The creek is lined with mangroves on both sides and if a hurricane threatened, I would choose to tie up in the creek just before it leads into the pond.

THE HOG CAYS

The Hog Cays lie just to the southeast of Allan's-Pensacola Cay, to the north of Angelfish Point, and just west of Spanish Cay. They offer little to the cruiser save some good conching. Hog Cay is private and visits ashore must be by invitation only. There is an entrance to a small cove on the north side of Hog Cay that is never used. I only mention it in that it might be a place to duck into in the event of a hurricane. The entrance takes 5' with 6' and more inside at MLW.

CRAB CAY AND ANGELFISH POINT

Angelfish Point lies at the northern end of Crab Cay, the small island that itself lies off the northernmost tip of Great Abaco Island. A 33' tall light that flashes white every 5 seconds marks the point. The anchorage in the lee of Crab Cay and Great Abaco Island is great in winds from north through east to south with good holding in sand mixed in with a few rocks.

Getting here is easy. A GPS waypoint at 26° 56.10' N, 77° 36.40' W places you approximately ½ mile north of Angelfish Point as shown on Chart #AB-8. If you're approaching from Moraine Cay, Allan's-Pensacola, Spanish Cay, or if you're heading north along the Great Abaco shoreline you can head directly for this waypoint. If you're approaching from Great Sale Cay or Fox Town, you can head more for the northern point of Crab Cay as you get within a mile or so. If you're paralleling the shoreline from Fox Town to Crab Cay, or in reverse, from Crab Cay to Fox Town, beware of the reefs a mile and more west of Crab Cay as shown on Chart #AB-8.

Crab Cay is bounded to the southwest by a large shallow bar and vessels wishing to access the anchorage have two options here. You can either go all the way around the bar to the southwest or pass close in along the Crab Cay shore and parallel it southeastward into the main anchorage area. There is a shallow bar with 6' over it at MLW just southeast of the light, but you'll have 7' or more the rest of the way along this route. You can anchor in the lee of Great Abaco in 6'-8' of water just off the small beach.

The small but very rocky beach is not worth exploring, but there are miles of shallow waterways that are worth exploring. You can even work your way back to where the locals keep their boats by the Bootle Highway bridge that connects Little Abaco Island with Great Abaco Island. Shallow draft vessels can even work their way up in here for excellent all-around protection, though there's a lot of current and it's buggy when there's no wind.

Abaco
The Hog Cays
Chart #AB-13
Soundings in feet at MLW

There is a little known shortcut between Crab Cay and Great Abaco Island, but it is only for skippers with an adventurous spirit, a high tide, and a vessel that draws less than 6'. Before I tell you about this one, I'm going to insist that you sound this passage first by dinghy, going in and out several times to familiarize yourself with it before you try it with your seagoing home. A good suggestion would be to set up a visual range for yourself. I use the small cay directly south of the cut and the small rock that lies east of Hog Cay directly north of the cut. I'll put the southern cay on my stern and the northern rock on my bow to get myself lined up with where the deeper water is. The hazards are a rocky bar that lies southeast of Crab Cay that dries a bit at low water and a few rocks lying northwest of Great Abaco Island. You must pass between the two in a narrow channel that is closer to the Great Abaco Island shoreline. As I said, try this with your dink first and if you don't feel comfortable, don't attempt this shortcut…it's not that far around Crab

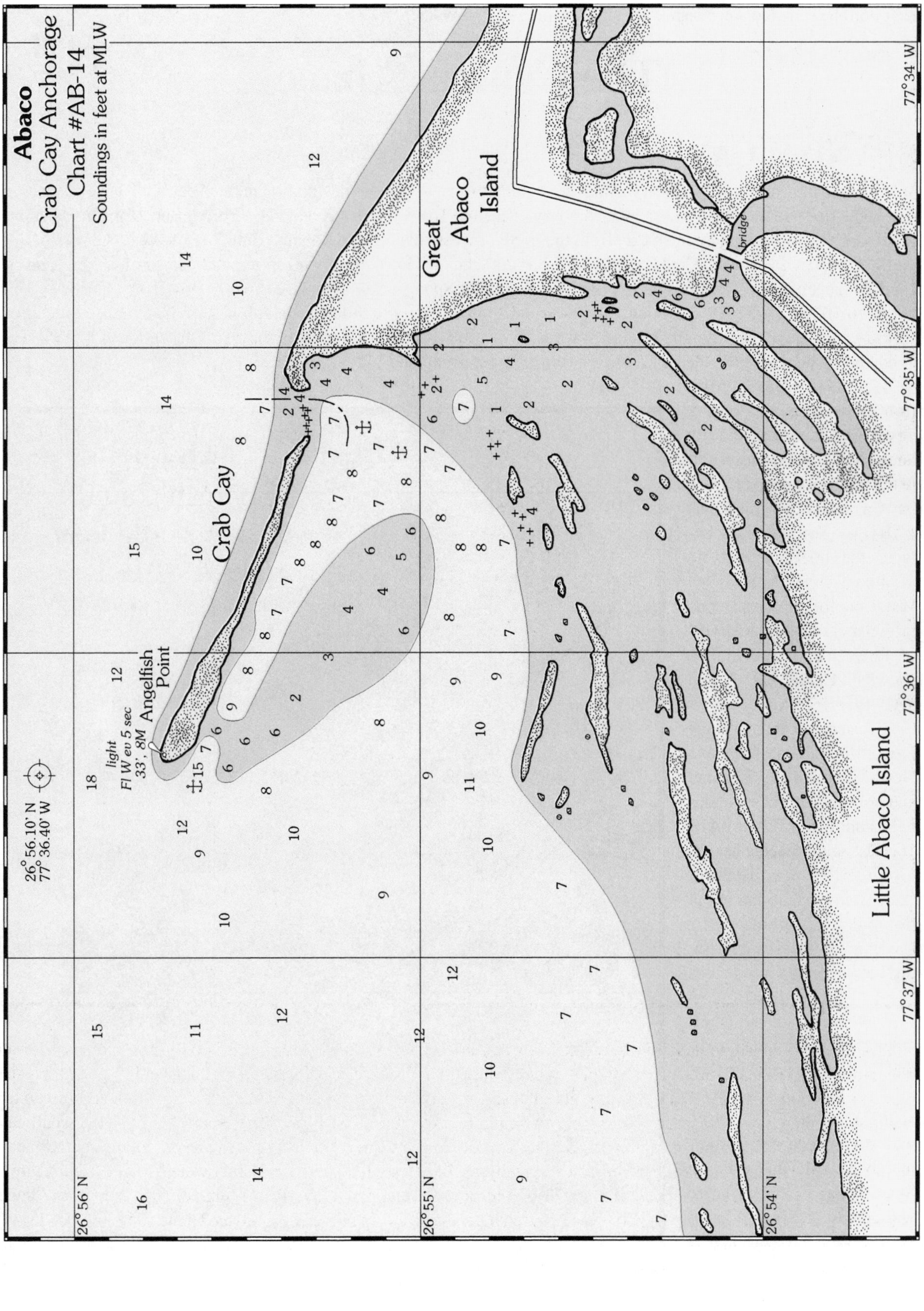

Abaco
Crab Cay Anchorage
— Chart #AB-14 —
Soundings in feet at MLW

26° 56.10' N
77° 36.40' W

Crab Cay

light
Fl W ev 5 sec
33', 8M Angelfish
Point

Great
Abaco
Island

Little Abaco Island

bridge

26° 56' N
26° 55' N
26° 54' N

77° 37' W
77° 36' W
77° 35' W
77° 34' W

Cay anyway. I only mention this route because it's fun to surprise people when they see you enter or leave by it. One time I was heading to this anchorage in company with another boat who was well ahead of me. He thought he had me beat until he rounded Angelfish Point and saw me setting my anchor.

The Central Abacos

SPANISH CAY

Over the past few years Spanish Cay has come into its own as a major destination in the Abacos. The new marina is one of the finest in the islands, the airstrip has reopened, and Spanish Cay has become a Port of Entry for The Bahamas.

If you're approaching Spanish Cay from the north or west on the Little Bahama Bank (as shown on Chart #AB-8), you'll need to pass between Crab Cay (Angelfish Point) and the Hog Cays as you approach Spanish Cay. You can pass south of the small shoal that lies off the northwestern tip of Spanish Cay to make a direct approach to a GPS waypoint at 26° 56.10' N, 77° 32.10' W, which will place you approximately ½ mile west/southwest of the entrance to *Spanish Cay Marina*. From the waypoint head in towards the marina entrance as shown on the chart; the entrance is marked by a red and green marker on the outer pilings (red, right returning here).

If you're approaching from Powell Cay or Coopers Town you need to avoid the large shoal that lies just south of the southeastern tip of Spanish Cay as shown on Chart #AB-15. You can pass between the shoal and Goat Cay as shown on Chart #AB-16. Watch out for the conspicuous brown reef that lies northwest of Powell Cay and that is shown on Charts #AB-16 and #AB-17.

Cruisers can enter or leave the Little Bahama Bank via North Spanish Cay Channel and South Spanish Cay Channel as shown on Chart #AB-16. The southern channel is a bit wider so let's discuss it first. Leaving the marina at Spanish Cay, parallel the shoreline southeastward passing between the conspicuous shoal to the south and Goat Cay as shown on the chart. Once clear of the small rocks that lie southeast of Goat Cay, turn and head for a waypoint at 26° 56.00' N, 77° 29.50' W, which will place you approximately ¼ mile inside South Spanish Cay Channel. There will be reefs off both sides of your vessel but you have a

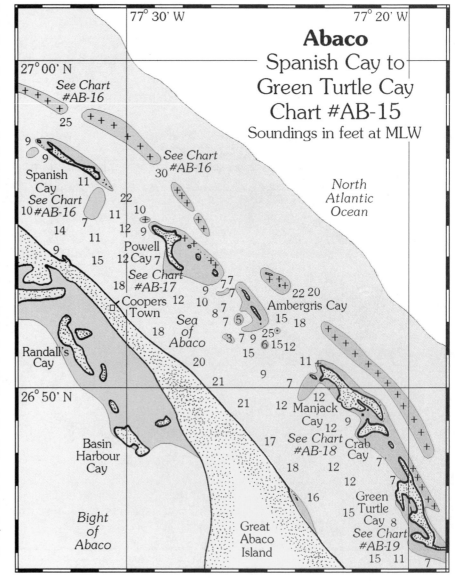

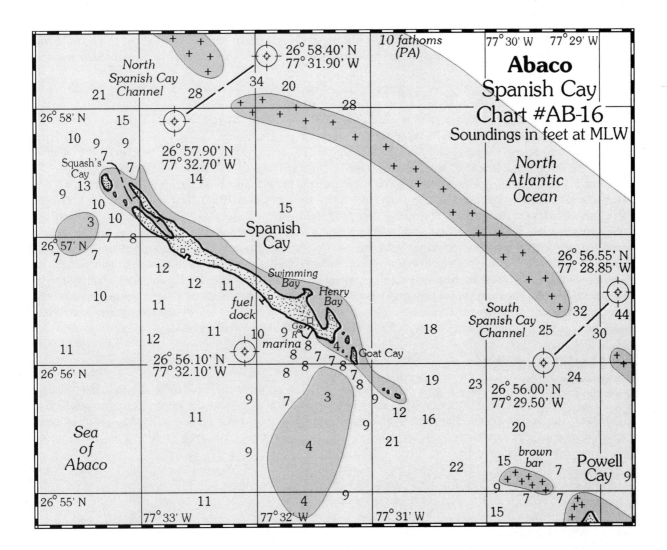

wide and deep cut here, 25' and more at MLW in places. Head through the cut on a northeastward course or head to the outer waypoint at 26° 56.55' N, 77° 28.85' W. The course here is not as important as staying between the reefs! If approaching from the North Atlantic Ocean, make your way to the outer waypoint at 26° 56.55' N, 77° 28.85' W. From here you can head southwest or make your way to the inner waypoint at 26° 56.00' N, 77° 29.50' W. Whatever way you choose to enter, just keep your eyes open, trust them and your depthsounder, not my charts!

North Spanish Cay Channel is narrower than the southern channel, but can be safely transited by the prudent skipper. From the marina at Spanish Cay, work your way northwestward around the northern tip of Spanish Cay, passing between the Spanish Cay and the shoal off its northwestern tip in 8'-10' at MLW as shown on Chart #AB-16. Round past Squashes Cay and head for the inner waypoint at 26° 57.90' N, 77° 32.70' W, which will place you approximately ¼ mile southwest of North Spanish Cay Channel. From here the reefs on both sides of the channel should be visible, you'll want to stay between them. Head for the outer waypoint at 26° 58.40' N, 77° 31.90' W keeping an eye out for the reefs. Once again, trust your eyes and depthsounder, not a chart when entering any cut in any island group. If you're approaching North Spanish Cay Channel from the deep waters of the North Atlantic Ocean, head for the outer waypoint at 26° 58.40' N, 77° 31.90' W and follow the above route in reverse.

Spanish Cay Marina offers 75 very nice slips that will accommodate vessels with drafts of 8' at MLW with full electric, ice, water, showers, a laundry, and restaurant on premises. *Spanish Cay Marina* monitors VHF ch. 16 and if you need to clear in give them a call and they'll notify *Customs* and *Immigration* for you. If you need shoreside accommodations try the Spanish Cay Inn. You can also dine at the *Pint House Restaurant* or enjoy your favorite beverage at the *Wrecker's Bar*, both of whom monitor VHF ch. 16.

There is a small, but well-protected anchorage at the northwestern end of Spanish Cay, but the entrance is shallow and tricky and the holding is poor. To enter the anchorage, round Squashes Cay as shown on Chart #AB-16 and then pass over the shallow bar 3' at MLW, favoring the eastern shoreline. Inside you'll find 6'-8' over a grassy bottom. Occasionally someone will place a small stake or piece of PVC pipe to mark the starboard side of the channel so use caution when entering.

Spanish Cay may have once played a part in a drama that began in Washington D.C. at the headquarters of the *Federal Bureau of Investigation*. For many years Spanish Cay was owned by Texas oil mogul Clint Murchison who built an airstrip on the deserted cay and imported over 1,000 palm trees. Murchison was a personal friend of *FBI* Director J. Edgar Hoover and several Mafia personnel such as Santos Trafficante, Carlos Marcello, and Sam Giancana, the trio that some believe were behind JFK's assassination. Murchison owned the *Del Charro* hotel in La Jolla, California near the Del Mar Racetrack and Hoover often stayed months at a time with Clint always picking up the tab.

Jimmy G.C. Corcoran, a former *Bureau of Investigation* (the Bureau did not acquire the term *Federal* until 1935 when it became the *FBI*) agent and close associate of J. Edgar Hoover, left the Bureau just after World War I. Over the next three decades Corcoran grew to become a very powerful figure in Washington political circles. Working as a lobbyist during World War II Corcoran attempted to collect a huge $75,000 fee, illegal at that time, and he received word that Hoover was going to "set him up." An enraged Corcoran confronted the Director, called him every type of SOB he could think of, and reminded him of the "favor" he had once done for him. Hoover, a closet homosexual, had been arrested in the late 1920's in New Orleans on sex charges involving a young man. Corcoran, who had by then left the Bureau and had several powerful contacts in Louisiana, stepped in and prevented Hoover's prosecution and the career ending scandal it would have produced. Hoover relented; Corcoran got his money and was not arrested. Several years later, in 1956, Corcoran died in a mysterious plane crash off Murchison's Spanish Cay.

POWELL CAY

Uninhabited Powell Cay has a great anchorage in the prevailing northeast through southeast winds, but it also has the advantage that if you need supplies you can shoot right across the Sea of Abaco to Coopers Town for fuel, food, or even a taxi to the airport at Marsh Harbour. There's great diving on the ocean-side reefs, nice beaches, plenty of land to trek around upon, great views from the hill, a marina nearby (at Spanish Cay), and even a submerged plane to explore when you've done everything else.

As shown on Chart #AB-17, a GPS waypoint at 26° 54.25 N, 77° 29.50' W, will place you approximately ¼ mile west of the main anchorage area. But don't simply plug in this waypoint and hit "Go To." If you're at Coopers Town, that would be fine, it's a straight shot, but if you're approaching from any other direction care must be taken.

If you're approaching from the north, from Spanish Cay or Angelfish Point, you must avoid the large shallow area that lies south of Spanish Cay as shown on Chart #AB-15. Most simply head south of it before altering course to Powell Cay. If you're leaving the marina at Spanish Cay bound for Powell Cay, you can pass between the shoal and Goat Cay as shown on Chart #AB-16. If you're taking this route keep an eye out for the conspicuous brown reef that lies just northwest of Powell Cay as shown on Chart #AB-17.

If you're approaching Powell Cay from the south, from Manjack or Green Turtle, simply parallel the shoreline of Great Abaco, deep water runs almost right up to the land, and head northwestward. Once you pass abeam of the southern tip of Powell Cay turn to starboard and head northward into the anchorage.

COOPERS TOWN

Coopers Town is the northernmost settlement on the island of Great Abaco. Coopers Town was originally settled in the 1870's by the Cooper family from Grand Bahama and the Bootle family from Green Turtle Cay. Although Coopers Town had no natural harbour, their intention was to create a transshipment point for the growing and exporting of produce. Today, many of Coopers Town 900 residents now work down the road at Treasure Cay and the town's principal claim to fame these days is that it is the home district of the Prime Minister of The Bahamas, The Right Honorable Hubert Ingraham.

A GPS waypoint at 26° 52.70' N, 77° 30.10' W, will place you approximately ½ mile off Coopers Town in the Sea of Abaco. Access is easy here, if you approaching from the north, from Angelfish Point, or from the south, from Green Turtle Cay, all you need do is parallel the shoreline of Great Abaco to arrive at Coopers Town. Don't fret the depths here, if you stay ¼ mile or more off Great Abaco you'll have 12'-20' of water (at MLW) the entire way. A mile or more north of Coopers Town is a small indentation in the Abaco shoreline that offers protection in south through west/northwest winds. The entrance is straightforward and will carry 3' at MLW with more inside.

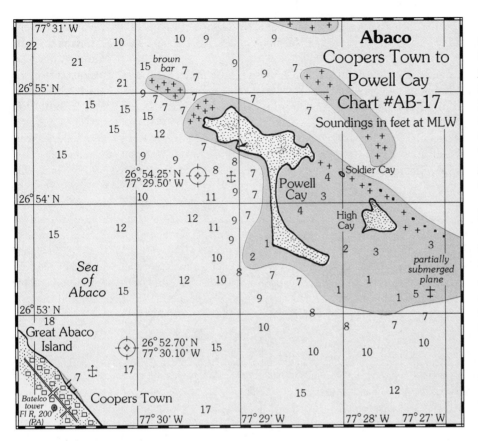

At the GPS waypoint off Coopers Town you can turn in and pull up the *Coopers Town Shell* dock (call ahead on VHF ch. 16) or you can anchor if conditions allow. This is a great lee anchorage in southwest to westerly conditions! *Coopers Town Shell* offers diesel, gasoline, water, and ice.

Ashore Cooper's Town has a large *Community Clinic*, a *Batelco* office, and a *Government Office* building. You can dine at *The Place Bakery and Souse House*, *Gelina's Pizza* (free delivery if you're at the dock), *M & M's*, the *Conch Crawl*, and at the *Same Ol Talk of the Town*. There are also two small grocery stores in Coopers Town. Visitors might wish to check out the *Albert Bootle Museum* where you'll learn a little about the early settlers, the Bootles and the Coopers, as well as sponging, sisal, and lumber.

A couple of years ago, a man believed he had struck oil in his yard. Digging down 100' through hard crystal, the bit brought up a dark substance that was believed to be oil. The owner, proclaiming that the oil led straight to the Persian Gulf, declared that God had led him to dig there and that the oil would be used to benefit the people and the government of The Bahamas. Unfortunately for The Bahamas, a Texas oil company took rock and water samples and announced that there was no presence of oil at the site. It is not known if the digger will keep trying in his quest.

MANJACK CAY

Manjack Cay, sometimes shown as Nunjack Cay on older charts, is home to a half-dozen lovely beaches and secluded coves, great hiking trails, and some interesting ocean-side reefs as well as a couple of wrecks for underwater explorers to investigate. The cay is popular with locals as well as cruisers as you can tell when you visit the "Manjack Hilton," a small collection of picnic tables that visitors have constructed.

The primary anchorage is found in the bight between Manjack Cay, Rat Cay, and Crab Cay. A GPS waypoint at 26° 48.80' N, 77° 22.80 W will place you approximately ½ mile west/southwest of this anchorage area. If you're approaching from Green Turtle Cay you can simply parallel the shoreline of Green Turtle Cay northward keeping the conspicuous shallow area between Crab Cay, Crab Rock, and Green Turtle Cay to starboard (see Chart #AB-18). Once past Crab Cay turn to starboard and anchor wherever your draft allows.

If you're approaching from the north you must avoid the large shoal area that lies south of the northwestern tip of Manjack Cay. You can either pass south of this shoal or, if you're feeling adventurous, you can pass over it with the tide in 4' at MLW as shown on Chart #AB-18. Approach the northwestern tip of Manjack Cay and Manjack Rocks keeping an eye out for the conspicuous brown bar as shown on the chart. Your course will parallel the shoreline of Manjack Rocks and Manjack Cay over the shoal area in 4' at MLW as shown on the chart.

There is great anchorage in a small cove off the northwestern tip of Manjack Cay as shown on Chart #AB-18. If approaching from the north you can round Manjack Rocks and head straight into the small cove, but if you wish to access this anchorage from the main anchorage you must once again avoid the large shoal that lies south of the northwestern tip of Manjack Cay. As previously mentioned, you may also choose to cross the shoal with the tide if your draft

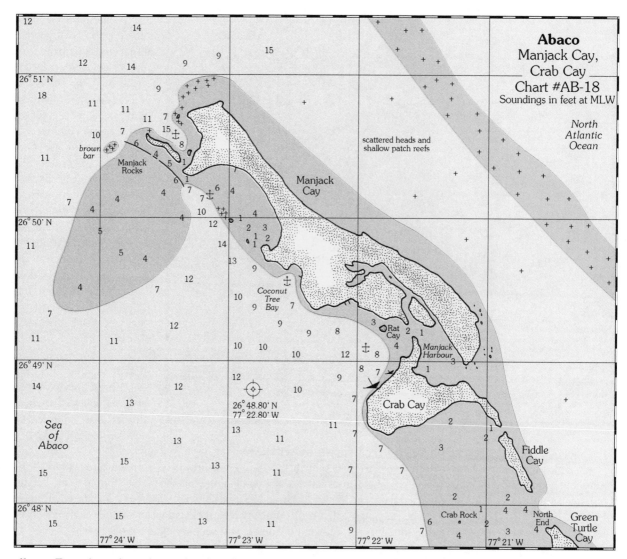

allows. From the main anchorage head northwestward paralleling the shoreline of Manjack Cay past Coconut Tree Bay, which is a nice little anchorage itself in north/northeast through east winds. As you proceed towards the northwestern tip of Manjack Cay you'll pass several small rocks where you can also anchor just off their northwestern side as shown on the chart. Continuing northwestward you'll take Manjack Rocks to starboard (as shown on Chart #AB-18) and cross over the bar with 4' at MLW. Once past Manjack Rocks, and clear of the brown bar that lies west of them, you can turn to the north to round Manjack Rocks and enter the small cove with 6'-15' at MLW. This anchorage is good in east through southwest winds, but it can get a bit rolly at times with strong northeast-east winds.

Those cruisers who wish to explore the cays they anchor off, will have an excellent opportunity to do just that at Manjack Cay. On the southeastern shore of the cay is a small dock that leads to a well-marked nature trail. The Manjack Nature Walk will give you a great chance to familiarize yourself with local flora from Poisonwood to Gummelemi Trees. There's also a "lookout tower" which will give you a great view of the windward side of the island and its long beach. Tiny Fiddle Cay is a popular spot with local boaters and the surrounding waters offer good shelling.

GREEN TURTLE CAY

New Plymouth, with it's pastel painted houses and their white picket fences and stone walls will remind you more of a quaint New England fishing village than a Bahamian out island. Most of the 500 or so residents of New Plymouth, the settlement perched on the southern end of mile-long Green Turtle Cay, can trace their roots back to the Loyalists that first settled here over two centuries ago. Many of these early settlers were skilled seaman and boat builders and a substantial bit of their history is documented at the *Albert Lowe Museum* in New Plymouth, a virtual treasure trove of

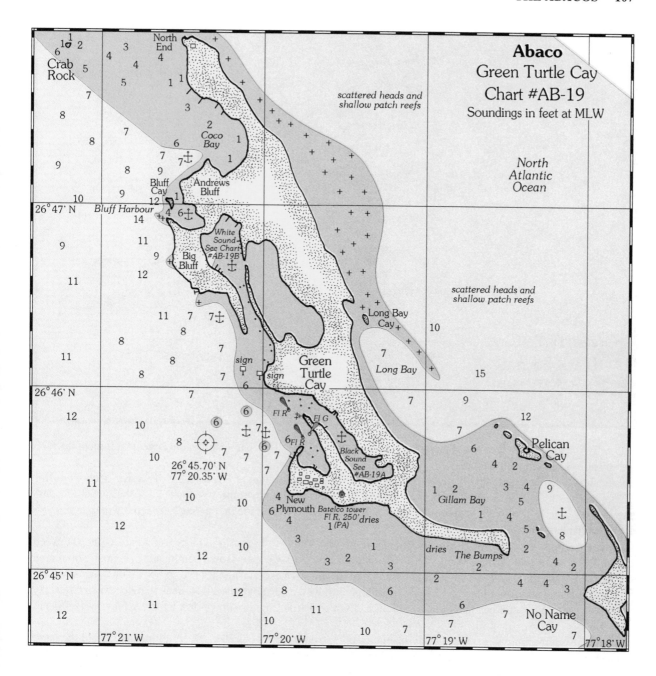

Chart labels (Chart #AB-19):

Abaco
Green Turtle Cay
Chart #AB-19
Soundings in feet at MLW

North
Atlantic
Ocean

Crab Rock
North End
Coco Bay
Bluff Cay
Andrews Bluff
Bluff Harbour
White Sound See Chart #AB-19B
Big Bluff
Long Bay Cay
Green Turtle Cay
Long Bay
scattered heads and shallow patch reefs
scattered heads and shallow patch reefs
sign
Black Sound See #AB-19A
New Plymouth Batelco tower Fl R, 250' dries
Pelican Cay
Gillam Bay
The Bumps
dries
No Name Cay
26° 47' N
26° 46' N
26° 45' N
77° 21' W
77° 20' W
77° 19' W
77° 18' W
26° 45.70' N 77° 20.35' W
Fl R
Fl G

momentos from the Loyalist years to more recent times. Here you'll find fascinating old photographs dating back a century or more alongside ship models of Abaco-built vessels that were used as gun-runners in the American Civil War years and later as rum-runners in the Prohibition years. The museum is housed in a restored 150-year-old mansion, and outside in the *Memorial Sculpture Gardens* you'll find bronze busts of some 30 Bahamians from all over the archipelago standing in a lovely, elegant, garden setting. If you'd like to rent a bicycle to explore New Plymouth, you can rent one from Ivy Roberts, the manager of the museum. Keeping in a historical vein you can explore the 200-year-old cemetery, the cay's original jail, and an amazing model schooner crafting shop. But Green Turtle Cay is much more than just a history lesson. Here you'll find a half-dozen anchorages along with several marinas and repair facilities including a haul out yard and quite a few choices for dining out.

Green Turtle is a "must" stop on nearly everyone's tour of the Abacos and access is fairly easy. As shown on Chart #AB-19, a GPS waypoint at 26° 45.70 N, 77° 20.35' W will place you about a half-mile west of the town of New Plymouth and the popular lee anchorage lying west of town (as also shown on Chart #AB-19B). This anchorage is good in winds from northeast through east and almost to southeast. I've found iffy holding in places here so make sure your

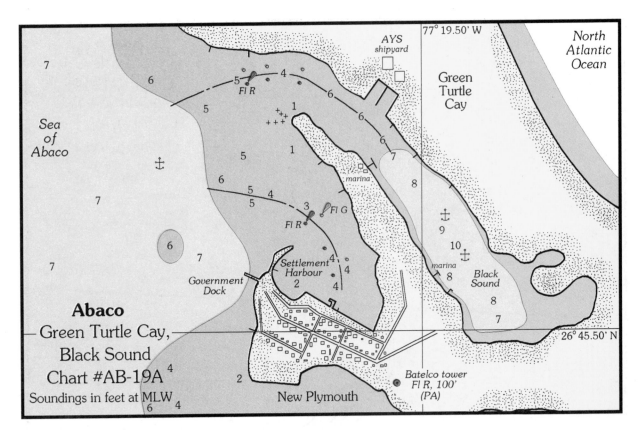

77° 19.50' W

North Atlantic Ocean

AYS shipyard

Green Turtle Cay

7

6

5   Fl R   4

5

Sea of Abaco

5

6

6

1   + + +   + + +

6

5   1

6

marina   7

6   5   4   5   5   3   Fl G   Fl R

8

6   7

7   *marina*   9

6   7   10

Settlement 4   Harbour 2   4   4   8   *Black Sound*

Government Dock

8

Abaco
— Green Turtle Cay,
Black Sound
Chart #AB-19A 4
Soundings in feet at MLW 4
6

7

26° 45.50' N

2   *New Plymouth*

Batelco tower Fl R, 100' (PA)

anchor is set before you leave your boat. If you need to clear in, you'll have to tie up to the large government dock on the western side of New Plymouth.

As shown on the chart, shallow draft vessels can also access Settlement Harbour and the town dock from this anchorage. I don't recommend this, but I show it because it's the best dinghy route into town. From the anchorage, pass between the outer pair of red and green markers (Fl R and Fl G) and continue on passing between the markers as you approach the large town dock.

If you're approaching Green Turtle Cay from the north you'll have few hazards as the Sea of Abaco is deep between Green Turtle and Great Abaco Island. The only real hazards from Coopers Town southward is a small shoal area southwest of Ambergris Cay and the large shoal south of the northern end of Manjack Cay as shown on Chart #AB-15. If you're approaching from Manjack Cay you can simply follow the edge of the shallow bank lying between Crab Cay and Green Turtle Cay and then parallel the shoreline of Green Turtle Cay (as shown on Charts #AB-15, #AB-18, and #AB-19).

If you're approaching Green Turtle Cay from the south, from Don't Rock Passage, you'll need to avoid the large shoal area that lies south and southwest of Green Turtle Cay (see Chart #AB-19) which blocks your courseline from the Sand Bank Cays. If you're approaching from Whale Cay Passage you'll need to keep Channel Rock, Two Rocks, No Name Cay, and the shoal south of Green Turtle Cay to your starboard side as shown on Charts #AB-21, #AB-20, and #AB-19. The hazards here are very visible and you can see the large shoal area well with good visibility. If in doubt, or if you just prefer deeper water, simply head more over to the Great Abaco Island side of the Sea of Abaco until you come abeam of the southern tip of Green Turtle Cay and can work your way east/northeast towards the anchorage and waypoint.

There are three more lee anchorages along the western shore of Green Turtle Cay. Just north of the anchorage off the settlement and north of the entrance to White Sound sits a nice lee anchorage as shown on Charts #AB-19 and #AB-19B. You can actually anchor anywhere along the shore here from Joyless Point northward, but if you tuck up as far north and east as you can you'll pick up some shelter from north winds as well as northeast through southeast winds. The *Bluff House* fuel dock lies to the west of this anchorage; you'll need to keep an eye out for the submerged rocks south of the fuel dock as shown on the chart.

A very protected anchorage lies in tiny Bluff Harbour as shown on Charts #AB-19 and #AB-19B. The entrance lies south of Bluff Cay between Bluff Cay and the mainland of Green Turtle Cay. The entrance bar has almost 4' over it at

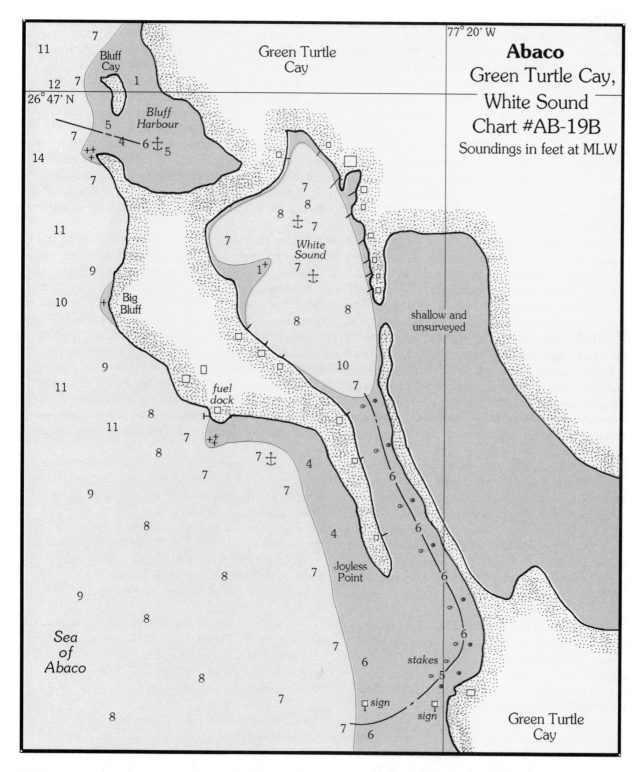

MLW and you'll find 6'-7' and more in a small pocket inside. Watch out for the submerged rocks off the point to the south of the entrance channel. As protected as this anchorage appears, it is no place to be in strong west to northwest winds. A bit further north cruisers can anchor in a small bight just to the west of shallow Coco Bay as shown on Chart #AB-19. This spot is good in winds from north of east through southeast and almost south.

Besides the above mentioned lee anchorages, there are two excellent well-protected anchorages, one in White Sound and one in Black Sound, that offer all-around protection and can be considered as shelter in the event of a hurricane. The entrance to Black Sound lies just north of the town of New Plymouth as shown on Chart #19-A. To enter

Black Sound from the lee anchorage west of New Plymouth you must pass between the outer red (FL R) and green markers that lie between the mainland to the north and the point of land to the south (as shown on Chart #AB-19A). Split the rest of the markers as you pass over the shallowest spot (4' at MLW) and continue past the large *Abaco Yacht Services* yard on your port side and the *Other Shore Club* dock on your starboard side. When you're back in deeper water anchor wherever your draft allows. The bottom is a quite grassy here so make sure your anchor is set well.

The entrance to White Sound, as shown on Chart #AB-19B, lies a bit north of the entrance to Black Sound (as shown on Chart #AB-19), between the two conspicuous signs, one of which sits well out into the water. The entrance is via a long, narrow (dredged to 30' wide), shallow (4½'-5'), but well-marked channel where you'll need the help of the tide. To enter you'll need to pass south of the outer sign, north of the inner sign (obviously!), and split the outer green and red buoys. You'll split a couple of pairs of makers here and then as the channel curves to the north you'll want to favor the eastern side of the channel, hugging the stakes as you proceed northward into White Sound. White Sound is a great anchorage in all conditions, but you must avoid the shallow bar that works out from its western shore and the rock at its eastern end (See Chart #AB-19B).

Now let's discuss the facilities found in Black Sound and White Sound. Black Sound has excellent facilities for the visiting boater, a good marina and a full-service haul-out yard. As you enter Black Sound you'll first pass the large *Abaco Yacht Services* on the northern side of the channel. This huge yard has been providing marine services and storage to Abaco boaters and yachtsmen for over twenty years; the owners are 7th generation Abaconians. Their 50-ton lift can handle boats up to 65', a 6½' draft, with a 21' beam. You can also arrange with *AYS* for dry storage for vessels up to that same size. *AYS* can haul your boat, pressure clean the bottom, and paint it with TBT anti-fouling paint. They also offer cleaning and waxing of hulls, factory trained *Yamaha* mechanics, welding, fiberglass work, and repairs of struts, props, and cutlass bearings. You'll also find showers, a laundry, ice, and water at their docks.

Directly across (almost) from *AYS* sits the *Other Shore Club and Marina*, a very friendly marina with 15 slips (full electric) as well as diesel, gasoline, water, ice, showers, and a short walk to town. A bit further in you'll find *Black Sound Marina* on the southwestern shore of Black Sound. This marina offers 15 slips accommodating boats up to 140' with drafts of up to 7' at MLW. The newly constructed docks boast 30-50amp electricity, water, ice, a laundromat, showers, and a barbecue/picnic area. "Downtown" is only a five-minute walk, but if you don't feel like walking you can rent a golf cart at the marina.

Also in Black Sound, *Roberts Marine*, a *Johnson* dealer, offers outboard and diesel repairs, boat rentals, batteries, ice, and the usual assortment of quality marine supplies. A bit further in Black Sound you'll find *Roberts Cottages and Dock* offering secure, private dockage for boats up to 65' with either short or long-term storage available. The docks are equipped with full electric, 30-50 amp and 110V/220V. *Roberts Cottages* monitors VHF ch. 16.

Not to be outdone by its southern neighbor, White Sound also offers the finest in Abaco amenities for the visiting boater. As you approach the end of the entrance channel as it opens up into White Sound you'll find *Dolphin Marine* on the western shore. *Dolphin Marine* is an *OMC* dealer and they monitor VHF ch.16. Their factory-trained mechanics and fully stocked parts department can help you solve any outboard problems you might be having. They also sell outboards at prices cheaper than U.S. and are dealers for *Carolina Skiff* and *Boston Whaler* and a line of inflatables as well.

On the western shore of White Sound sits the *Bluff House Club Hotel & Marina*. *Bluff House* can accommodate boats with drawing up to 7' though part of the marina has only 4' at MLW. Their docks have full electric hookups, water, ice, showers, a laundry, the *Bluff House Boutique* and a restaurant and bar on location. The *Bluff House* fuel dock sits on the western shore of Green Turtle Cay as shown on Charts #AB-19 and #AB-19B. The *Bluff House Restaurant and Bar* serves lunch from 11:00am and seats for dinner at 7:30pm with reservations a must. Dockage also includes use of the facilities of the *Bluff House Hotel*.

At the northern end of White Sound resides the *Green Turtle Club and Marina,* proud owners of a four-star rating from *Fielding's Travel Guide* in 1992. The marina can accommodate vessels with a beam of up to 25' and a draft of 5'-7'. They offer 35 slips with full electric hookups and satellite TV, fuel, water, ice, showers, a laundry, marine supplies, a grocery/liquor store, the *Green Turtle Club Boutique* and an excellent restaurant on site. Try breakfast or lunch on the patio of the restaurant and then enjoy dinner in their Queen Anne style dining room (reservations before 1700 are a must). The *Green Turtle Club* also hosts live music on Monday and Saturday nights.

The *Green Turtle Club* has a unique history. An old wooden boathouse was converted into a yacht club style pub and became the cornerstone for today's Green Turtle Club. Even in its infancy the *Green Turtle Club,* under the leadership of its owner Allen Charlesworth, gained an international reputation THE spot to escape from the daily rigors and trappings of civilization. Mr. Charlesworth passed away in 1989, but his family has continued to maintain the timeless charm of the tradition-filled *Green Turtle Club*. Today the Club is proud of its newest addition, the *Green*

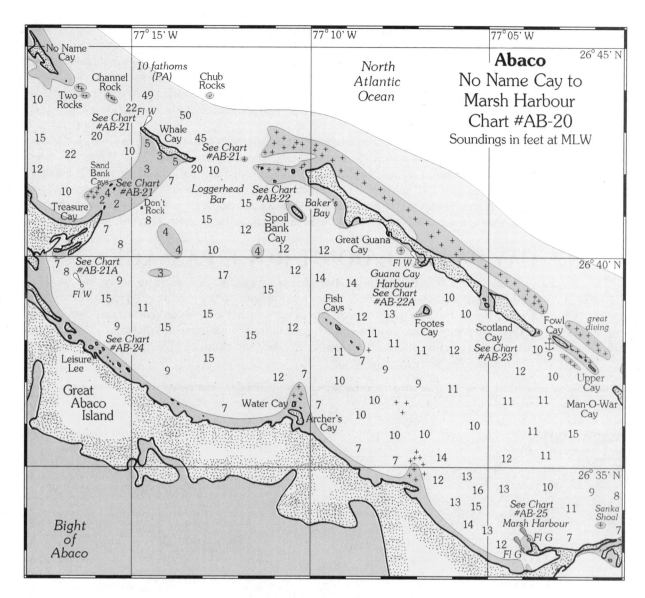

The chart shows: Abaco, No Name Cay to Marsh Harbour, Chart #AB-20, Soundings in feet at MLW.

Turtle Club Divers operation. The dive shop offers Scuba and snorkel trips as well as island tours to other Abaco Cays. *GTC Divers* is a complete PADI and NAUI affiliated dive shop with sales, rentals, and air fills. But this isn't the only dive shop around; you can also visit *Brendal's Dive Shop* on Green Turtle Cay. Brendal is the dean of the Green Turtle Cay diving operations, he's been doing this for over 20 years. Brendal offers Scuba certification, daily snorkel, Scuba, and glass bottom reef trips, wreck and cavern dives, stingray and grouper feedings, and he has full service retail store. Give Brendal a shout on VHF ch. 16.

Now that we've covered White Sound and Black Sound, let's check out what's in store for you in New Plymouth. If you're coming into the town dock in Settlement Harbour by dinghy you find several stores right on the waterfront or just around the corner from it. There's *Robert's Hardware*, *New Plymouth Hardware*, *Sid's Food Store*, *Lowe's Food Store*, *The Island's Restaurant and Grill* (breakfast, lunch, and dinner; they monitor ch. 16), *Curry's Food and Liquor Store*, *B & M Seafood*, and *Laura's Kitchen*. At the popular *Wrecking Tree Bakery and Restaurant* you can order breakfast, lunch, and dinner; they specialize in seafood (and they also monitor VHF ch. 16). *Curry's* and *Sid's* can fill your propane tanks for you. Part of the charm of New Plymouth is walking the narrow streets and finding interesting little shops, you'll love it!

In the center of town you'll find the *New Plymouth Club and Inn* where you can have breakfast, lunch, and dinner daily or partake in their Sunday Brunch. The inn is a restored colonial inn, an intimate place with a beautiful garden, pool, and restaurant that offers candlelight dinners. *Plymouth Rock Liquors and Café* is open Mondays-Thursdays from 0900-1800 and Friday and Saturdays from 0900-2100. The store proudly stocks over 50 different brands of rum and they will deliver! Next door, the *Ocean Blue Gallery* offers Bahamian inspired artwork with over 50 artists represented. *Barclay's Bank* is open on Tuesdays and Thursdays from 1000-1300.

Two places you must not miss are *Mike's Bar*, on the southern side of New Plymouth, and the world famous *Miss Emily's Blue Bee Bar*. If you're an aficionado of quality alcoholic concoctions, you will bask in the history that surrounds you at *Miss Emily's Blue Bee Bar*, the birth place of the *Goombay Smash*, that world famous rum punch that is today served throughout the Caribbean basin. *The Rooster's Nest*, near the school, hosts live music on Friday and Saturday nights.

South of Green Turtle Cay lies No Name Cay whose beaches are popular with cruisers as well as Green Turtle-ites (yes I know, that probably isn't a word, but it could be…couldn't it?). There is a large, deep (7'-10') pocket of water between No Name Cay and Green Turtle Cay that is a pleasant anchorage, especially in southeast winds. The entrance is gained by crossing the shallow bar (2'-4' at MLW in places) between No Name Cay and "The Bumps," the southern tip of Green Turtle that until recent history was only a sandbar. Check out the route with your dinghy first as the deeper water here changes from time to time. Shell collectors will want to investigate the shallow waters of "The Bumps."

WHALE CAY PASSAGE/DON'T ROCK PASSAGE

Whale Cay Passage, although far from difficult in good weather, is always a major concern for Abaco cruisers. The problem with Whale Cay Passage occurs when seas build up and make the cuts north and south of Whale Cay downright dangerous. You don't need strong winds for a rage to occur here, a storm far to the north can generate sufficient seas to close Whale Cay Passage. Do not try Whale Cay Passage in a rage, it is not a playground; Whale Cay Passage has a history of wrecks and has earned every bit of its nasty reputation. For daily information on the conditions in Whale Cay Passage, listen in to the *Cruisers Net* every morning on the VHF.

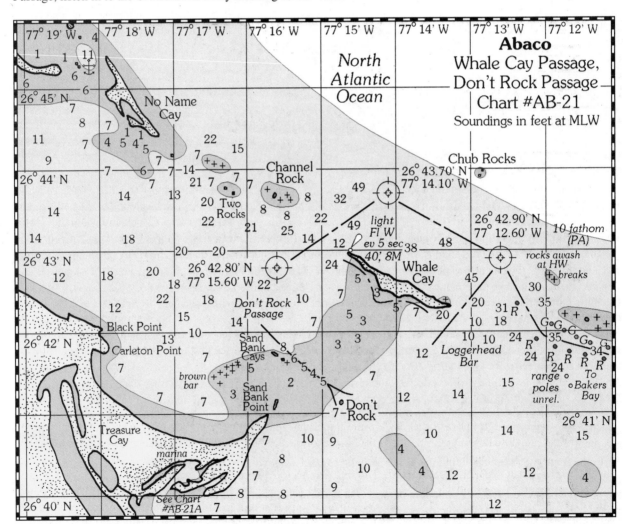

Whale Cay Passage really doesn't require waypoints, it is so very easily run simply by eyeball navigation, but for those folks that need a waypoint I'll offer a few for your use in a moment, first let me tell you how to do the Whale Cay Passage by eye. If you're approaching from the north, as you head out into deeper water in the cut between Whale Cay and Channel Rock you can turn to starboard to parallel the shore of Whale Cay staying at least ¼ mile off the island. On the other hand, don't go so far out into the North Atlantic Ocean that the Chub Rocks become a hazard to navigation. When you approach the cut between Whale Cay and Great Guana Cay you can take the southeastern tip of Whale Cay to starboard to head for *Treasure Cay Marina*, or follow the marked pilings that will lead you into Bakers Bay on Great Guana Cay as shown on Chart #AB-21. Take care if you plan to cross the Loggerhead Bar, seas can pile up on that shallow area and make for a very rough ride. Northbound cruisers can follow the above directions in reverse. Now for those of you that feel a bit better with a waypoint to head for, let's see what we can do about that.

If you're approaching this route from the north, make your way to a waypoint at 26° 42.80' N, 77° 15.60' W, which places you approximately ¾ mile southwest of the but between Whale Cay and Channel Rock as shown on Chart #AB-21. From this inner waypoint, head to the outer waypoint at 26° 43.70 N, 77° 14.10' W. This position places you in deep water about halfway between Whale Cay and Chub Rocks. From this point, turn to starboard and head for your next GPS waypoint at 26° 42.90' N, 77° 12.60' W. This is the outer waypoint that lies north of the cut between Whale Cay and Great Guana Cay. From this waypoint you can head in towards *Treasure Cay Marina* keeping the southeastern tip of Whale Cay to starboard in about 20' of water. (Use caution if you plan to enter back onto the banks by crossing the Loggerhead Bar.) Skippers bound for Bakers Bay on Great Guana Cay will see a red piling to the south/southeast of the waypoint. Take it to starboard and follow the rest of the pilings (marked red and green) right into Bakers Bay. Northbound cruisers should follow the above route in reverse.

An alternative to Whale Cay Passage, and really only just a shortcut for shallower draft vessels, less than 4½', is the route in the lee of Whale Cay as shown on Chart #AB-21. The route starts at either end of Whale Cay by paralleling the shoreline of the cay in 5'-7' at MLW. The shallowest area is mid-cay where a large shallow area exists with barely 3' over it at MLW. The channel through here is undefined and skippers will just have to hunt and pick their way over the shoal. You probably won't get close enough to Whale Cay in a rage to try this route, as I said, it's only an alternative shortcut and a fair weather one at that.

If Whale Cay Passage is impassable, there is always the chance that Don't Rock Passage is possible. In normal conditions Don't Rock Passage is simply a shortcut across the Sand Bank, the shoal that lies between Whale Cay and Treasure Cay as shown on Chart #AB-21. The controlling depth for Don't Rock Passage as of the time of this publication was 4' at MLW so a 6' draft is passable at most high tides. The depths here may change, and usually do every so often, so use care when traversing the bank here. When a rage is occurring at Whale Cay Passage, some swells will work their way through to Don't Rock Passage, so if it looks rough at Don't Rock Passage, don't try it!

Southbound cruisers should make their way to a position just north of the Sand Bank Cays as shown on Chart #AB-21. From this position, take the Sand Bank Cays to starboard as you head for Don't Rock (once called Don't Ye May Rock). You'll have 6'-8' just north of the Sand Bank Cays, but the depths will shallow to about 4' (at MLW) or so halfway between the Sand Bank Cays and Don't Rock. Stay on your courseline for Don't Rock and when the water starts getting deeper you can actually pass north or south of Don't Rock. Once past Don't Rock you can alter course to *Treasure Cay Marina*, Baker's Bay, or even Marsh Harbour (watch out for the shallow bank just southeast of Don't Rock on this route).

Northbound cruisers should make for a position just off Don't Rock as shown on Chart #AB-21. Though you can pass either south or north of Don't Rock, I prefer to start the Don't Rock Passage from the northern side of Don't Rock; it gives me a better view of my courseline past the Sand Bank Cays. So, as you pass just to the northern side of Don't Rock, you'll want to keep the Sand Bank Cays on your port side, aiming for a spot about 50-100 yards north of the northernmost of the cays. The rest is as described above, but in reverse. Once past the Sand Bank Cays you'll be in deeper water and can take up a course for Green Turtle or other points north.

TREASURE CAY

Treasure Cay, although not really a "cay" in the traditional sense of the word, it's more of a peninsula, has an absolutely first-rate upscale marina, moorings for rent, one of the prettiest beaches in The Bahamas, and several small canals where you could hide in the event of a hurricane.

As shown on Chart #AB-21, the entrance to *Treasure Cay Marina* lies along the southern shore of Treasure Cay just south of Whale Cay Passage and west of Great Guana Cay. As shown on the enlarged Chart #AB-21A, a GPS waypoint at 26° 39.53' N, 77° 17.00' W, will place you approximately ¼ mile southeast of the entrance channel to the Treasure Cay complex. Use caution when approaching this position as just south of the waypoint stands a light (Fl W) that marks

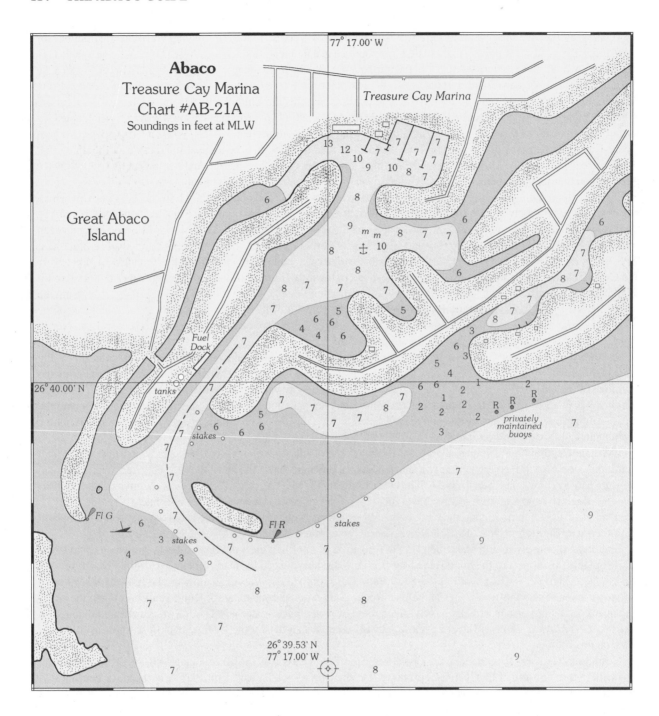

Abaco
Treasure Cay Marina
Chart #AB-21A
Soundings in feet at MLW

Treasure Cay Marina

Great Abaco
Island

77° 17.00' W

13
12
10
9
7
7
7
10
8
7
8
9
m m
8
7
7
⚓ 10
8
6
6
6
8
6
7
5
7
6
6
5
4
5
6
4
3
6
5
3
6
6
2
1
2
5
4
1
2
R R R
2
2
2
2
2
3
8
8
7
7
7
8
7
7
7

Fuel
Dock

26° 40.00' N

tanks

7

5
6
6
7
stakes

7

7

Fl G
6
3 *stakes*
4
3

7

7
stakes

Fl R

7

7

privately
maintained
buoys

7

7

9

9

8

8

7

8

26° 39.53' N
77° 17.00' W

9

8

the entrance area. From the waypoint you will see a string of stakes leading past a small spoil island with a few trees on it. The entrance channel is to the west of this small spoil island as shown on the chart. Enter between the two rows of stakes, one to port and one to starboard, and follow them as they curve around to the northeast where you'll parallel the shoreline past the fuel dock and into the marina and canal area. Just before the marina you'll see some moorings to starboard, if one is available go ahead and pick it up and give the marina a call on VHF ch. 16 to inform them of your arrival.

If you're approaching Treasure Cay from Baker's Bay or Great Guana Cay Harbour (as shown on Chart #AB-20), your course needs to avoid the small shoals lying east of the entrance to the marina as shown on the chart. If you're approaching from Man-O-War Cay you must detour around the Fish Cays as you make your way to the waypoint. If you're approaching from Marsh Harbour you can simply follow the shoreline as shown on Chart #AB-20, but you must

Photo by Nicolas Popov.

Scenery at the Treasure Cay Beach Hotel, Abacos.

make certain that you give a wide berth to Water Cay and the point just southeast of it as submerged rocks stretch out a bit into the Sea of Abaco.

Treasure Cay Marina offers 150 slips with a minimum depth of 7' at MLW with full electric hookups (20/50/100 amp), water, ice, showers, repairs, wet and dry storage, and luxury accommodations at the new $30 million *Bahamas Beach Club*. If you walk across the road from the marina you'll find the beautiful curving Treasure Cay Beach, absolutely superb! If the beach doesn't keep your full attention, you can always try a round of golf on the Dick Wilson designed course at the *Treasure Cay Golf Club*. You also find other amenities such as tennis courts, boat rentals, and facilities for fishing and Scuba diving. If you have guests flying in or leaving, Treasure Cay has its own airport.

One of the best ways to tour the Treasure Cay area is by golf cart and you can pick one up at *Cash's Resort Carts*, *Blue Marlin Golf Cart Rentals*. If you prefer, you can rent an automobile from *McKenzie's Car Rentals*, *Triple J Car Rentals*, *Cornish Car Rentals*, and *R&A Rentals and Tours* (they monitor VHF ch. 16). You can even get your teeth cleaned or repaired at the *Treasure Cay Dental Clinic* (365-8625/8425, in U.S. 800-224-6703). If you need someone to do your laundry, check out Annie's Laundry.

If you have shopping to do you can choose from the *Treasure Cay Mini Market* where you'll find fresh meat, veggies, frozen foods, dairy products, and all sorts of staples. There's also a branch of *Abaco Markets, Ltd.* and the *G&M Variety Store*. For your dining pleasure you have *Hudson's Restaurant and Bakery,* as well as the *Touch of Klass Restaurant* at the Bootle Highway entrance to Treasure Cay. The *Island Boil Restaurant and Sports Lounge* offers true Bahamian cuisine specializing in souse, fish, and lobster. There's also *Lee's Diner*, a fairly new restaurant located in Madera Park at *Parker Plaza*, they're open from 7:30 till late serving breakfast, lunch, and dinner. The *Flour House Bakery* in Marsh Harbour will deliver fresh bread for you to *Lee's Diner* so be sure to ask about it. The most popular places around are probably *Café Florence*, the *Coco Bar*, *The Spinnaker Restaurant* and *The Tipsy Seagull Bar*. The *Spinnaker*, and *The Tipsy Seagull* were both damaged by the remnants of Hurricane Mitch in November of 1998, but they should both be up and running again by the time you read this. You must not miss a visit to the fashionable *Spinnaker Restaurant* or the livelier *Tipsy Seagull Bar*, especially if you need a place to unwind.

77° 11' W   77° 10' W   77° 09' W   77° 08' W   77° 07' W   77° 06' W   77° 05' W

Abaco
Great Guana Cay
—Chart #AB-22—
Soundings in feet at MLW

10 fathoms (PA)

26° 43' N

1 fathom

6

Gumelemi Cay

6

6

North Atlantic Ocean

26° 42' N

7

Great Guana Cay

G. G. R. R.
pilings R
7   6   G. G.
9   6   R   30   G.   12
8   2   pilings   5
stakes   1   pilings   7
15   29   12   Bakers   Joe's
        buoys   Bay   Creek

tower
Fxd R
50' (PA)

26° 41' N
15   9   9
                4
12   stake   1
        11
Spoil Bank   7   1 + Crossing   3
Cay   7   7   Bay   7
                7   7   8   7
26° 40.50' N   7 + 7 +   8
77° 09.80' W   + +   6 +   10
4   9   8   9   8

26° 40' N   17
15   15   12   8
18   13   14   12   8 Fl W
                Guana Cay
18   15   14   Harbour
                See Chart
        15   10   #AB-22A   15
        11   15   private
                13   8   marina
                                12

26° 39' N   14   8
15   11   12   7   8   11   9
                14   9   Scotland Cay
18   Fish   9   7   See Chart
14   Cays   8   rock   7   Footes   #AB-23
        12   awash   Cay
                at LW   9   11

26° 38' N   10   10
14   12   9   11
14   10   12   12

GREAT GUANA CAY

Great Guana Cay has long been known for having one of the longest and most beautiful beaches in the entire Bahamas. Couple that with some great diving on the offshore reefs and easy access from any of several anchorages and you'll probably come to appreciate Great Guana Cay as one of your favorite stops in the Abaco chain. Ashore at Bakers Bay, probably the most popular of the Guana Cay anchorages, are the remains of the old cruise ship depot, now long deserted and a haven for cruisers that like to poke around that sort of place. Some of the docks are deep enough to allow you to tie up if you need to do some work on your vessel. Explorers might wish to investigate the small mangrove creek southeast of Baker's Bay as shown on Chart #AB-22. And if you don't want to take your boat to Great Guana Cay, you can always hop on a ferry.

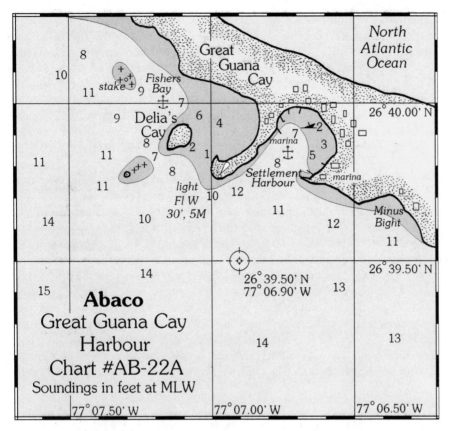

Abaco
Great Guana Cay
Harbour
Chart #AB-22A
Soundings in feet at MLW

Bakers Bay lies at the southern terminus of the Whale Cay Passage at the northwestern end of Great Guana Cay. A lovely curving sand beach offers good protection from north/northeast through southeast winds but does allow a little swell to work in sometimes causing a bit of a roll. If you're approaching from the north, from Whale Cay Passage, head for the GPS waypoint at 26° 42.90' N, 77° 12.60' W (keep an eye out for the rocks awash about ¾ mile east of this position). This waypoint is approximately ½ mile northwest of the well-marked entrance channel leading into the old cruise ship mooring basin at Bakers Bay as shown on Charts #AB-21 and #AB-22. From the waypoint you will see a red marker to the southeast; take it to starboard and turn to enter the marked channel, red markers to starboard and green markers to port. There are the remains of an old range west of Spoil Bank Cay that leads you southeastward towards this marked channel, but the range is hardly needed here. As you head generally south of east down the marked channel (see Chart #AB-22) you will pass south of some small rocks and between Gumelemi Cay and Spoil Bank Cay (created when this basin was dredged for cruise ships in the late 1980's, and now a great spot for shelling). As you pass to the east of Spoil Bank Cay you will be in the old mooring basin, you'll see the old mooring buoys, and you can weave your way between the buoys and the pilings to the east of the basin to head into the anchorage at Bakers Bay. Though most of the depths in Bakers Bar are 7'-8', there are a few scattered 6' spots, small sandy humps here and there. If you don't wish to make use of the old cruise ship channel, you can pass to the west of Spoil Bank Cay and round its southern tip to anchor in Bakers Bay.

If you're approaching Bakers Bay from the south, from Marsh Harbour, you can head for a GPS waypoint at 26° 40.50' N, 77° 09.80' W. This position lies approximately ¾ mile south of Bakers Bay as shown on Chart #AB-22. Use caution here, don't just plug in the waypoint at Marsh Harbour and head straight for it, you must avoid the Fish Cays and Foots Cay as shown on Charts #AB-20 and #AB-22. If you're approaching Bakers Bay from Guana Cay Harbour, keep an eye out for a pair of rocky areas, one only 6' deep at MLW, the other not much better at 7' at MLW; both are shown on Chart #AB-22. Southeast of Bakers Bay lies Crossing Bay as shown on Chart #AB-22. Crossing Bay is now the home of the new *Guana Seaside Village Resort and Restaurant*. The resort plans to dredge their dock area so look forward to that opening up soon.

There are two other nice harbours along the southern shore of Great Guana Cay. As shown on Chart #AB-22A, a GPS waypoint at 26° 39.50' N, 77° 06.90' W will place you approximately ¼ mile south of Great Guana Cay Harbour and about ½ mile southeast of the anchorage at Delia's Cay. From the waypoint you can head west and round the small, unnamed rock lying southwest of Delia's Cay to enter the Fishers Bay anchorage north of Delia's Cay. You can also pass between Delia's Cay and this rock in 7' at MLW as a shortcut. Keep and eye out for the submerged rocks that stretch towards Delia's Cay from the small rock, you'll see the deeper, hazard free water. If in doubt, it only takes a couple of minutes to go around the rock, don't take a chance in bad visibility. When anchoring north of Delia's Cay you must keep an eye out for the shallow rocky bar that is sometimes marked with a stake. This anchorage is good in winds from north/northeast through east to southeast and almost south if you can tuck in far enough. Rumor has it that moorings may be in place in this harbour sometime in 1999, so keep an eye open for them.

If you wish to enter Guana Cay Harbour (sometimes shown on charts as Settlement Harbour) from the waypoint, simply head north/northeast into the cove and anchor where your draft allows a shown on Chart #AB-22A. Once you manage to get your anchor to set in the grassy bottom, this spot is good in winds from west through north to southeast. At the western side of the harbour is the *Guana Beach Resort and Marina* dock where you can pick diesel or gasoline, and rent one of their 22 full-powered slips. The marina can accept boats with drafts of up to 7' with beams of up to 20'. *Guana Beach Resort* monitors VHF ch. 16 and also offers limited water, ice, and showers. Saturday afternoons you can delight in live music at the resort. At the southeastern end of the harbour, protected by a jetty, is the new *Orchid Bay Marina,* a *Texaco Star Port*. They offer 32 slips (up to a 7½' draft) with full electric and a 24-hour weather service.

Ashore you'll find the *Guana Beach Boutique*, the *Guana Harbour Grocery*, and *My Two Sons Liquor Store*. The *Guana Beach Resort* is the home of the infamous *Guana Grabber*; try one, no, on second thought, try two, or three, or… if you're looking for a place for lunch you can slide over to the *Sand Dollar Café* Monday through Saturday from 10:00am -2:00pm One of the more interesting stops is *Milo's Art Gallery/Gift Shop*; you MUST meet Milo. Milo's shop offers unique native crafts, gifts, and clothing and the bright yellow shop itself is an old Loyalist cottage. Nearby you'll want to stop under the Fig Tree to take a load off your feet and chat with whomever is present and enjoy the view. Also nearby are *Guana Hardware*, the *Bikini Hut*, and *Tom's T-shirts* where you can indulge in Great Guana Cay information while smoking a Cuban cigar and browsing through all the shirts and hats that are for sale.

The newest and most popular spot on Great Guana Cay is *Nipper's Beach Bar*. *Nipper's* is set upon a sand dune overlooking the beautiful North Atlantic Ocean, an absolutely spectacular view. *Nipper's* hosts a fantastic wild boar roast right on the beach on Sundays and Wednesdays and will pick you up in town in one of their golf carts. The place is rapidly becoming the party spot in Abaco and the ambiance is definitely "pirate." The bar has a pirate wind vane and the new pool has a pirate's face painted on the bottom with painted fish surrounding it. The solar heated 4' deep pool is divided into two levels by a waterfall with a pirate's cannon standing sentinel. *Nipper's* has added a new deck next to the bar and sun-weary party animals can enjoy the shade provided by beach umbrellas while lounging around the pool in chairs and hammocks.

WHAT DO YOU DO WITH A DRUNKEN SAILOR? A TALE OF GUANA CAY

My first time in Nassau harbor I made the mistake of anchoring off *Club Med*, the long pink building along the north side of the channel on Paradise Island. Normally this would not have been too unbearable but this particular night was *Karaoke Night* at the *Club Med* bar. If there is one thing our old beleaguered and troubled world did not need (next to PWCs in a quiet anchorage) it is *Karaoke*. Who discovered and unleashed this wretched, foul-smelling curse upon us? I personally am not fond of beautiful, noble, stirring melodies and questionable standards being used to showcase a vacuum of talent by slightly to fully-inebriated pseudo-entertainers, most of whom couldn't carry a tune if it had a handle and instructions. Yes, yes, I know…it's all in the name of fun. Needless to say my first mate Kelly and I immediately raised anchor and moved across the harbor. After resetting our CQR three more times we finally moved east of the Paradise Island Bridge to find a little peace and quiet. I really must compliment *Club Med* on their tremendous sound system that puts out decibels of bad taste at a level just shy of Gabriel's horn.

Ah, but such is the miracle of alcohol consumption. It brings out the inner man (or woman as the case may be) who immediately becomes the Hyde to our Jekyll. The weak become strong, the old young, the timid brazen, and those who lack any sort of natural talent insufferable in their attempts to display just the opposite, albeit for their own pleasure and not ours so who the hell cares what we think anyway?

Now hold on there Pardner, as the old TV cowboys would say. Don't take this the wrong way. This is not a Carrie Nation attack on one of the few pursuits of freedom that we are still allowed. I enjoy a sundowner as much as the next person and have more than paid my dues getting bottle emptying, falling down, knee walking, room spinning, toilet hugging drunk. I have been five exits past Margaritaville and countless sheets to the wind in "no class dives" where nobody cares where you puke (as long as it's not on them), to "high class establishments" where all the other drunks look down their noses at you as you barf all over the turkey buffet causing a stream of patrons to rush to the head to stick perfumed or cologned fingers well down their incredibly cultured throats. Proof that an overindulgence of distilled or fermented beverages can make a normally intelligent human being into an unthinking hazard to themselves and others. Such is the story of Gus.

Gus, which may or may not be his name, is a South African cruising sailor whose acquaintance I first made while on a repair layover in Jacksonville, Florida. Later that same year I saw Gus at Green Turtle Cay and in Marsh Harbour,

Abaco, and witnessed his Hyde's misdeeds. Gus is normally a very fair and conscientious person, the sort of person who believes in righting wrongs, his inner man unfortunately believes in wronging rights.

At that time there was a concession on the northern end of Great Guana Cay in the Abacos that featured a dolphin exhibition. Dolphins, as we all know, are highly intelligent creatures and most sailors look forward to their appearance alongside their vessels, delighting in their frolicking and cavorting with us as we share the miles. We feel a certain kinship with these pelagic roamers, and who among us can look in their eyes and deny their intelligence? I personally feel about dolphins the way I feel about birds. They are beautiful creatures to behold but not in captivity. Birds can only be birds when they are free to fly, that is their nature. Dolphins can only be dolphins when they are free to roam the open waters. I do not care to witness the antics of either one in captivity; it is saddening to my soul. Gus felt this same way as did some of his friends. After numerous concoctions of one sort or another I retreated to the sanity of my own boat as Gus and his fellow conspirators gathered in secret and a plan was hatched. "Free the Dolphins" became the mantra for these self-styled activists, these bottle-nosed freedom fighters.

The next day around noon, as we dropped anchor in Marsh Harbour, I noticed a commotion over by the town dock. There were two dolphins in the water and about 15 people gathered around taking pictures. By the time Kelly and I hopped in the dinghy and cruised over, a couple of people were already in the water swimming with the gentle creatures. One of the dolphins was very friendly and could be petted, the other was a little standoffish, yet he knew what a camera was and gleefully posed for pictures. People were feeding them pieces of bread and even slices of watermelon. . . I never knew dolphins ate watermelon. These were obviously very well trained and, it seemed, very hungry dolphins. Someone mentioned that the dolphins from Great Guana Cay escaped the night before and another person said that this pair had followed his trawler from Baker's Bay to Marsh Harbour earlier that morning. A cruiser got in touch with the dolphin's trainers on Great Guana Cay, and relayed the message back to everyone gathered to give the dolphins plenty of attention and to keep them occupied until they could get to Marsh Harbour within the hour.

A little over three hours later the trainers had the dolphins safely loaded aboard their boat and thanked everyone who helped out. It seems that this pair of dolphins was raised in captivity and had never been in the wild. They had been hand fed for over 12 years by their trainers, and did not know how to fend for themselves much less protect themselves from sharks. They would have starved to death very quickly had it not been for their fans in Marsh Harbour. When asked how they escaped the trainers had no answers, it seemed as if someone had released them. Imagine that Mr. Hyde.

I talked to Gus later that day and related to him all that had transpired in Marsh Harbour. He shrugged his shoulders and for the first time I found Gus with little to say. In the painfully sobering hours of the morning after, while Gus' Jekyll paid for Hyde's amusement, the only consolation his aching mind found was in the realization that another wrong had been righted, justice was served, and the world was now a better place in which to live. Even when Gus came to realize what the consequences could have been from the Great Great Guana Cay Raid he still insisted it was right and muttered something about a damn good idea, high ideals, courageous hearts, and excellent execution. I agreed on the latter parts and then added poor planning due to a lack of intelligence. We both decided it was time for a drink.

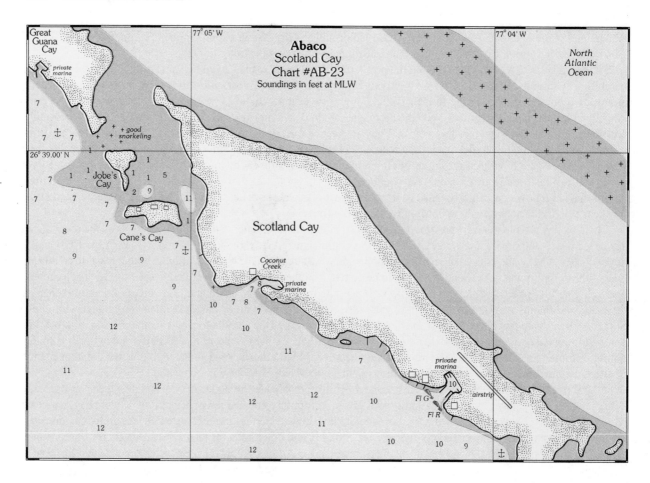

SCOTLAND CAY

Scotland Cay, once called Cotland Cay, lies just southeast of Great Guana Cay as shown on Chart #AB-23. Scotland Cay is private and visits ashore must be by invitation only. Although you can anchor anywhere in the lee of Scotland Cay in winds from northeast through east, the best spot is off the northwestern tip south of Cane's Cay or even in the lee of Cane's Cay south of Jobe's Cay. There are some deeper pockets of water that offer good shelter between Jobe's Cay and Scotland Cay, but access to them is limited as you must cross a 2' bar (MLW) to avail yourself of their protection. If you're shallow enough to get in there you'll need to anchors, there's quite a bit or current here. There's good snorkeling in the cut between Scotland Cay and Great Guana Cay. The two small marinas shown on the chart are private.

Southeast of Scotland Cay, as shown on Chart #AB-20, lies the Fowl Cay Preserve, protected by *The Bahamas National Trust*. You'll find excellent reef diving on the reefs off Fowl Cay, but nothing can be taken. You can anchor in the lee of Fowl Cay or Upper Cay in settled weather and investigate the reefs full of holes and tunnels at your leisure, either snorkeling or by Scuba. Watch out for tidal currents here north and south of the reefs and especially at the mid-reef break.

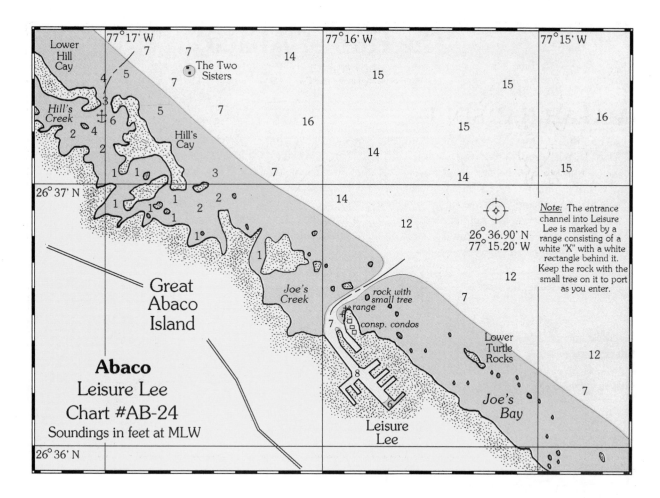

Lower
Hill
Cay

77°17' W

The Two
Sisters

77°16' W

77°15' W

Hill's
Creek

Hill's
Cay

26° 37' N

Note: The entrance
channel into Leisure
Lee is marked by a
range consisting of a
white "X" with a white
rectangle behind it.
Keep the rock with the
small tree on it to port
as you enter.

26° 36.90' N
77° 15.20' W

Great
Abaco
Island

Joe's
Creek

rock with
small tree

range

consp. condos

Abaco
Leisure Lee
Chart #AB-24
Soundings in feet at MLW

Lower
Turtle
Rocks

Joe's
Bay

Leisure
Lee

26° 36' N

LEISURE LEE

Leisure Lee is a small canal community just south of Treasure Cay that is a wonderful hurricane hole, certainly one of my first choices for protection. As shown on Chart #AB-24, a GPS waypoint at 26° 36.90' N, 77° 15.20' W, will place you approximately ¼ mile northeast of the entrance channel into Leisure Lee. A range that sits northwest of the conspicuous condos marks the entrance channel to Leisure Lee. The range consists of a white "X" in front and a white rectangle behind it. As you enter keep the rock with the small tree on it to port and head on it. As you approach the point of land northwest of the condos give it a wide berth if you can; there are submerged rocks just off the point. Round this tip of land to port and you can enter the canal complex. Quite a few of the lots have not been sold and there are plenty of places to secure your vessel in the event of a hurricane. You will probably have to set your anchors ashore as the bottom has been dredged and the holding is not very good. Please don't tie up your vessel so as to block the owners of the homes here and certainly don't tie up to their docks.

There is small and seldom used anchorage north of Leisure Lee at Hill's Creek. The entrance is between Hills' Cay and Lower Hill Cay and will barely take a 5' draft at high water. Inside is a small area of deeper water in which to anchor. I strongly urge you to check out this route by dinghy first before entering. Look for bonefish on the flats here.

The Hub of Abaco

MARSH HARBOUR

Well, this is it, the Mecca of Abaco cruising, the hub of the Hub of Abaco, the George Town of the Northern Bahamas. Whatever moniker you hang on it you will most likely stay a while in Marsh Harbour and make it your base of operations while in the area…and why not? It's got everything you need. There are more marinas here than in the entire Exuma chain. There's little you cannot find when shopping. *UPS* delivers here (but not *Airborne Express*!). There's usually a happy hour special somewhere every night of the week. The international airport is perfect for guests that wish to visit you…the holding is superb…you'll have the camaraderie of numerous other cruising boats…I'm running out of things to say! You'll have to go there and decide for yourself the reasons that keep you there. I can guarantee that you won't regret it.

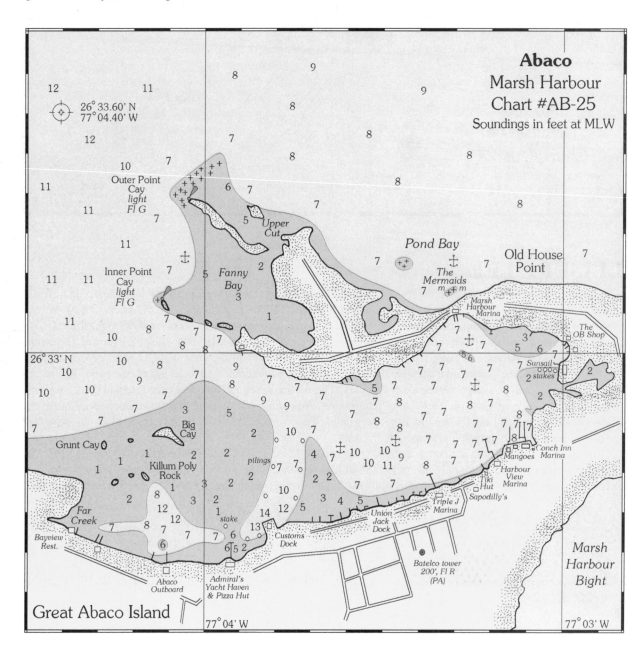

As shown on Chart #AB-25, the entrance to Marsh Harbour is fairly easy. The GPS waypoint at 26° 33.60' N, 77° 04.40' W will place you approximately ¼ mile northwest of the shallow reef off Outer Point Cay (light-Fl G). If you're approaching this waypoint from Great Guana Cay you'll wish to avoid the Fish Cays and Footes Cay as shown on Chart #AB-20. If you're approaching from Treasure Cay or Leisure Lee, you can parallel the shoreline of Great Abaco but you must give Water Cay and the reefs off the point southeast of Water Cay a wide berth, also as shown on Chart #AB-20. Vessels approaching on this route need not head directly to the waypoint. Once clear of the reefs off the point you can take up a course to take you south of Inner Point Cay (put Inner Point Cay just on your port bow). Your aim here is to stay south of Inner Point Cay and north of the shoal area off Big Cay as shown on Chart #AB-25.

If you're approaching from Man-O-War Cay, either from the harbour, from North or South Man-O-War Channel, or from the lee of Dickie's Cay, you can head for this waypoint once you clear Garden Cay and Sandy Cay as shown on Chart #AB-26. If you're heading to Marsh Harbour from Hope Town on points south, you can head for this waypoint once you clear Point Set Rock (also as shown on Chart #AB-26). When approaching from either Man-O-War or Point Set Rock, use caution and make sure that as you arrive at the waypoint you are well clear of the reef at Outer Point Cay (Chart #AB-25), this reef can be difficult to make out. If you happen to be approaching Marsh Harbour at night (not recommended), be advised that the Marsh Harbour *Batelco* tower flashes red. Do not confuse this tower with the tower in Dundas Town, 2 miles west of Marsh Harbour, which displays a fixed red light at night, or the fixed tower east of Marsh Harbour, which also displays a fixed red light at night.

From the waypoint the entrance into Marsh Harbour is straightforward. Head south/southeast and take Inner Point Cay well to port to pass between Inner Point Cay and the shoal are north of Big Cay. As you proceed eastward you will notice a marked channel to starboard. This leads to the *Customs* dock and if you need to clear in, that is where you must go. This is also the route to Silbert Mill's *Yacht Haven Marina* and the *Pizza Hut*. Head down the channel and turn as you approach the *Customs* dock to make your way to the marina. You can even head further west here (stay south of the privately maintained stake) to anchor in 8'-14' of water south of Killum Poly Rock and north of the large *Abaco*

Photo by Nicolas Popov.

Conch Marina, Marsh Harbour, Abaco.

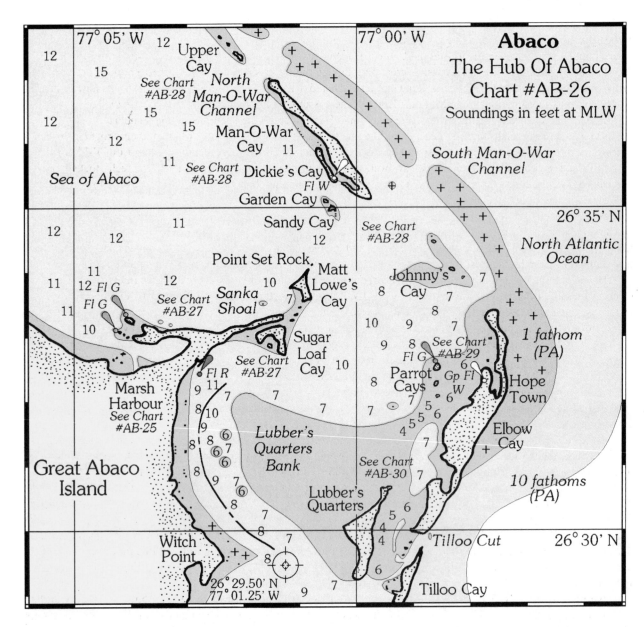

77° 05' W   12   Upper Cay

North Man-O-War Channel
See Chart #AB-28

15

15

15

Man-O-War Cay   11

11   See Chart #AB-28   Dickie's Cay
Fl W

Garden Cay

Sea of Abaco

12

12

12

Sandy Cay   12

See Chart #AB-28

South Man-O-War Channel

26° 35' N

North Atlantic Ocean

77° 00' W

Abaco
The Hub Of Abaco
Chart #AB-26
Soundings in feet at MLW

Point Set Rock.

Matt Lowe's Cay

Johnny's Cay   7

7

8

12   11

11   12 Fl G

Fl G

11

10

11   12   10

Sanka Shoal   7
See Chart #AB-27

Sugar Loaf Cay   10

See Chart #AB-27

9   11   7

7   7

8   10

9

8   8   6

8   7   6

6

8   6

8   7   6

7

8   7

8

10   9   7

9   8   See Chart #AB-29   6
Fl G

Parrot Cays   Gp Fl W   6

8   7

7   5   6

4   5

7   1 fathom (PA)

Hope Town

Elbow Cay

10 fathoms (PA)

Marsh Harbour
See Chart #AB-25

Fl R

Great Abaco Island

Lubber's Quarters Bank

Lubber's Quarters

See Chart #AB-30   7

5   6

5

4

4   Tilloo Cut   26° 30' N

Witch Point   8

8   7

26° 29.50' N
77° 01.25' W   9

7   6   Tilloo Cay

Outboard facility. In a strong westerly, when the rest of Marsh Harbour is getting choppy, this area is well protected by the shallows and cays surrounding it.

If you bypass the channel to the *Customs* dock and continue eastward you'll enter Marsh Harbour proper and you can anchor wherever you prefer. Most of the harbour is only about 7'-8' deep at MLW, but there is a deeper trough where the water is 10'-14' deep in places. This area lies east of the large shoal off the *Customs* dock and just north of the *Union Jack Dock*; the large dock with all the dinghies tied to it. Please try not to anchor so close to the marked channel to the *Customs* dock that the large freighters cannot enter or depart…they need room! By the way, the *Union Jack Dock* is probably where you'll wind up tying your dinghy while you explore Marsh Harbour. I must inform you of some of the local folks that may to try help you tie up your dinghy, and watch it for you while you're gone. They'll also hand you down your bags or boxes of supplies after you climb into your dink. They may also remind you of services rendered if you fail to tip them. They mean well, they're only trying to make a few bucks. I cannot advise you to pay them or not, that choice is yours.

As you set your anchor take a look and check out your neighbor's ground tackle arrangements. If they're all laying to two anchors, that's a good hint that you should also. If they're laying to only one, and the holding is so good here that one is often all you need, then you should consider a similar arrangement. This decision also depends on your estimated length of stay and the upcoming weather forecasts.

If you decide to take a slip instead of anchoring you have a great selection from which to choose. As I mentioned earlier, just west of the *Customs* dock is *Admiral's Yacht Haven Marina* and the *Pizza Hut* (with great lunch specials- a very popular spot you'll come to find out). *Yacht Haven* does not sell fuel, but they offer 20 slip with full electric, showers, and restrooms. The protection is great here though the water shallows as you approach the shore. Silbert Mills, once seen on a more regular basis at the marina and heard daily on the Cruiser's Net (weather), can now be heard on Abaco's only radio station, 93.3 FM, *Radio Abaco*. There is another FM radio station that you can pick up in Abaco, 100 JAMZ. There is from Nassau via satellite to a Marsh Harbour receiving and transmitting antenna.

In Marsh Harbour itself, the first marina you'll come to lies on the southern shore of the harbour, popular *Triple J Marina*. *Triple J*, sells diesel, gas, water and ice, as well as offering 26 slips with depths ranging from 5'-7' at MLW with full electric, cable TV, and telephone. Showers and laundry facilities are also available. The well-stocked *Triple J Marine Store*, just across the street from the dock, sells marine supplies, bait, tackle, gifts, and offers sales and service on *Garmin, Furuno, Simrad*, and *ICOM* electronics!

Just a bit east of *Triple J* you'll come to *Harbour View Marina*, home to the floating *Tiki Hut*, a popular restaurant and bar in Marsh Harbour for over ten years. *Harbour View* sells fuel, water, ice, and offers 36 slips with depths ranging from 5'-over 6' at MLW. All slips have full electric and the marina has a nice laundry, good showers, and some of the best dining in Marsh Harbour is right next door at *Mangoes*, which is also a marina (no fuel available).

The last marina on the southern shore of the harbour is the huge and extremely popular *Conch Inn Marina*. Besides offering diesel, gas, 75 slips with depths of 9' (MLW) and full electric, *Conch Inn Marina* is now owned by *The Moorings* and houses their fleet of charter boats as well. You can have your mail sent here and use their phone service in the office for your Internet connection. The hotel offers air-conditioned rooms if you wish to get away from the water for a night or if you have guests arriving. The marina's restaurant, *Bistro Mezzomare*, specializes in Italian cuisine and is open daily for breakfast, lunch, and dinner; call *Bistro* on VFH ch. 16 for reservations. They have a daily happy hour from 6:00pm to 9:00pm. There is also a great new deli on site with delicious baked goods and food items. Just across the street from the *Conch Inn* is *Sharkey's Pizza* with pizza, subs, homemade ice cream, and pies (they'll deliver to your slip). Right next door is *Barefoot Gifts* where you can pick up all types of resort-wear, gifts, and island-made jewelry and music.

On the northern shore of Marsh Harbour you'll find the *Marsh Harbour Marina*. With 57 slips and dockside depths of 7' at MLW, the marina also offers fuel, water, ice, showers, a laundry, and a great restaurant and bar, the *Jib Room*. The *Jib Room* has daily happy hours from 5:00pm to 7:00pm and great BBQs on Wednesdays and Sundays.

There is one more marina in the Marsh Harbour area, large and upscale *Abaco Beach Resort* and *Boat Harbour Marina*, but it must be accessed from Marsh Harbour Bight as shown on Chart #AB-27. We will discuss *Boat Harbour Marina* and its access later.

At the eastern end of Marsh Harbour, just south of the old *Sunsail* docks, is the shallow entrance to a small creek. This creek is good for drafts of less than 4' at high water only and is an excellent hurricane hole for small, up to 40', shallow-draft vessels. If you need this protection better plan on getting there very, very early or the charter boats may beat you to it.

There are so many businesses in the Marsh Harbour area that I cannot list them all here, but I will give you the basics. If you're looking for a charter boat, a small boat rental, bicycle, scooter, or car rentals, you'll have to look them up in *Appendix C: Service Facilities*. But as far as getting around town goes, walking will take you most places. Taxis can be hailed on VHF ch. 16 and they often hang out around the *Conch Inn* and at the *Union Jack Dock*. The locations for some of these businesses will be shown here or in the section *Abaco by Car*.

To begin with, if you need medical help you'll find it 24/7 in Marsh Harbour. The local doctors, Dr. Lundy and Dr. Boyce, have excellent clinics and provide great health care service. The *Agape Family Dental Centre*, 367-4355, is a few blocks south of the traffic light. If you need to fill a prescription head for the *Chemist Shoppe* or *Lowe's Pharmacy*. If you need pet supplies, for dogs, cats, or even parrots, check out *Pets R Us* just off Don Mackay Blvd.

On Great Abaco you'll find the very professional *Trauma One* ambulance team who have been providing emergency service to Abaco residents and visitors for no fee, they are supported entirely by contributions. *Trauma One* had been operating since September of 1995 and your help is needed. Donations may be sent to *Trauma One*, P.O. Box AB 20594, Marsh Harbour. All contributions are recorded and acknowledged.

If you need electronic, marine, outboard engine and related repairs, Marsh Harbour has more of these facilities than any other city in the Bahamas except Freeport and Nassau. At the northern end of Marsh Harbour, east of *Marsh Harbour Marina*, sits the *Outboard Shop,* Marsh Harbour's *OMC* dealer. They can be reached on ch. 16, (*Outboard Shop*) or by phone at 367-2703. *Abaco Outboard* is the local *Yamaha* dealer and their dock is west of *Admiral's Yacht Haven* in Dundas Town. You can reach them on ch. 16 (*Abaco Outboard*) or by phone at 367-2452. *Abaco Outboard* can haul small boats up to 30' and 8 tons.

If you need a *Suzuki* dealer, try *B & D Marine, Ltd.* at the traffic light in Marsh Harbour. *B & D* offers fine marine products, dive gear, Petit paints, *Suzuki* parts and service, *Standard Horizon* VHF radios, and fishing supplies. They can be reached on ch. 16 or by phone at 367-2622. *National Marine* is the local *Mercury* dealer and they can be reached at 367-2326.

For diesel work try *Asterix*. They can be reached on ch. 16 (*Asterix*) or by phone at 367-3166. *Pinder's Marine and Auto* also specializes in diesel repairs and can be reached by phone at 367-2274. Another option is *Sea Services* at *Boat Harbour*. Their phone number is 367-6805.

If you need prop work (up to 36") see the folks at *Abaco Marine Prop* on Don MacKay Boulevard next to the *Western Auto*. Their phone number is 367-4276. *Abaco Marine Props* also does sandblasting and stainless and aluminum welding.

If you require the services or goods of a hardware store try *Abaco Hardware* (367-2170). *Abaco Hardware* carries some marine supplies as well as hardware, lumber and power tools. If you need propane you can pick it up at the *Corner Value Hardware*, one block east of the traffic light. *Standard Hardware* sits two blocks east of the same light. There's also a *Western Auto* in town on Don Mackay Blvd. You'll want to visit *Doug's Place*, a dealer for *RCA* and *GE* TV's, for *Shakespeare* antennas, satellite systems, CD's and tapes. The *Snap Shop* is Marsh Harbour's one-hour photo developing lab. Their number is 367-3020. If you need a coin laundry try the *Classic Coin Wash*, just off Don Mackay Blvd. next to *Kool Scoops Ice Cream Parlour*.

If you need to do some banking while in Marsh Harbour, you have several to choose from and they are all open Monday –Thursday from 9:30am to 3:00pm and Fridays from 9:30am to 5:00pm. *Barclay's Bank* and the *Commonwealth Bank* can be found at the light while *CIBC* is one block south of the light next to the *Shell* station. *Scotia Bank* and the *Royal Bank of Canada* are both a couple of blocks south of the *Shell* station.

If you need office products and the like try *Abaco Office Products*, formerly *The Loyalist Shoppe*, and now next to the *Texaco* station on Don Mackay Blvd. *Abaco Office Products* sells magazines books, newspapers, gifts, and office supplies. The newest addition in office supplies is the *Bellevue Business Depot* in the *B & L Plaza*. The *Bellevue Business Depot* is modeled after the U.S. chain that we know as *Office Depot*. They offer faxes, copies, computer supplies, printer supplies, and office machines. If you need computer supplies or repairs see the folks at *Abacom, Ltd.*, the owners of oii.net.

For groceries you have several good choices. From the *Union Jack Dock* walk two blocks south and you'll find the large *Golden Harvest Supermarket*, a great full-service supermarket. Another block south and east is *Solomon Brothers* where you can buy in bulk at wholesale prices. *Abaco Market*, located in the Abaco Shopping Center, carries groceries, meats, and canned goods and fresh produce. *Abaco Wholesale* offers full galley stocking with free delivery to marinas or the *Union Jack Dock*. The *Bahamas Family Market* is located near the traffic light and offers grocery and gourmet items. *Roderick's Convenience Store* on Crockett Drive sells wild boar meat as well as fresh baked breads and a full selection of groceries. There is a small store, *Wilson's Quick Trip*, in *Memorial Plaza* behind *Triple J Marina*. They offer fresh produce and meats as well as dairy products.

Chelsea's Choice drinking water and ice, will deliver water, water coolers, and bottle pumps. *Abaco Ice, Ltd.* sells ten pound block and cubed ice and will deliver with a ten bag minimum. *Sawyer's Soft Drinks* located near the traffic light sells bulk quantities of soft drinks.

Located on Bay Street in Marsh Harbour, just down the road from *Triple J Marina* and across the street from the *Straw Shop*, is *The Flour House*, one of, if not the busiest bakery in town. Here you can choose from all types of breads, from French, to Italian, white, rye, wheat to honey bran and eight grain, all baked on site fresh daily. Owners Terell and Leona Russell also serve up cheesecakes, pies, cookies, and other sweet treats. *The Flour House* is the only bakery in town to serve up wheat bread on a regular basis, every Thursday. You'll find *Lovely's Bakery* in town.

If you wish to dine out for a change, Marsh Harbour has more choices than you could sample in a couple of week. Surrounding the harbour you can of course sample the offerings at the *Pizza Hut*, *Mangoes*, *Sapodilly's*, *Wally's*, the *Tiki Hut*, *Bistro Mezzomare*, the *Jib Room*, and *Sharkey's Pizza*. At the extreme southwestern end of the harbour you'll definitely want to try the *Bayview Restaurant* right on the waterfront in Dundas Town, west of *Abaco Outboard*. They have an excellent Sunday Champagne Brunch.

The Castle Café sits high on the hill overlooking Marsh Harbour and serves lunch daily on the terrace of the old house. *The Castle Café* was once the home of Dr. Evans Cottman (*Out Island Doctor*).

Another one of the best spots to dine out in the Marsh Harbour area is, without a doubt, *Mother Merle's Fishnet* in Dundas Town. The *Fishnet* is a down–home, family-style restaurant that opened in 1968 and has been going strong ever since. Mother Merle Swain is the proprietor and chef, and will serve you one of the finest meals you will ever eat in The Bahamas.

Downtown you'll find the *Golden Grouper Restaurant* in the *Dove Plaza* and *Kool Scoops Ice Cream Parlour* behind the *NAPA* near the traffic light. The *Ranch Sports Bar and Lounge* on Don Mackay Blvd. has a pool table, darts, and satellite TV. Just outside Marsh Harbour is *Kipco's Place*. Kipco is a tall Bahamian "Rastafarian" whose little bar and restaurant sits amidst a mass of wrecked cars and other items of salvage. Kipco loves to talk and his eloquent style and flowing commentaries on anything you wish to discuss is entertaining to say the least. *Nettie's Museum Restaurant* offers fantastic sunset views from their decks 18 miles south of the airport.

Cruisers seeking live entertainment have a pretty good choice in Marsh Harbour. *Abaco Towns by the Sea* has live music on Sunday's, Tuesday's and Fridays, while the *Abaco Beach Resort* offers live music every afternoon except Sunday and Wednesday. You can catch live music at *Mangoes* on Tuesday nights and at *Wally's* on Wednesday and Saturday nights. Estin Sawyer is the granddaddy of the Abaco music industry having been in the business for over 30 years. Mr. Sawyer has performed in Marsh Harbour at *Abaco Towns by the Sea* for the past 14 years, every Sunday, Tuesday and Friday from 6:30pm until... He also performs at *Wally's* every Wednesday and Saturday from 6:30pm to 9:30pm, and at *The Green Turtle Club* on Green Turtle Cay every Monday night from 7:00pm until...

REGATTA TIME IN ABACO

By far, the biggest party in Abaco is held during late June/early July...*it's Regatta Time in Abaco*! The first *Abaco Regatta* was held September 1, 1976 with 4 workboats and 10 cruising boats participating. After a couple of years of hosting the event in early September, the organizers realized that few cruising boats were actually in Abaco in the middle of hurricane season and in 1978 the event was moved back to a late June-early July time frame.

Thirty boats participated in the Regatta that year, and many of them then moved on to Green Turtle for what was considered to be the second regatta. From Green Turtle, the fleet moved just a bit to Treasure Cay for what was called the third regatta. The number of participants began to grow as word of the event spread throughout the southeastern US. A major change was taking place, the end of Bahamian work-boat participation. Traditionally those crews were paid to participate and unless there was compensation they would not show up. This was not the case with the cruisers whose only motto was "Will sail for fun and beer."

In the early 1980's, the three-race format was the norm and the schedule was set for the next decade. The Regatta kicks off in Marsh Harbour, then the fleet moves to Treasure Cay, and finished up at Green Turtle Cay. By now participation was nearing 150 boats and climbing.

A unique sideline event to watch was the annual dinghy tow from Marsh Harbour to Treasure Cay. The race to Treasure Cay is usually a spinnaker run and since it was not fair to have sailors tow their dinghies during the race a dinghy tow was organized. It often took as long to arrange and tow the dinghies to Treasure Cay that the racing fleet was already at Treasure Cay waiting to enter the marina. What may have been the largest dinghy tow in the event's history, some 80 dinghies, was hauled by singer David Crosby's schooner *Mayan*.

The bronze "lost-wax" castings of Little Harbour artist Pete Johnston (see the section on *Little Harbour*) that were given as trophies soon approached cult status. Racers soon found themselves competing not only for the line honors, but for Pete's castings, too. In the 1990's the regatta picked up sponsorship from *Mount Gay Rum* and *Beck's Beer*. Pretty soon the *Mount Gay* hats became almost as sought after as Pete's castings.

Soon the racing became more and more competitive, and the cruising boats found themselves vying for honors against true racing boats. The powers that be came up with an idea, a "Mother Tub Class." This allowed the cruisers to still compete and have a chance at the awards. Over the years the MTC became the largest fleet in the race, and it is still based on the principle of "FUN," or if you prefer, "PARTY!" *Regatta Time in Abaco* spans two grand holidays, Independence Days for both the United States (July 4th) and The Bahamas (July 10th), which certainly helped the party spirit.

In 1991, the organizers reversed the schedule of the races and dropped the Treasure Cay race entirely. The regatta then started with the Green Turtle race, moved on to Guana Cay, and then to Marsh Harbour. The dates and schedules changed, but the racing and parties remained the same. *Regatta Time in Abaco* is still rolling along, is still the number one summer attraction in Abaco, and it's still attracting sailors from far and wide. If you can plan to be in Abaco during regatta, by all means do so, don't miss it! How could you go home from your Abaco cruise, with all those wonderful memories, and not have a single one of *Regatta Time in Abaco*?

Photo by Mimi Rehor.

THE WILD HORSES OF ABACO

If you're an animal lover, particularly a horse lover, you'll probably want to try to catch a glimpse of the wild horses of Abaco while you're in the Marsh Harbour area. Nobody is really sure of their origin, some say they were left behind by the Conquistadors and probably settled in Abaco in the late 1500's to the early 1600's. Still others say they are descendents of the horses that the Loyalists brought with them. However they came to be here, their herd once numbered in the hundreds and they lived contentedly in the pine barrens of Great Abaco.

The opening of the Queen's Highway in the 1960's brought an increase in the number of hunters into their habitat and the wild horses were almost eradicated, some captured to work on other islands, some killed for no reason at all. Finally, three horses were found, a stallion and two mares, and they became the core of the current herd on Abaco. They were sheltered and cared for and as soon as the herd built up to a dozen, they were released into the wilds of Abaco again. By 1994, the wild horses of Abaco numbered 30, not a lot, but certainly much better numbers than two decades earlier.

In 1992, an American, Mimi Rehor, visited the area and took up their cause. She discovered that in 1996-1997 the herd was decreasing again. One mare died while giving birth and the foal was killed when only ten days old. Corpses of horses once again began appearing and the herd shrank to an alarming 16 rather quickly. Nobody is really sure what killed the horses, some say wild dogs, some say traps, some say humans. In all of 1998, only one wild horse was born…this is not the way to build a herd.

In 1998, representatives of the *U.S. Humane Society Equine Protection Division* and the *Pegasus Foundation* visited Abaco to see these magnificent creatures. The experts concluded that the horses are indeed of the Spanish Barb Type with only five lumbar vertebrae, all other domestic horses have six. Pending DNA testing, the researchers announced that they are potentially unique in that they have not been tampered with by man for several hundred years and are genetically very close to the first horses imported into the New World. Some of the horses have been linked to the Narragansett Pacer, a breed developed in the U.S. during the Revolutionary War years and who were exported all over the Caribbean. These are most likely the horses that the Loyalists would have had with them.

Whatever their origins, the wild horses of Abaco have been called a National Treasure that needs to be preserved. In 1994, Mimi Rehor started the *Abaco Wild Horse Fund*, a non-profit organization dedicated to preserving the wild horses of Abaco. A grant and donations from supporters have enabled her to continue to publicize the plight of the herd. She works with a variety of people to map out ways to preserve and protect the horses. I urge people to support her in her cause. Donations can be sent to *The Abaco Wild Horse Fund, Inc.*, c/o Mimi Rehor, General Delivery, Marsh Harbour, Abaco, Bahamas. Mimi, who lives aboard her sailboat in Marsh Harbour, can be faxed at the local *Batelco* office at 242-367-4756. Contact Mimi if you wish to take a tour to see the horses.

GREAT ABACO BY CAR

If you wished to drive around Abaco in years past you had to put up with hellish roads that ate tires, shocks, and mufflers for breakfast. Until about the mid-1950's there was no highway to carry motorists from one end of Abaco to the other. There were only logging roads, cut out of the scrub brush so timber could be hauled to waiting ships. Today, the roads from south to north are newly paved, fairly smooth, and almost pothole free. They are a delight to cruise on at almost any speed, and one of the best ways to see the island of Great Abaco. Formerly called the Great Abaco Highway, the road is now known as the Scherlin Bootle Highway, or just the Bootle Highway.

You'll most likely start your trip in Marsh Harbour where, at the time of this writing there is only one traffic light, but that will soon change. The government is making plans to improve road safety in Central Abaco so you can expect to see some new road signs including named roads and dangerous curves, as well as new centerline stripes and turning arrows. Six more traffic lights will be installed in Marsh Harbour, which will certainly be a change for this place! For now, let's start with what you'll find in the immediate Marsh Harbour area.

At the light you'll find a *NAPA*, a couple of banks, a *Shell* station and several other businesses. If you head east from the traffic light, you'll pass the *Batelco* tower and office just north of the road. Two blocks east of the light is *Standard Hardware,* and then continuing on to the east you'll pass the marinas on the waterfront and places like *Wally's*, and *Mangoe's*. As you pass *Conch Inn* you'll find the *Island Breezes Motel*, and the *Sanddollar Shop*. Up the hill to the left will be the *Castle Café*. A little further on is the turnoff to *Boat Harbour Marina* and a *Little Switzerland* outlet. A bit further east you'll come to the *Albury Ferry* dock and the end of the road at the eastern shore.

Heading west from the traffic light you'll find the *Royal Harbour Village*, the *Juliette Art Gallery*, and *Tropical Treasures*. If you're heading west from the *Union Jack Dock* you'll pass the *Customs* dock, *Admiral's Yacht Haven*, *Pizza Hut*, *The Ambassador Inn and Restaurant*, *Abaco Outboard*, a Police station, the *Bayview Restaurant*, and finally come to a *Shell* Station.

If you head south from the traffic light you'll be on Don Mackay Blvd. and you'll quickly come to *Dove Plaza* where you can eat at the *Golden Grouper* or rent a video at *Hit Video*. The *Immigration* office is here, and right across the street is the dental clinic. This section of highway is full of businesses of interest to cruisers. There's *Marsh Harbour Auto Parts*, *Abacom Computers*, *The Chemist Shoppe*, *Abaco Markets*, *National Marine*, *UPS*, *KFC*, *Scotia Bank*, the *Island Bakery*, *Maria's Restaurant*, the *Royal Bank of Canada*, *Abaco Family Medical Center*, *Texaco*, *Abaco Hardware*, *Pets R Us*, *K&S Auto Service*, an *Esso* station, *Abaco Saver's Mart*, *Abaco Wholesale*, *Western Auto*, the *Airport Hotel*, and a propane fill station.

At the roundabout at the far southern end of Don Mackay Blvd. you'll find the entrance to the *Marsh Harbour Airport*, the *Seventeen Shop*, and the site of the new *3 Screens Theater*.

Well, we've fairly well covered the Marsh Harbour area so let's see what else lies outside the limits of town. Let's begin our tour of Great Abaco by heading south to Cherokee Sound, Little Harbour, Sandy Point, and Hole in the Wall. Please note, for navigational information to the settlements on Great Abaco, see their relevant section in this chapter. For your information, Sandy Point lies approximately 49 miles south of the airport roundabout at Marsh Harbour via the Bootle Highway.

Beginning at the roundabout at the Marsh Harbour Airport on Don Mackay Blvd. and heading south you will quickly come to the *Abaco Big Bird Poultry Farm*. Here the owners raise all of Abaco's chickens, some 30,000 a month. This company had become so popular and successful that they are now able to ship many of their charges to Freeport, Nassau, and Eleuthera. A little further on you will come to the turn-off to Snake Cay, the old lumber port for the *Owens-Illinois Company* that was still active into the 1960's. The creek at Snake Cay is an excellent hurricane hole.

A bit further south on the main highway is the well-marked turn-off to Cherokee Sound, and Little Harbour. Eight miles down this winding but well paved road is the turnoff to Little Harbour where you can drive right up to *Pete's Pub* for a cold one while you explore the gallery. Check out the small "blue hole" on the side of the road on your way in. Forget the turnoff to Little Harbour and in three miles you'll approach Cherokee Sound. Take a left at the small *BEC* generator building and drive up and over the hill to the parking lot to leave your car. Cars are not used in Cherokee Sound as the roads are little more than wide sidewalks, but if you take the time to investigate, you will find that you have entered a marvelous little settlement. Cherokee Sound was once a thriving boat building and fishing community, and its population welcomes visitors. There is a small grocery store here as well as a *Batelco* station.

South of the Cherokee Sound turn-off is the road to Casaurina Point, a small residential community that was once the residential area for the executives of the *Owens-Illinois* Company. On the road leading in you'll find the *Different of Abaco* bonefishing resort with its bar and restaurant. Owner Nettie Symonette's forty-plus years of experience has enabled her to open a unique hotel/eco-tourist resort/bonefishing club along Abaco's eastern shore. Here you'll stroll the preserved grounds alongside a friendly donkey, chickens, ducks, geese, rock iguanas, and even pink flamingos. Ms. Symonette once had a dream of nesting flamingos on Abaco, and with that in mind, several years ago she brought 15 flamingos to her resort, but several died right away and most of the survivors were scattered during a hurricane. Some survivors are said to be doing well in the marls north of Casuarina Point. The two remaining birds are still there, in full plumage and looking great as they slowly make their way through the water, feeding, preening and watching the people who stop to admire them. Last year Ms. Symonette imported nineteen young West Indian Pink Flamingos from Inagua in the hopes that they will be the beginning of a breeding colony. Good luck Ms. Symonette.

A few miles further south on the Great Abaco Highway is the road that leads to Bahamas Palm Shores, a small residential community with a beautiful beach. About 11 miles south of Bahamas Palm Shores is the town of Crossing Rocks, a small community located on the eastern shore of Great Abaco island where you'll find a small restaurant and bar right on the highway.

Once back out on the Bootle Highway the next stop is Sandy Point. About 7 miles south of Crossing Rocks is the Sandy Point/Hole in the Wall junction. If you wish to visit Hole in the Wall, a truly rough trip whose 15 miles requires at least an hour or more each way as well as a high-clearance vehicle, take a left here (southeast) to get to the lighthouse. Keep an eye out for the rare Bahamian parrot on this route, you're in the vicinity of the *Abaco National Park*, a 20,000-acre site encompassing the nesting area and habitat of the Abaco Parrot. The paved Bootle Highway continues on another 6 or so miles to Sandy Point.

If you continue on to Sandy Point you will follow the highway to the end where you'll find *Pete and Gay's Guest House* right next to the town dock. If you're looking for a good spot to spend the night in Sandy Point, they have eight rooms that are usually booked by serious bonefishermen. Nearby are the *Seaside Inn Restaurant and Bar* and *Oeisha's Resort* for your dining pleasure.

Okay, now we've been south of Marsh Harbour all the way to Sandy Point, and you're probably wondering what's to the north of Marsh Harbour. Well, we're heading there right now. From the light on Don MacKay Blvd. in Marsh Harbour, head towards the airport roundabout and take a right on the Bootle Highway at *Abaco Wholesale* and you'll find yourself heading north on the Scherlin Bootle Highway. Your first stop will probably be Treasure Cay. On the way north you'll pass a small stretch where you can view the beautiful waters of the Bight of Abaco on the western side of the Bootle Highway. Heading north you'll be driving down a well-paved highway between two pine forests. You might think you're in south Georgia instead of The Bahamas.

The entrance road to Treasure Cay is well-marked and lies just north of *Hudson's Restaurant and Bakery* and the *Touch of Klass Restaurant*, roughly about 20 miles or so north of Marsh Harbour. As you turn in and head east you'll find *Abaco Ceramics*, a gift shop, and the *Treasure Cay Golf Course*. As you approach the entrance to the marina you'll find the signs that direct you to the *Tipsy Seagull* and the *Spinnaker Restaurant*, and the marina office. As you turn in you'll find several small shops such as the *Treasure Cay Variety Store*, *JIC Boat Rentals*, *Triple J Car Rentals*, *Blue Marlin Golf Cart Rentals*, *Annie's Laundry*, and *R&A Rentals and Tours* (they monitor VHF ch. 16). Heading north again on the Bootle Highway you'll pass *McKenzie's Car Rentals*, *Cornish Car Rentals*, and the Treasure Cay Airport.

A few miles or so north of Treasure Cay is the small community of Blackwood where you'll find the *Poinciana Restaurant and Bar*. Just past Blackwood is Fire Road where you can dine at *Lankin's Restaurant* or *Pizza World*. *Murray's Service Station* has better prices on cases of sodas than you'll find in Marsh Harbour (as of this writing). Fire Wood is almost a suburb of Cooper's Town, the next stop to the north.

Cooper's Town is well known to boaters…it has a *Shell Fuel Dock* and navigational information for the area will be found elsewhere in this chapter. Cooper's Town has a large *Community Clinic*, a *Shell* station, a *Batelco* office, and a *Government Office* building. You can dine at *The Place Bakery and Souse House*, *Gelina's Pizza* (free delivery if you're at the dock), *M & M's*, the *Conch Crawl*, and at the *Same Ol Talk of the Town*. There are also two small grocery stores in Coopers Town. Visitors might wish to check out the *Albert Bootle Museum* where you can learn a little about the early settlers, the Bootles and the Coopers, as well as sponging, sisal, and lumber.

Leaving Cooper's Town you'll cross a small bridge and find yourself on the island of Little Abaco heading west now instead of northwest. The first stop is Cedar Harbour whose only amenity is a small *Batelco* office. Five miles west is the *Wood Cay*, an excellent spot for lunch or to stay overnight. The *Tangelo Hotel* offers very nice accommodations (12 rooms) and great food at a good price. The community also has an *Esso* gas station and a good mechanic at *Chuck's Auto Service*. The next community is Mount Hope where you can treat yourself at *Trippers Ice Cream Shoppe* or grab a meal at the *BJ Restaurant and Bar*. Try the *V & M Grocery Store* if you need to pick up a few supplies for the road.

The next stop is the largest one on the island of Little Abaco, Fox Town, and is very accessible by big boat. Fox Town is in the middle of a bit of a construction boom - they are building a huge new *Community Clinic*. There is a *Shell* station on the water's edge next to the *Valley Bar and Restaurant* (with a pool table folks). Just west of the *Shell* station is the *Texaco Star Port* dock where you can fuel up and purchase oil if needed. If you plan to stay overnight, check out *Mimi's Guest Cottages* or the *Tangelo Hotel*.

Okay, next stop, the end of the road folks. Crown Haven. Crown Haven is really little more than a good walk west of Fox Town and offers a phone, the *Black Room Bar and Restaurant*, and *E&J's Ice Cream Parlour and Video Tape Rental*, quite a bit to put on one sign I assure you. If you're hungry and have forgotten to call ahead for a meal, simply stop by and see Bookie Butler at the *Chili Bar Restaurant*, he's pretty handy in emergencies. Crown Haven, like so many communities in The Bahamas, has an interesting past. Many of the residents remember when they lived on nearby Cave Cay in the Bight of Abaco. A hurricane in the 1930's destroyed their homes and the Government moved them to the island of Little Abaco, at the end of the road and today we have Crown Haven; a haven courtesy of the Crown.

MATT LOWE'S CAY TO MARSH HARBOUR

The area between Matt Lowe's Cay and Marsh Harbour offers a fairly nice anchorage, first rate snorkeling, some private dockage, and a shortcut to Marsh Harbour Bight for vessels that draw less than 5'. Snorkelers will marvel over the beauty and ease of access at the Mermaids, a small protected reef in Pond Bay as shown on Chart #AB-25. Guests of *Marsh Harbour Marina* can visit this reef simply by crossing the road from Marsh Harbour Marina to the small beach and then swimming out to the reef. But if you're anchored out, or if you're the guest at another marina, the best way to visit the Mermaids is by dinghy. There is a small mooring where you may tie up your dink to while you investigate the undersea life.

There is a nice anchorage just inside the small cove on the southwestern shore of Matt Lowe's Cay as shown on Chart #AB-27. You can anchor here in 6'-8' at MLW over a nice sandy bottom where you'll find shelter from northeast through southerly winds. There is a bit of small boat traffic coming and going through the cut south of Matt Lowe's Cay, and the ferries use the small channel that lies between Sugar Loaf Cay and the Eastern Shore of Great Abaco Island. If you're transiting the waters between Matt Lowe's Cay and Marsh Harbour, be sure to keep an eye out for the well marked (a conspicuous stake) Sanka Shoal as shown on Charts #AB-26 and #AB-27.

As I mentioned earlier, there is a shortcut between Sugar Loaf Cay (once called Hall's Point) and Great Abaco that the ferries use on a regular basis. Vessels with drafts of less than 5' can also use this passage, but it helps if the skipper can read the water a bit and has a high tide on his side. If you're attempting to use this passage as a shortcut into the Bight of Abaco, make your way around Sanka Shoal and pass northeast of the small rock that lies just off the eastern tip of Great Abaco. The channel lies between this rock and the string of rocks that stretch between Matt Lowe's Cay and Sugar Loaf Cay. The entrance carries 6' at MLW and should be easy to make out. If in doubt, anchor and watch the ferries as they come through here or check the route with your dinghy first. As you pass to the north of Sugar Loaf Cay you'll see several nice houses and private docks and the water depths will vary from 6'-9' and more in places. As you approach the southwestern tip of Sugar Loaf Cay you'll see two small rocks lying to the southwest of Sugar Loaf Cay. Take these two rocks to port and you'll pass over a shallow area that barely carries 3' at MLW. Don't stray too far either way here as the water will just get shallower. As soon as you're over the shoal you can make your way to *Boat Harbour Marina* or wherever else you choose.

If you prefer the safer and deeper long way around into Marsh Harbour Bight this route will be far less of a test on your nerves and a simple bit of eyeball navigation. From Marsh Harbour take Point Set Rock to starboard as shown on Charts #AB-26 and #AB-27. Point Set Rock is hard to miss; it's the small rock just off the northern tip of Matt Lowe's Cay that has a conspicuous white shack upon it. Keep at least 100 yards off the rock and never anchor in its vicinity. Once past Point Set Rock you can simply follow the shoreline past Sugar Loaf Cay and onward to the waypoint for *Boat Harbour Marina*.

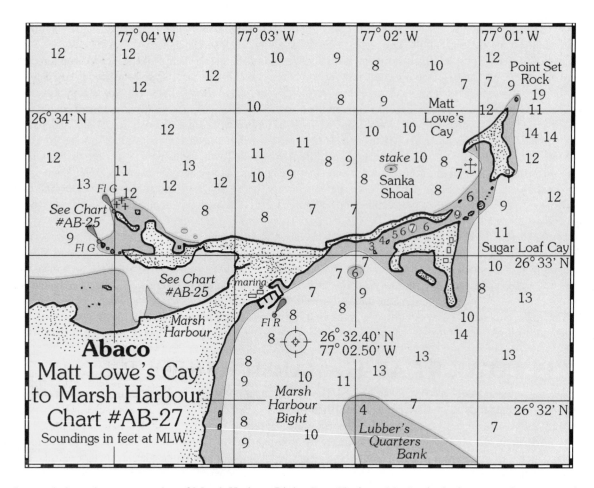

Located along the western edge of Marsh Harbour Bight, *Boat Harbour Marina* is the largest and most upscale of Abaco's marinas. As shown on Chart #AB-27, a GPS waypoint at 26° 32.40' N, 77° 02.50' W, will place you approximately ¼ mile southeast of the entrance to the marina. There is a large piling with a light (Fl R) that will lie between the waypoint and the marina entrance. Enter the wide opening passing between the two jetties into the marina proper. *Boat Harbour Marina* offers 160 slips and can accommodate large vessels with a draft of 9' and a beam of up to 33'. The marina boasts full electric hookups, satellite TV, water, ice, showers, laundry, a restaurant, a swim-up bar (*The Sand Bar*), and several shops. Repairs can also be arranged and guests can stay at the lush *Great Abaco Beach Hotel*, also on site.

Private *Carambola Cottage* is located on the southwestern tip of Sugar Loaf Cay at Parrot Point, approximately one mile east of the entrance to *Boat Harbour Marina*. While the cottage is just one of many fine places for rent throughout the Abacos, cruisers will be interested in the private dockage at the 54' by 70' L-shaped dock. Dockage includes fresh water and 30-amp or 50-amp electricity in a very protected little harbour. Dockage is free for cottage guests.

Vessels heading southward, towards Witch Point, North Bar Channel, Lynyard Cay, or Little Harbour, can follow the shoreline of Great Abaco Island staying between it and Lubbers Quarters Bank as shown on Chart #AB-26. Stay outside the small string of rocks lying off Great Abaco and you'll have 7'-10' all the way. If you favor Lubbers Quarters Bank you find several areas where the water shallows to 6' at MLW in spots. Once past Witch Point you can take up your course for Snake Cay, Tilloo Pond, or Tilloo Bank as you wish. Northbound cruisers can head for a GPS waypoint at 26° 29.50' N, 77° 01.25' W, which will place you approximately ¼ mile east of the shallows off Witch Point. From here follow the above directions in reverse to head to *Boat Harbour Marina* and the Hub of Abaco.

MAN-O-WAR CAY

Man-O-War Cay is the traditional boat building center of the Abacos, in fact of the entire Bahamas. As you probably know by now, Loyalists settled in the islands of The Bahamas in the 1780's. Those that settled farther south, in Exuma, tended to be farmers. Those that settled in Abaco tended to be merchants and boat builders and these traditions

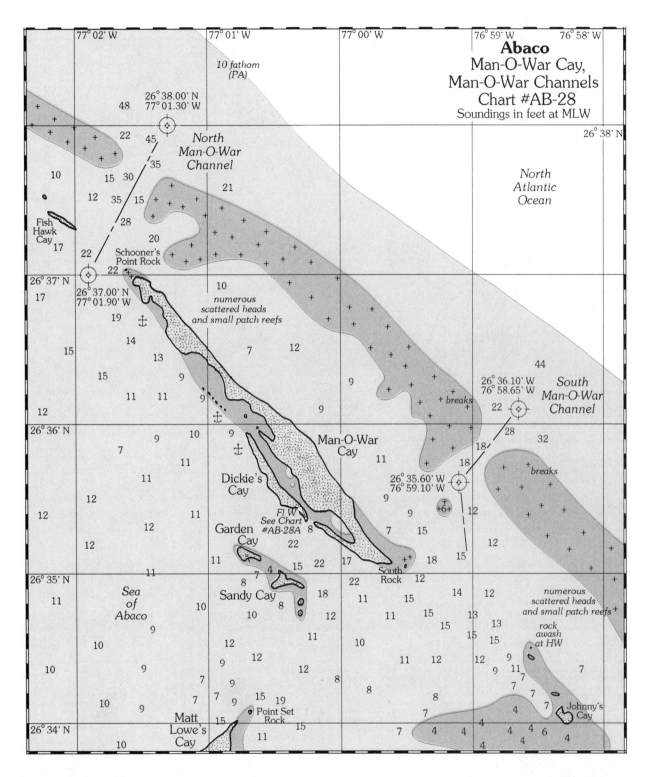

Abaco
Man-O-War Cay,
Man-O-War Channels
Chart #AB-28
Soundings in feet at MLW

have endured. There are no descendants of Loyalists in Exuma, but there are in Abaco. Almost all the residents of Man-O-War Cay can trace their roots back to Nellie Archer and Ben Albury. Nellie Archer used to visit Man-O-War Cay to farm a plot of land that her family owned there. On hot days she and her family would visit the beach for a break from the heat. One particular day they heard voices coming from the beach and when they investigated, Nellie found several survivors from a wreck on the reef offshore being led ashore by 16 year old Ben Albury. True love being what it is, the rest is history so they say.

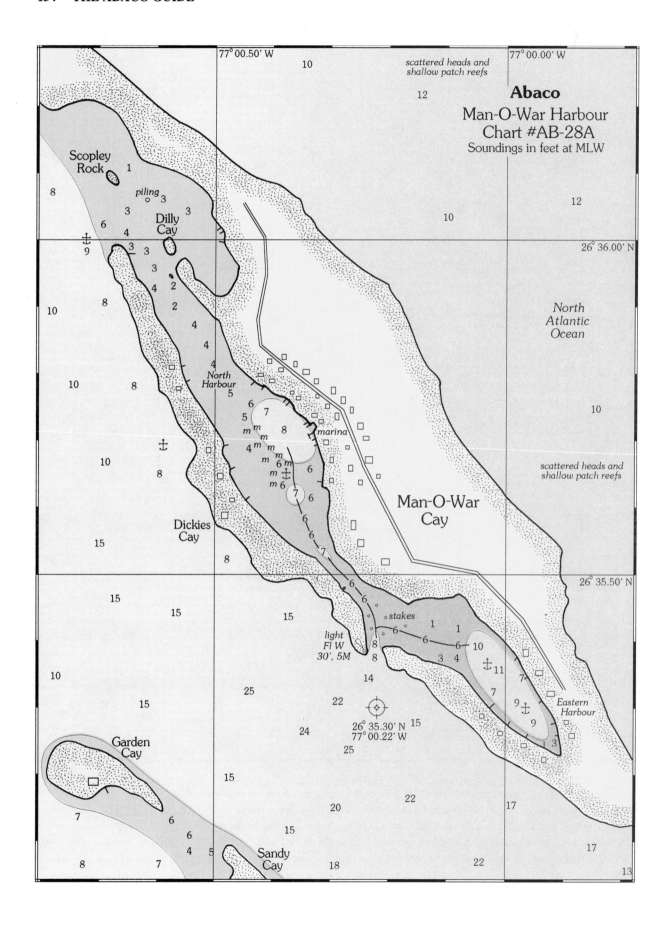

Scopley
Rock

1

piling 3

3

3   Dilly   3
     Cay

6
    4
    3   3   3

    3

    4   2

        2

        4

        4

        4

North
Harbour   5

        5   7
        5 m
           m m
        8   m
            m
        4 m m
            m 6 m
            m   6 m
            m 6
                7   6

                6

                6

                7 1

Dickies
Cay

        8

        6
         6
             stakes
                    1   1
    light   6
    Fl W   6   6
    30', 5M   8   6   10
                 8   3 4
                        11
        14   7
                              7
        25   7   9
                            9
        22   9   Eastern
    26° 35.30' N 15   Harbour
    77° 00.22' W   3
        24

        25

Garden
Cay

        15

    7   6
            6
            4   5
Sandy
Cay
    8   7   18

77° 00.50' W   10   77° 00.00' W

        12

Abaco
Man-O-War Harbour
Chart #AB-28A
Soundings in feet at MLW

8   12

        10

‡
9   26° 36.00' N

10   _North_
                                     Atlantic
8   _Ocean_

10   8

                    marina

        6   10

            6

                                    scattered heads and
                                    shallow patch reefs

10   8

15

        Man-O-War
        Cay

        8   26° 35.50' N

15

15   15   15

10

15   22   20   22   17

        18   22   17

                                              13

Photo by Nicolas Popov.

Man-O-War Cay, Hub of Abaco.

Man-O-War Cay offers excellent all-around protections, a quality marina, a nice lee side anchorage, and two passages through the reef into the ocean. As shown on Chart #AB-26, the cay lies north of Point Set Rock, northwest of Elbow Cay, and northeast of Marsh Harbour…within an hour or two sail from each of those places. As shown on Charts #AB-28 and #AB-28A you can anchor in the lee at the northern end of Dickie's Cay or n the lee of Man-O-War Cay just north of Dickie's Cay. Vessels wishing to enter the harbours at Man-O-War Cay should make for a waypoint at 26° 35.30' N, 77° 00.22' W, which will place you approximately 250 yards south of the entrance channel. It is imperative that you don't just plug in this waypoint and hit "GO TO," especially if you're approaching from Marsh Harbour. The waypoint lies between the entrance channel and the offlying Garden Cay and Sandy Cay. From the waypoint enter the channel midway between the two points of land as shown on Chart #AB-28A. The point of land to port is actually the southern tip of Dickie's Cay and is marked by a white flashing light. If you're heading into the Eastern Harbour, once you split the first pair of markers, you can turn to starboard and keep the next marker to port as you avoid the shoal area off the northern shore of the harbour and head into Eastern Harbour proper. Eastern Harbour is primarily used for vessel storage and there are a lot of moorings here.

If you intend to enter North Harbour, enter the main channel as described above and instead of turning to starboard to head into Eastern Harbour, bear more to port splitting the next pair of markers and following the channel into North Harbour. You'll find that North Harbour is usually crowded and the best idea is to pick up a mooring or get a slip at *Man-O-War Marina*. The northern entrance to the harbour is shallow and should be avoided by all but the shallowest draft vessels and small outboards.

Man-O-War Marina, well known for its service and hospitality offers the visiting yachtsman all of the comforts of home in a very protected harbour setting. The marina can accommodate yachts to 115' with drafts of up to 8'. The marina's 60 slips have full electric hookups and cable TV as well as showers, a laundry, a fuel dock, and they can handle cosmetic, mechanical, and even refrigeration repairs. The marina is home to the *Pavilion Restaurant* featuring barbecue nights on Fridays and Saturdays. The marina also sends and receives e-mail for cruisers. The marina dive shop rents and fills Scuba tanks and has a great selection of beach and casual wear.

Northwest of *Man-O-War Marina* lie two of the best boat yards in The Bahamas...*Edwin's Boat Yard #1* at the northwestern end of the harbour next to *Albury's Sail Shop*, and *Edwin's Boat Yard #2* which is located closer to the center of the waterfront. It is my firm belief that this is the best place to take your vessel for repair in The Bahamas. The prices are right, the service is the best, and the only problem is the wait; everybody seems to be lining up for this quality service. Just northwest of *Edwin's #2* is *Albury Brothers Boat Building*, makers of high quality fiberglass outboard boats.

As I mentioned earlier, there are two cuts to the ocean at Man-O-War Cay. The best by far is the North Man-O-War Channel as shown on Chart #AB-28. This is the preferred channel by veteran Abaco boaters as it is wide, deep, and because it will be open when most others are closed. If approaching from the sea, head for a GPS waypoint at 26° 38.00' N, 77° 01.30' W, which will place you about ¼ mile north/northeast of the channel. Head generally south/southwest to a GPS waypoint at 26° 37.00' N, 77° 01.90' W, your courseline bringing you approximately halfway between Schooner's Point Rock off the northern tip of Man-O-War Cay and Fish Hawk Cay. Once clear of Schooner's Point Rock you can parallel the shoreline of Man-O-War Cay southeastward towards the entrance to the harbours. If outbound via North Man-O-War Channel, simply use the waypoints mentioned and follow the course in reverse. The channel is wide here and you'll likely see the seas breaking on the reefs on either side.

South Man-O-War Channel is narrower and a bit more complicated, I much prefer North Man-O-War Channel and highly recommend it over its southern counterpart. If approaching from the ocean, head for a GPS waypoint at 26° 36.10' N, 76° 58.65' W, which will place you approximately ¼ mile north of the entrance to this channel as shown on Chart #AB-28. Use caution when approaching this waypoint; to the southeast of this waypoint lies a vast area of shallow reefs stretching for over a mile off the northern shore of Elbow Cay. From the outer waypoint head in towards the inner waypoint at 26° 35.60' N, 76° 59.10' W, keeping between the obvious reefs on both sides. Once at the inner waypoint you must avoid a rocky patch with only 6' over it at MLW that lies between the inner waypoint and South Rock as shown on the chart. Detour around this rocky patch and South Rock and pass between Sandy Cay and Man-O-War Cay to head for the harbour entrance channel. If you seek to head outbound via the South Man-O-War Channel, you must work your way to the inner waypoint by avoiding South Rock and the rocky patch north/northeast of it. Follow the above directions in reverse and watch out for the reefs off Elbow Cay!

Okay, now let's discuss what you'll find on Man-O-War Cay, but perhaps I'd better start with what you won't find on the cay. You won't find alcohol or tobacco for sale on the cay so you'd better have enough for your stay at Man-O-War Cay. There are two fine grocery stores on Man-O-War Cay. *Albury's Grocery Store* is right on the harbour while the *Man-O-War Grocery* sits behind *Man-O-War Marina*. Both will deliver your order to the dock. Across the street from *Man-O-War Grocery* is *Albury's Bakery* where you can pick up fresh baked goods daily. There is a branch of *CIBC* bank in town that's open only on Thursdays from 1000-1400. You can get your propane filled at *Man-O-War Gas*.

If you're in search of someplace besides the *Pavilion Restaurant* for dining while here, try *Sheila's Deli* or *Ena's Place*. *Sheila's* is on the waterfront while *Ena's* sits on the road southeast of the settlement. At *Ena's* you can eat in on the porch or take it with you. *Ena's* is open for lunch every day and every night for ice cream; Wednesday and Saturdays are dinner nights (other nights by reservation only). *Man-O-War Hardware* carries marine supplies and can handle all your hardware needs; they can deliver to Hope Town, Green Turtle, and even Little Harbour. *Joe's Studio and Emporium* is a must while at Man-O-War Cay. Here Joe Albury crafts fine wooden gifts such as beautiful half-hull models and, art objects, and even chairs. Joe also sells books, T-shirts, and jewelry. *Mary's Corner Store* also sells T-shirts, books, gifts, postcards, jackets, and bags.

One of the must stops here is *Albury's Sail Shop*, a misleading name as you will come to find out. They no longer build or repair sails here, their primary business is the construction of fine canvas bags, hats, and purses. If you need sail repair, look up Jay Manni at *Edwin's Boat Yard*, he might be able to help you.

Southeast of Man-O-War Cay lies Johnny's Cay. You can anchor in the lee of Johnny's Cay and enjoy the fishing and diving opportunities on the reefs that lie about a mile or so off the cay. With the help of the tide you can cross the shoal area south of Johnny's Cay if you're bound for Hope Town, controlling depth is 3'-4' here at MLW and it is sometimes marked by a stake to the south of Johnny's Cay.

ELBOW CAY

Most cruisers who visit Elbow Cay come for one reason...Hope Town. Hope Town is another one of those Abaco locales that if you haven't been there, well, you just haven't been to Abaco. Well marked by its candy-striped lighthouse, Hope Town is so popular among the boating community that some folks make it the focus of their Abaco cruise.

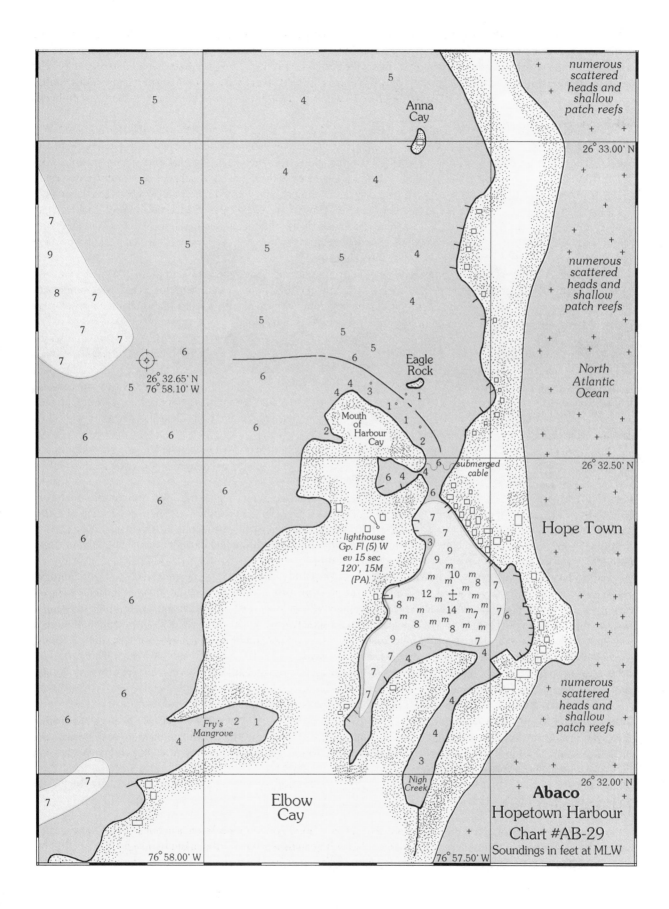

numerous
scattered
heads and
shallow
patch reefs

5

Anna
Cay

26° 33.00' N

numerous
scattered
heads and
shallow
patch reefs

North
Atlantic
Ocean

Eagle
Rock

26° 32.65' N
76° 58.10' W

Mouth
of
Harbour
Cay

submerged
cable

26° 32.50' N

Hope Town

lighthouse
Gp. Fl (5) W
ev 15 sec
120', 15M
(PA)

numerous
scattered
heads and
shallow
patch reefs

Fry's
Mangrove

Nigh
Creek

26° 32.00' N

Elbow
Cay

Abaco
Hopetown Harbour
Chart #AB-29
Soundings in feet at MLW

76° 58.00' W

76° 57.50' W

Photo by Author.

Hope Town Lighthouse.

Hope Town is an excellent hurricane hole and there are several marinas where you can tie up, or if you prefer, you can take one of the many well-maintained moorings in the harbour (and with the popularity of moorings in Hope Town harbour, anchoring is getting harder to do, I suggest a mooring).

The entrance to Hope Town is fairly shallow and should be done on a high tide if you draw over 4'. From Point Set Rock you can head north of the Parrot Cays (the northernmost cay is marked by a Fl G light) for a GPS waypoint at 26° 32.65' N, 76° 58.10' W, which will place you approximately ½ mile west of the entrance channel to the harbour as shown on Chart #AB-29. From the waypoint head eastward as if to pass north of Eagle Rock. Use caution in this area as it's pretty shallow...deeper draft vessels can proceed towards the conspicuous quarry on the western shore of Mouth of Harbour Cay before turning northeast towards the entrance channel to avoid some 5' at MLW spots. This part of the Elbow Cay shoreline is also a popular anchorage and a good spot from which to dinghy over to Parrot Cay where you'll find *Island Marine*, an *OMC* dealer.

As you approach the channel between Eagle Rock and Mouth of Harbour Cay, take a look down the channel towards the shoreline of Elbow Cay where you'll see a concrete road leading away from the water's edge. Steer your vessel as if to head straight down this road (148° mag.) and you'll spot a range on shore consisting of two white poles with red reflectors. Favor the Eagle Rock side of this channel; there may be some markers here to show you the channel, but don't count on their being there the same time you are as they're privately maintained. When Hope Town harbour opens up to starboard, turn and enter the harbour mouth staying approximately mid-channel. Before you actually enter Hope Town harbour you'll see a small cove to starboard, this is used primarily for storage of vessels and haul outs at *Lighthouse Marina*.

As you enter the harbour proper you can head for one of the marinas, pick up a mooring, or anchor where your draft allows. The community of Hope Town requests that visiting yachtsmen leave a channel approximately 200' wide along each shore of Hope Town harbour. As I mentioned, I suggest that you pick up a mooring, as the harbour is almost

Photo by Nicolas Popov.

Hope Town, Elbow Cay, Abaco.

always full. Call *Lucky Strike*, *Club Soleil*, or *Abaco Bahama Charters* on VHF ch. 16 for a mooring. All of the marinas in Hope Town also monitor VHF ch. 16.

Directly to starboard upon entering the harbour is *Lighthouse Marina* offering 6 slips with full electric hookups, water, ice, showers, a laundry, fuel, and 7' at MLW. *Lighthouse Marina* also offers wet and dry storage, a well stocked marine supply store, and a selection of fishing tackle and bait. A restaurant/bar is on site and groceries can be picked up in town. *Lighthouse Marina* can help you with *Yamaha* outboard repairs, they're a *Yamaha* dealer. If you need *OMC* help, *Sea Horse Marine* is the local dealer (they monitor VHF ch. 16).

Just past *Lighthouse Marina* is *Club Soleil Resort and Marina*, the old *Hope Town Marina*, with 16 slips, 7½' at MLW, full electric hookups, fuel, water, ice, showers, and fishing tackle and bait. Minor repairs and cosmetics can be handled here. *Club Soleil* has an excellent restaurant that is open for breakfast, lunch, and dinner Monday through Saturday featuring Bahamian and European cuisine. *Club Soleil* can also handle e-mail for cruisers. *Club Soleil* can help you with *Nissan* outboard repairs.

Just past *Club Soleil* are the docks of *Hope Town Hideaways*. Primarily featuring vacation homes and waterfront property, they also have a 12-slip marina with a freshwater pool.

There are several places for moored or anchored cruisers to gain shore access in Hope Town. The large government dock sits in the southeastern end of the harbour at the northern end of Nigh Creek. If you tie up here please don't block the Ferry access. By the way, cruisers can find some excellent hurricane protection up the creeks at the southern end of Hope Town harbour. You can tie your dinghy up at the *Harbour View Grocery* dock where you can stock up on groceries, sundries, meats, veggies, and even get your propane filled. *Harbour View* is open Monday-Friday from 0800-1300 and then from 1400-1800. Saturdays they're open from 0800 until 1900.

Photo by Nicolas Popov.

View at sea level, Hope Town, Elbow Cay, Abaco.

One of the more popular waterfront hangouts is the *Harbour's Edge Restaurant* that opens daily at 1000. Here you can dine while gazing at your lovely yacht, can shoot some pool, rent a bike, buys some ice, or catch the latest news or weather on satellite TV. Saturday night is pizza night with live music; Sunday's there's live music too.

Every bit as popular is *Capt. Jack's* right on the water's edge. You can get breakfast, lunch, or dinner here in an extremely casual atmosphere. The specialties are Bahamian dishes and you can watch satellite TV and listen to live music on Wednesday and Friday nights.

There is so much to see and do in Hope Town, the first place to start might be with *Island Cart Rentals*, they'll deliver right to your marina and they monitor VHF ch. 16. In town you can shop at *Vernon's Grocery and Upper Crust Baker*, where if you can't find what you want at *Harbour View*, you'll probably locate it here. You must sample their fresh baked pies and breads. I remember sitting in the harbour one morning when an announcement came over VHF ch. 16 saying that fresh bread was available at *Vernon's*. All of sudden a mass of dinghies made their way to shore in a mad rush to share in the tasty treats that the bakery is famous for.

Also in town you'll find the *Abaco Ocean Club*, the *Bike Shop*, a *CIBC* bank that is open Wednesdays from 1000-1400, the *Water's Edge Studio*, the *Island Gallery*, and high on the hill is the *Hope Town Harbour Lodge* with its excellent restaurant. The restaurant serves breakfast and lunch Mondays-Saturdays while the *Reef Bar and Grill* at the *Lodge* serves lunch Monday-Saturday from 1130-1430, with a happy hour from 1600-1700 Monday-Saturday. You can also satisfy your appetite by visiting *Munchies, Hollywood Temptations*, and *Rudy's Place* just outside of town. Call *Rudy's* on VHF ch. 16 to arrange transportation.

A wonderful spot to spend an hour or three is at the *Wyannie Malone Historical Museum*. Here you'll learn the secrets of Hope Town's history dating back to Lucayan times. The museum was founded in 1785, and is maintained by the community.

One thing that you MUST DO while in Hope Town is climb to the top of the lighthouse. Many, many years ago the folks of Elbow Cay made their living off the salvaging of wrecked vessels that came to grief on the reefs of Elbow Cay. A popular tale recounts how a minister was preaching to his congregation when he spied a ship on the reef. His flock

Photo by Author

Tower at Tavern Cay.

had their back to the sea and could not see this windfall. The minister asked everybody to bow their heads for a few minutes of silent retrospection and prayer. After a few minutes of this silence, some of the members started raising their heads and they noticed that the preacher was nowhere to be seen. Suddenly he was spotted in his boat heading to the wreckage. The next day the congregation turned the altar around so that they had the view of the sea.

When the lighthouse was scheduled to be built in 1864, Abaconians who lived off salvaging protested but to no avail. Today, the candy-striped landmark still stands as sentinel for Abaco, but it has been a long uphill battle to keep its distinct and historical flavor. This symbol of Bahamian maritime heritage is one of the last three oil-burning, hand-wound lighthouses in the world. The lighthouse keeper must climb the 101 steps to the top every two hours to hand crank the weights that operate the beacon. The light mechanism sits in mercury and its five bulls-eye lenses focus its kerosene fueled light once every 15 seconds. Faced with modernization, the community of Hope Town pulled together and managed to preserve the lighthouse in its original state. This involved a huge fund raising effort as well as immense difficulties in finding much needed out-dated parts. Help came from some of the oddest places…a group of professional bridge painters agreed to repaint the lighthouse in exchange for room and board and today the lighthouse absolutely gleams in her new paint job.

Lovely White Sound lies about a mile north of the southern end of Elbow Cay and Tilloo Cut. Here you'll find a dredged entrance channel, the *Abaco Inn*, the *Sea Spray Resort Villas and Marina*, and a fair sized residential community. The entrance is fairly straightforward as shown on Chart #AB-30. A GPS waypoint at 26° 31.10' N, 76° 59.00' W, will place you approximately ¼ mile west/northwest of the entrance channel to White Sound. If you're approaching from Hope Town, simply parallel the shoreline of Elbow Cay southward passing between the Parrot Cays and Elbow Cay (see Chart #AB-26). If you're heading for this waypoint from Point Set Rock you'll pass west of the Parrot Cays, and you'll have to avoid the small rock that lies southwest of this group as shown on Chart #AB-26. Once abeam of that small rock you'll pass over a shallow area (5' at MLW) before getting back into deeper water at the waypoint (7').

East of the GPS waypoint you'll see a turning mark indicating the beginning of the dredged channel (6' at MLW) into White Sound as shown on Chart #AB-30. At the time of this writing the marker was a red ball, but I have been told that an amber flashing light will replace it some time in 1999, so keep your eyes peeled for the new marker. The entrance channel lies south of the marker and a range at the *Abaco Inn* (two red disks-lit red at night) will lead you in on a bearing of 123°. There really isn't any room to anchor here, you can't anchor in the channel and the rest of White Sound is too shallow, but the *Abaco Inn* offers complimentary dockage for guests of their restaurant and bar. Dockage here is Med-style, drop a hook and back in to tie up stern to. Cruisers wishing to anchor and enjoy White Sound by dinghy can anchor south of the entrance as shown on Chart #AB-30 in prevailing east/southeast winds.

The *Abaco Inn* sits on a dune with views of both White Sound and the North Atlantic Ocean. Their restaurant offers elegant gourmet Bahamian and American cuisine in a casual setting. Cruisers in Hope Town can contact the *Abaco Inn* for a free pick up at the Government Dock.

If a slip is more to your liking, you can take the dredged channel south in White Sound to the *Sea Spray Resort Villas and Marina* located at the extreme southern end of White Sound. The well-marked channel turns sharply southward (as shown on the chart) and as you approach the marina you will pass to the west of a jetty that protects the marina.

Sea Spray Resort Villas and Marina boasts 24 slips with full electric, water, ice, showers, and a laundry on site. They can handle boats with a maximum beam of 22' and the docks carry 6' at MLW. *Sea Spray* monitors VHF ch. 16 and is a *Texaco Star Port*. Guests can dine at the *Boat House Restaurant* (breakfast, lunch, and dinner) or have a beverage at the *Garbonzo Bar* before or after taking a dip in their fresh water pool. For a real treat, try some of their fresh baked goods.

LUBBERS QUARTERS, TAHITI BEACH, AND TILLOO CUT

Remote but accessible Lubbers Quarters lies just to the west of Tilloo Cut as shown on Charts #AB-26 and #AB-30. What is *Yahoe's* you may ask? Well *Yahoes Sand Bar* is the principal attraction for cruisers these days on Lubbers Quarters. Named after the legendary elusive *Yahoo*, a half-bird half-man creature which is said to have inhabited Lubbers Quarters, *Yahoes* is unique in its location as well as being quite unusual in its construction. The main structure is constructed of native pine logs and is covered with old sails that have seen both the Pacific and Atlantic Oceans. Norwegian chef Hans Hinrichsen and his staff prepare a daily menu of various Caribbean and Continental cuisine. When he is not concocting some tasty dish Chef Hans loves to mingle with the customers. Hans wants all his guests to have a good time and that's not hard to do at *Yahoes*. Tuesday night's menu is primarily hamburger and hot dogs as the dining area is cleared to become a dance floor with live music. This is locals night as *Albury's Ferry* offers service from the surrounding cays. Sunday's between 1600 and 1900 there is a barbecue buffet with live music. But the high point of the month is usually the full moon buffet, crowded but not to be missed. *Yahoe's* is open daily except Monday, from 1100 with dinner after 1800. Call *Yahoe's* on VHF ch. 16 for reservations. The best way to access Lubbers Quarters by boat is to anchor in White Sound or at Tahiti Beach and dinghy over and tie up at *Yahoe's* dock. You can anchor to the east of *Yahoe's* in 4'-6' but only in westerly winds. How do you get to Tahiti Beach you might ask? Well dear reader, move on to the next paragraph for instructions.

If you're approaching Tilloo Cut from the north, from White Sound, once out of White Sound turn south paralleling the shoreline of Elbow Cay between Elbow Cay and Lubbers Quarters, but favoring Elbow Cay as shown on Chart #AB-30. Once past Aunt Pat's Creek and the conspicuous three story house (once owned by Burl Ives), put the house on your stern and steer approximately 230°. Continue on this course for about ¼ mile and you'll see Bakers Rock and Tahiti Beach at the extreme southwestern tip of Elbow Cay as shown on the chart. Head in towards Tahiti Beach and anchor where your draft allows.

Tilloo Cut is a viable passage to the ocean, but usually only local boats use it. Cruisers normally opt for North Man-O-War Channel or North Bar Channel, which lies a bit further south. If you're approaching Tilloo Cut from the south in the Sea of Abaco you can round Tavern Cay as shown on Chart #AB-30, and head in along the western shoreline of Tilloo Cay. You'll be passing between Tilloo Cay and the conspicuous sandbank to its west where you'll find 7' and more all the way out through Tilloo Cut. As you approach Tilloo Cut itself, favor the southern side of the cut where you'll have 7'; the northern side of the cut is shallow. By all means, once outside give the northern end of Elbow Cay a WIDE berth. Shallow reefs here stretch seaward for over a mile.

If you're approaching Tilloo Cut from White Sound or Tahiti Beach, clear Bakers Rock as shown on Chart #AB-30 where you'll pick up some water that's about 7' at MLW. Your aim is to round south of the string of cays lying west of Tilloo Cut in a narrow, but deep channel that is easily seen with good visibility. You'll cross a spot with only 6' at MLW,

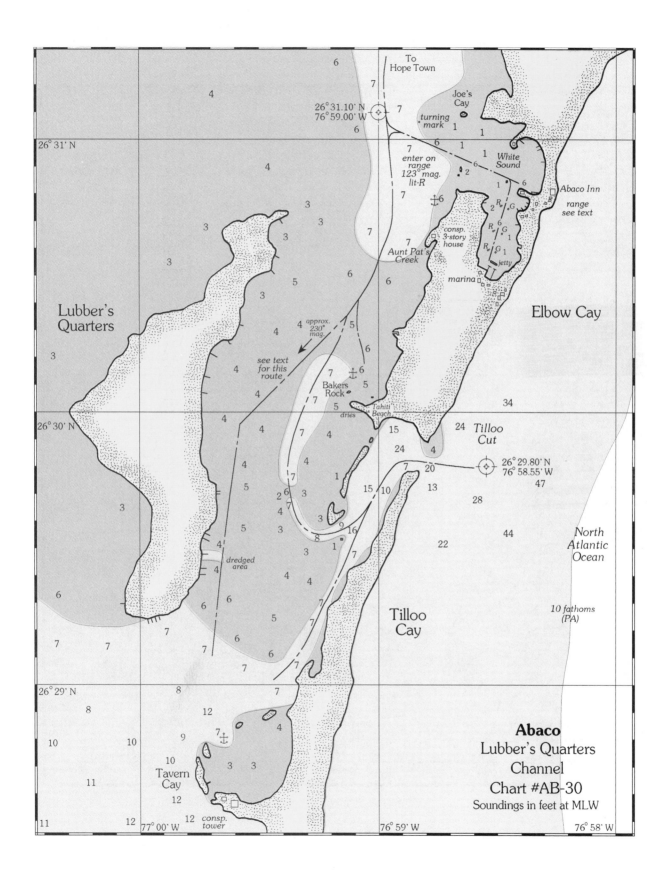

To
Hope Town

6

4

7

26° 31.10' N
76° 59.00' W

7

7

6

Joe's
Cay

turning
mark   1

1

1

White
Sound

26° 31' N

7

enter on
range
123° mag.
lit-R

6

2

Abaco Inn

range
see text

7

1

R   G

2   6

7

Aunt Pat's
Creek

7

consp.
3-story
house

R   G
6

R   G
1

jetty

Lubber's
Quarters

3

4

4

3

3

3

3

5

6

6

marina

Elbow Cay

3

3

5

4

approx.
230°
mag.

5

6

see text
for this
route

4

5

7   6

Bakers
Rock

5

5
dries

Tahiti
Beach

34

26° 30' N

4

4

4

7

15

24

Tilloo
Cut

26° 29.80' N
76° 58.55' W

47

3

5

4

7

1

24

4

20

13

28

44

North
Atlantic
Ocean

3

5

2   6

3

15   10

4

8

3

9   16

1

22

4

6

3

1

7

4

4

dredged
area

6

6

5

Tilloo
Cay

10 fathoms
(PA)

6

7

6

7

7

7

6

7

7

26° 29' N

8

7

8

8

12

Abaco
Lubber's Quarters
Channel
Chart #AB-30
Soundings in feet at MLW

10

10

9

7

4

11

10

Tavern
Cay

3   3

11

12

11

12

77° 00' W

12   consp.
tower

76° 59' W

76° 58' W

77°03' W 9 10 77°02' W 13 77°01' W 14 77°00' W 7 76°59' W 76°58' W

Cormorant Cay 10

26°28' N

12

⚓

North Atlantic Ocean

13

14

See Chart #AB-33 12

⚓ 3 6 7

13

14

14

Snake Cay 13

13

15

14

11

7

12

14

9

26°27' N

12

12

13

Tilloo Pond

See Chart #AB-32

7

7

10

11

14

11

12

Soap Point 1

Deep Sea Cay

Note:
Route through Middle Channel, Tilloo Bank. Line up the tip of Snake Cay, the northern tip of Channel Cay, and the northern tip of South Pelican Cay.

11

2

Tilloo Bank
(consp. bright green) 2

Tilloo Cay

9 9

7

11

2

Mockingbird Cay

12

14

11

26°25.90' N
77°01.10' W ⊕

11

11

4

7

1

26°26' N

11

7

11

5

7

9

9

1

breaks

Ironwood Cay

7

12

Middle Channel

10 5

7 7 6

7

8

20

9

9

10

5

12

4

6 8

8 26°25.38' N
77°00.20' W ⊕

8 11 10

9

13

7

8

7

9

4 1

11

12

4

Bob's Cay

6

8

10

9

7

4

7 ⚓

17

12

26°25' N

2

Channel Cay

12

13

breaks

7

3

3

2

Approx. boundaries:
Pelican Cays Land and Sea Park

2

6

3

11

26

Bucaroon Bay 6

6

6

3

7

Gaulin Cay

9

Pelican Harbour

12

20

9

South Pelican Cay

5

4

6

7

9

9

15

Angel Cay

Black Point

Devil's Teatable

Sandy Cay ⚓

⚓ 7

4

18 14

26°24' N

Great Abaco Island

Black Point Cay

2

4

1

1

m m
m
26

28

18

12

+ Channel Rock

22

Abaco
Cormorant Cay to Pelican Point
Chart #AB-31
Soundings in feet at MLW

5

6

7

Cornish Cay

7

12

dinghy moorings

11

26°23.60' N
76°59.00' W ⊕

North Bar Channel

15

Spencer's Bight 12

18

16

20

26°23.45' N
76°58.10' W

18

33

7

Spencer's Point

Pelican Point 17

7

Lynyard Cay 26°23' N

but elsewhere in this channel you'll have deeper water as shown. Follow the channel between the last cay and a small rock as shown on the chart and you can head right on out Tilloo Cut.

If you're approaching Tilloo Cut from offshore you can head for a GPS waypoint at 26° 29.80'N, 76° 58.55' W, which will place you approximately ¼ mile east of Tilloo Cut. From the waypoint head westward towards the cut favoring the northern tip of Tilloo Cay, rounding it about 50 yards off. Watch out for the shallow area on the northern side of Tilloo Cut.

Skippers wishing to head southward from White Sound or Tahiti Beach, between Lubbers Quarters and Tilloo Cut may find that this short passage is the most challenging of their Abaco cruise. The waters between Lubbers Quarters and Tilloo Cut have shallowed a bit over the last few years and you must have a high tide to transit this area. When heading south, I much prefer to follow the channel between Great Abaco and Lubbers Quarters Bank as shown on Chart #AB-26. It's a lot easier and less stressful…but if you insist on passing east of Lubbers Quarters here's how. (I don't recommend this route if you draw over 5'.)

If you're heading south from White Sound, once out of White Sound head generally south paralleling the shoreline of Elbow Cay between Elbow Cay and Lubbers Quarters, but favoring Elbow Cay as shown on Chart #AB-30. Once past Aunt Pat's Creek, and with the conspicuous three story house bearing approximately 50°, put the house on your stern and steer approximately 230°. As you follow your 230° course you'll soon find the waters getting quite shallow, 4' or less in places at MLW. You'll approach the shoreline of Lubbers Quarters quite closely and when the western shore of Tavern Cay bears 205° you can turn and head directly for it until you're back in deeper water just past the southern tip of Lubbers Quarters. Please use extreme caution on this route, it gets very shallow, I don't like to use it, but you might. Trust your eyes and your depthsounder here.

A quiet anchorage can be found in a small bight northeast of Tavern Cay as shown on Chart #AB-30. This spot is good in winds from northeast through east to southwest, but do not plan on staying here for a frontal passage; it's wide open to the northwest.

The Southern Abacos

TILLOO POND

Tilloo Pond is a wonderful, well-protected little anchorage about halfway down the western shore of Tilloo Cay as shown Chart #AB-31. Tilloo Pond will accept boats with drafts of less than 6', vessels drawing more than 3½'-4' will have to wait for the tide to enter and leave. This anchorage is a good spot to ride out a front, especially if you can duck in far enough behind the Shearpin Cay as shown on the blowup on Chart #AB-32. A strong west wind will create a bit of a surge in here at times as it funnels in through the entrance and bounces around inside, nothing dangerous mind you, but you might find it a bit uncomfortable. The docks in the pond are all private so don't tie up your dinghy there.

If approaching Tilloo Pond from the north, from the northern end of Tilloo Cay or Lubber's Quarters, you can parallel the shoreline of Tilloo Cay southward to a GPS waypoint at 26° 27.00' N, 77° 00.50' W. This will place you approximately ¼

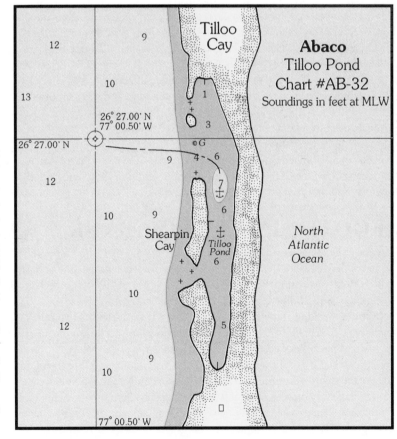

mile west of the entrance into the pond. The western shore of Tilloo Cay has several small coves that are good for anchoring in easterly winds. If you're approaching from Witch Point on Great Abaco, you can make a beeline for the waypoint given and be in good water all the way.

If approaching Tilloo Pond from the south, from Middle Channel at Tilloo Bank, once clear of Tilloo Bank you can head for the GPS waypoint at the entrance to the anchorage. Be careful to avoid the northern edge of Tilloo Bank, it's easily seen and avoided. If you're approaching from Snake Cay, simply head straight for the waypoint at Tilloo Pond, almost due east in good water all the way.

From the waypoint, the entrance to Tilloo Pond is fairly straightforward. Heading east, the entrance lies between Shearpin Cay and the small rock north of the cay. At the time of this writing there was a green marker just south of the small rock and if that is there when you arrive, keep it to port. The entrance channel lies roughly halfway between the small rock and Shearpin Cay. Once over the bar turn to starboard to anchor behind Shearpin Cay, do not turn to port as the water shallows almost immediately there.

SNAKE CAY

In the 1960's, Snake Cay was a hustling, bustling little port that was operated by the Owens-Illinois Company for their lumber operations. Today the equipment lies unused and the bottom is littered with pieces of concrete, steel, and who knows what else. Snake Cay's best attribute is that it is one of the best hurricane holes in the Abacos.

If approaching from the north, from Witch Point or Lubbers Quarters Channel, you can head straight for a GPS waypoint at 26° 26.90' N, 77° 02.70' W, which will place you approximately ¼ mile southeast of the southeastern tip of Snake Cay. If approaching from the south, from Middle Channel at Tilloo Bank, once clear of Tilloo Bank you can steer straight for this waypoint, Snake Cay will be clearly visible and bearing about 310°.

If the winds are southeast to southwest you can head north just a bit to anchor in the small bight formed by the "foot" of Snake Cay, but be advised, there are several submerged obstructions here, especially the closer you get to shore and the old dock. You might foul your anchor on old pilings, beams, or even a piece of heavy equipment; use caution when setting your hook here.

As I mentioned, Snake Cay is one of the best hurricane holes in the Abacos. There is a small, deep channel close in to the southern shore of Snake Cay that will take you back between Snake Cay and Deep Sea Cay and, if your draft allows, to a small deep pocket to the west of Deep Sea Creek. To access this area, follow close in along the southern shore of Snake Cay as shown on Chart #AB-32. You'll pass between the shoal that lies northeast of Deep Sea Cay and the southern shore of Snake Cay in good water from 8'-20' in depth. There is a bit of current here so be prepared. You can anchor in the deep cut between Snake Cay and Deep Sea Cay or, if your draft allows, cross over the 3' bar (MLW) to head south/southwest to the conspicuous blue patch of water (7' at MLW) that lies west of Deep Sea Creek.

It's possible to anchor in the bight at the southern end of Cormorant Cay (Chart #AB-33) in winds from west to almost north when this small anchorage will be calm. The flats to the west of Cormorant Cay and Snake Cay, like most in Abaco, offer excellent bonefishing. A GPS waypoint at 26° 27.45' N, 77° 02.75' W will place you roughly a quarter-mile east/southeast of this small bight.

Well south of Snake Cay lies Bucaroon Bay as shown on Chart #AB-31. In winds from southwest to northwest you can anchor in the lee of these cays and take the opportunity to do some flats exploring. This harbour is not good in a blow; the bottom is a mixture of hard sand and rocks.

NEGOTIATING TILLOO BANK

Vessels heading southward to North Bar Channel or Little Harbour, who are not wishing to go outside into the deeper waters of the North Atlantic Ocean must instead negotiate the very shallow and conspicuous Tilloo Bank. Tilloo Bank presents no real difficulties for the average skipper; it can be rounded by following its very visible edge or bisected by using Middle Channel as shown on Chart #AB-31.

If you're heading south in the Sea of Abaco from Lubber's Quarters, Witch Point, or Snake Cay, steer for a GPS waypoint at 26° 25.90' N, 77° 01.10' W. This position will lie approximately ¼ mile northwest of Middle Channel and roughly in line to pass across the Tilloo Bank in 6'-7' at MLW. From the waypoint you can take up a course of approximately 130° or follow a very easy and visible range. The courseline through here is not as important as staying between the two shallow areas of the Tilloo Bank and staying on the range. When heading south the range consists of putting Snake Cay on your stern and lining up the northern tip of Channel Cay and the northern tip of South Pelican Cay on your bow. Once past the highly visible Tilloo Bank you can round Channel Cay to starboard and proceed southward

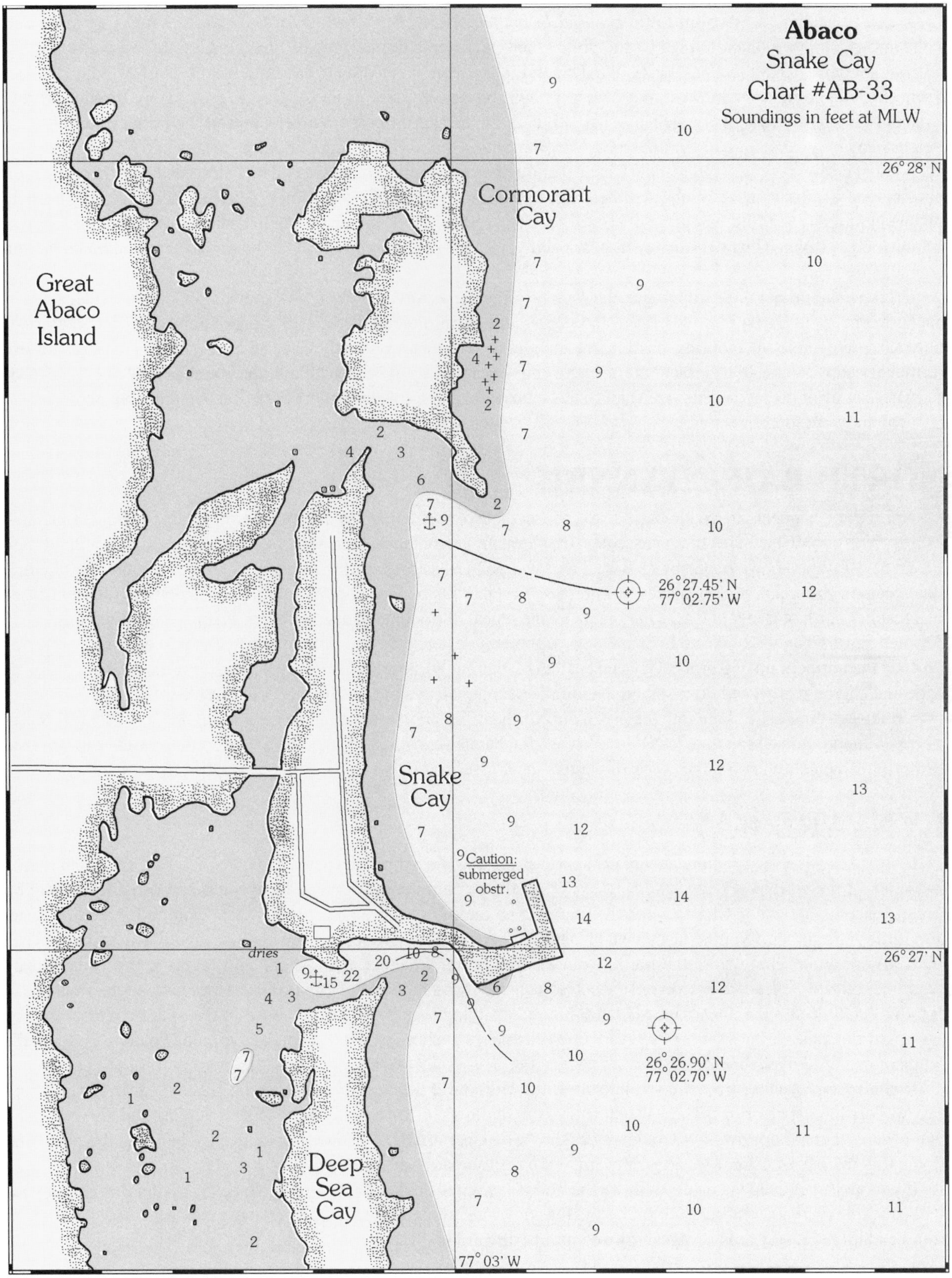

Abaco
Snake Cay
Chart #AB-33
Soundings in feet at MLW

26° 28' N

Cormorant
Cay

Great
Abaco
Island

Snake
Cay

9 Caution:
submerged
obstr.

26° 27.45' N
77° 02.75' W

26° 27' N

dries

26° 26.90' N
77° 02.70' W

Deep
Sea
Cay

77° 03' W

to anchor off Sandy Cay and enjoy the *Pelican Cays Land and Sea Park* or head further south to Lynyard Cay or Little Harbour.

If you're heading north from Little Harbour or perhaps North Bar Channel, pass between Sandy Cay and South Pelican Cay, and then take Channel Cay to port. Once clear of the northern tip of Channel Cay, turn to port to head to a waypoint at 26° 25.38' N, 77° 00.20' W. This will place you approximately ½ mile southeast of Middle Channel. From this waypoint you can take up a course of approximately 310° on Snake Cay to pass safely through Middle Channel. It's best to use the range here also. Line up the northern tip of Channel Cay and the northern tip of South Pelican Cay on your stern and put Snake Cay on your bow…this should bring you safely across in 6'-7'.

A lot of cruisers opt to avoid Middle Channel altogether and simply round the end of Tilloo Bank and this is fine; the bank is very visible and easy to follow. If heading south, from the northern waypoint of Middle Channel simply keep the visible bar to port and follow it around. You'll pass between Tilloo Bank and a smaller sandbar that lies northwest of Channel Cay. Round Channel Cay to starboard and you're on your way to Little Harbour. Northbound boats run this course in reverse.

Cruisers should not miss stopping at the *Pelican Cays Land And Sea Park*. As shown on Chart #AB-31, you can anchor in the lee of Sandy Cay in Pelican Harbour and dinghy around to the eastern shore of Sandy Cay where you can tie your dinghy up to the moorings there. The anchorage to the west of Sandy Cay can often get a bit rolly as the seas from the ocean find their way around the northern end of Sandy Cay. The chart shows the boundaries of the *PCLSP* and no marine or plant life, and no coral or shells may be taken from the confines of the Park. Take nothing but photographs, leave nothing but footprints.

NORTH BAR CHANNEL

North Bar Channel is an excellent route to or from the North Atlantic Ocean. When Little Harbour Bar is too rough to cross North Bar Channel is often passable. If approaching from the ocean-side, head to a GPS waypoint 26° 23.45' N, 76° 58.10' W as shown on Chart #AB-31. This waypoint places you approximately ½ mile east/southeast of North Bar Channel. From this waypoint head just north of west passing between tiny North Channel Rock and the submerged reef that lies north of Lynyard Cay. Once again let me repeat, the course in degrees is not as important as passing safely between North Channel Rock and Lynyard Cay. A good range here is to line up your bow with the southern tip of Sandy Cay and the northern tip of Cornish Cay and head in on that range, approximately 295°. I never use the range, the cut is wide and all you really need do is stay in the middle keeping an eye out for the reef off Lynyard Cay.

Vessels wishing to head out into the ocean via North Bar Channel can head to a GPS waypoint at 26° 23.60' N, 76° 59.00' W, approximately ½ mile WNW of North Bar Channel. From the waypoint ocean-bound vessels can head out North Bar Channel following the above directions in reverse.

LYNYARD CAY

Lynyard Cay is a very popular anchorage in prevailing northeast through southeast winds. My favorite anchorage is just south of the westward lying sandbar that lies off the northern end of Lynyard Cay southeast of Pelican Point on Great Abaco (as shown on Chart #AB-34). There are no facilities ashore here, but if you're waiting for the tide to get into Little Harbour, or if you've just arrived from Eleuthera and want to rest for the night, Lynyard Cay is the spot.

If you're approaching from the north, from the North Bar Channel area, head south favoring the Great Abaco shoreline south of Pelican Point to avoid the not-so-conspicuous sandbar off Lynyard Cay. Once clear of the shoal, head east and tuck up into the anchorage shown on the chart lying southwest of the house in the small cove. Actually, anywhere along the western shore of Lynyard Cay is a fine lee anchorage, but that small cove, and two more closer to the southern end of Lynyard are the best.

If you're approaching from the south, from Little Harbour, head north/northeast after leaving Little Harbour and pass well to the east of Bridges Cay. Watch out for the shallows on the eastern shore of Bridges Cay and also avoid the shallow area that lies northwest of Goole Cay as shown on Chart #AB-34. You can actually pass between this shoal and Goole Cay in 7'-9' of water to head northward along the Lynyard Cay shore.

If you've just entered via Little Harbour Bar and you want to anchor for the night, you can parallel the reef on your starboard side and pass between Goole Cay and the above-mentioned shoal. If this is not to your liking you can keep on your heading (345°) towards Bridges Cay and turn northward to clear the shoal lying west of Goole Cay as shown on Chart #AB-34.

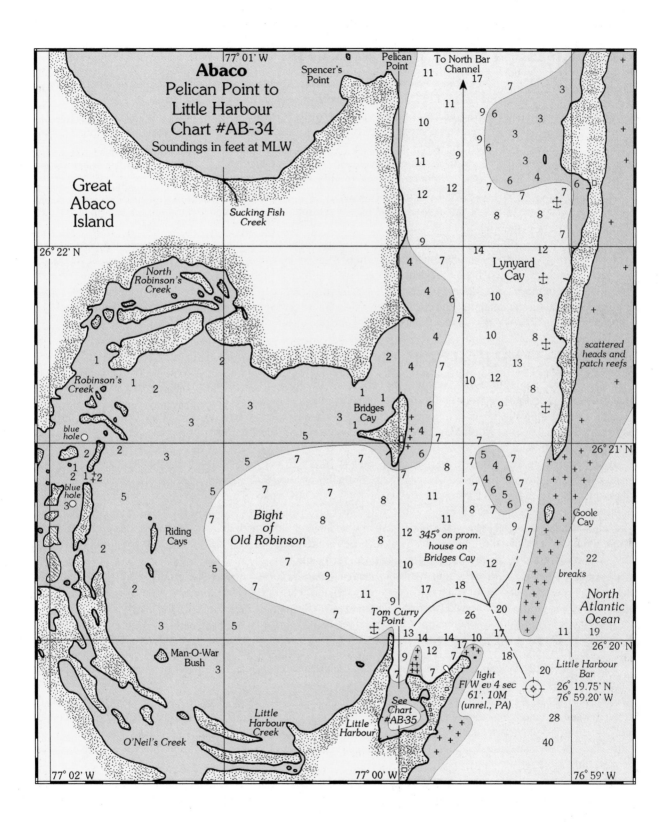

Abaco
Pelican Point to
Little Harbour
Chart #AB-34
Soundings in feet at MLW

77° 01' W

Spencer's Point

Pelican Point

To North Bar Channel

Great Abaco Island

Sucking Fish Creek

26° 22' N

North Robinson's Creek

Lynyard Cay

scattered heads and patch reefs

Robinson's Creek

blue hole

Bridges Cay

Riding Cays

Bight of Old Robinson

Goole Cay

blue hole

North Atlantic Ocean

breaks

345° on prom. house on Bridges Cay

Tom Curry Point

26° 21' N

Man-O-War Bush

Little Harbour Creek

O'Neil's Creek

Little Harbour

See Chart #AB-35

light
Fl W ev 4 sec
61', 10M
(unrel., PA)

Little Harbour Bar
26° 19.75' N
76° 59.20' W

26° 20' N

77° 02' W

77° 00' W

76° 59' W

When heading north or south along here, keep an eye out for the shallow bar that works out from the southern tip of Bridges Cay northward to about 26° 22' N along the Great Abaco shoreline.

Just east of Goole Cay lies an old VW van in about 12' of water. It once knew life as Taxi 18 in Marsh Harbour.

THE BIGHT OF OLD ROBINSON

The Bight of Old Robinson, once known as Little Harbour Bay, lies just west of Little Harbour Cut and the entrance to Little Harbour, between the mainland of Great Abaco and Bridges Cay as shown on Chart #AB-34.

If approaching from the north, you can head west just after you pass south of Bridges Cay. You can anchor wherever your draft allows, but be advised that a strong easterly swell will make the Bight uncomfortable. The Bight of Old Robinson is best explored by dinghy while anchored at Lynyard Cay or Little Harbour but if you insist on anchoring inside the bight, by all means do so. In general, depths in the center range from 7'-9' and gradually shallow as you approach the shore of Great Abaco. Some folks have trouble getting a hook to set here, there are a lot of large grass clumps and some scattered rocks about. If your anchor gets a good bite it's a fine overnight anchorage, and the Bight of Old Robinson can be a bit of a haven in winds from the south through north, though I would much prefer to be in Little Harbour for a blow of any consequence.

In a curve from south through west to north lies a string of small rocks and cays that you will not want to miss exploring. Using a rising tide, you can enter the mouths of some of these small creeks and you will delight in the marine life you'll find there. Bonefish are everywhere! In a few short hours I found and dove on two blue holes and cruiser John DeCarion of the S/V *Packadreams* tells me that he has discovered 10 blue holes tucked up in there. I found some large grouper and lobster inhabiting the cracks and crevices lining the sides of these holes. Just inside Tom Curry Point you can anchor in 5'-7' at MLW, a good spot to wait on the tide to enter Little Harbour.

LITTLE HARBOUR BAR

Little Harbour Bar is either the last exit to the ocean for a southbound vessel, or the first entrance to the Abacos for an northbound one. Either way, this cut is heavily used by cruising vessels. In most conditions it is an easy entry, the reefs that border it break and are easily seen (but not always!), but in heavy seas it would be prudent to head north to North Bar Channel or even North Man-O-War Channel, which is the safest in most conditions. Never try to cross the Little Harbour Bar at night!

If you're arriving from offshore, head to a waypoint at 26° 19.75' N, 76° 59.20' W, which will place you approximately ¼ mile southeast of the cut between the reefs. From this position take up a heading of approximately 345° on the conspicuous house on Bridges Cay as shown on Chart #AB-34. Once again let me remind you that the course here is not as important as staying between the reefs (obviously!), but the opening between the reefs is actually very wide here. Many folk make this cut out to be worse than it really is, but in good light, moderate seas, and with a reasonable amount of caution it is a piece of cake. Once inside you can head for the waypoint to Little Harbour or head north to Lynyard Cay. See the appropriate text for each destination for more details.

If you're outbound at Little Harbour Bar, head south and put the conspicuous house on Bridges Cay on your stern and take up a course of 165° until you pass between the reefs and are in deep water. If heading south keep at least a mile off shore between Little Harbour and Cherokee Sound to avoid the dangerous reef known as "The Boilers."

LITTLE HARBOUR

Picturesque Little Harbour is an almost land-locked anchorage and one of THE MOST popular stops on an Abaco itinerary; no cruise to Abaco would be complete without a stop here. Approaching from the north or from Little Harbour Bar, head to a GPS waypoint at 26° 20.10' N, 76° 59.95' W, which will place you approximately ¼ mile north of the marked entrance channel into Little Harbour as shown on Chart #AB-35. If approaching from the north make sure you clear the shallow areas off Great Abaco and Bridges Cay as shown on Chart #AB-34. If approaching from Little Harbour Bar make sure that you don't drift south, keeping clear of the reef that lies north of the eastern entrance point to Little Harbour.

From the waypoint, head generally south/southwest past Tom Curry's Point as shown on Chart #AB-35. Here you'll be in deep water that gradually shoals to about 3½' in the marked channel just before you enter the deeper water of Little Harbour. This passage will require a rising tide for most boats and if you need to wait for the tide to come up, a good spot is inside Tom Curry's Point in the Bight of Old Robinson as shown on the chart.

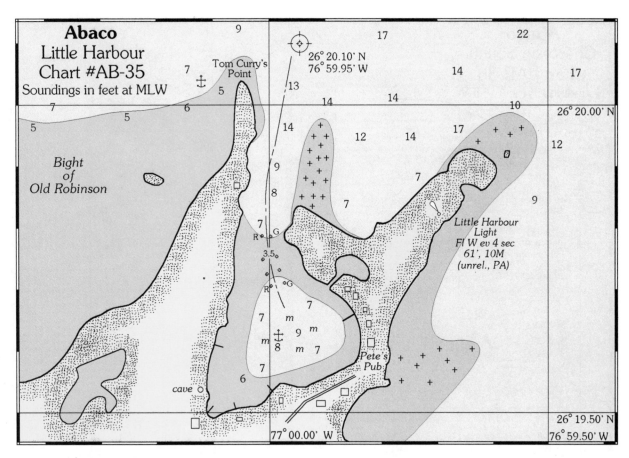

The entrance channel into Little Harbour is marked (at the time of this writing) by four pairs of red and green markers (red, right, returning here!) and is easy to follow. Once inside Little Harbour anchor wherever you desire, but it's so much easier to pick up one of Pete's moorings. If you do anchor please make sure that when you swing you'll not collide with the moored boats.

I'm sure that by now most people are aware that the recent history of Little Harbour and the family of internationally acclaimed sculptor Randolph Johnston are entwined…if you're not, then let me try to fill you in. The history of this remarkable family could fill a book, and does. *Artist on his Island, A Study in Self-Reliance* by Randolph W. Johnston sells in several places in Marsh Harbour as well as Little Harbour. The book is basically an autobiography, and chronicles the Johnston family's exodus to a better life and their eventual choice of Little Harbour as their own little bit of Heaven on earth. The book has been primarily compiled from Johnston's diary, which he called "The Escapist's Notebook" or "The Good Life for Those Who Can Take It."

In 1950, Randolph Johnston was an assistant professor at Smith College in Massachusetts. He was also a sculptor who wanted to spend his time sculpting. Little Harbour was completely deserted save for the lighthouse keeper and his family. On New Year's Day of 1951, at the age of 46, Randolph Johnston and his family left behind what he described as the "Megamachine" and arrived at Man-O-War Cay in the Abacos 16 days later. They immediately set up house-keeping and began a life on this quiet boat-building cay.

Seven months after their arrival at Man-O-War, Randolph Johnston purchased a 47' schooner that was used to convey crawfish to market. The family hastily moved aboard *Langosta* and spent the next six months converting the commercial boat into the family home. Then in February of 1952, their shakedown cruise took them to Nassau. The plan was to putt about the Caribbean and then perhaps on to the South Pacific, sounds like any normal family of cruisers today doesn't it? Shortly they set off for the Exumas and began to realize that the Bahamas offered much of what they sought. When they sailed into Little Harbour on Abaco it was like love at first sight, Randolph's quest for a bit of Eden was fulfilled. These few paragraphs do no justice to the tales that Randolph Johnston weaves in his autobiography. You'll marvel at how the family lived in the huge cave at the southwest end of the harbour and the hardships they endured in transforming Little Harbour into a home and foundry for sculptor Randolph and son Pete.

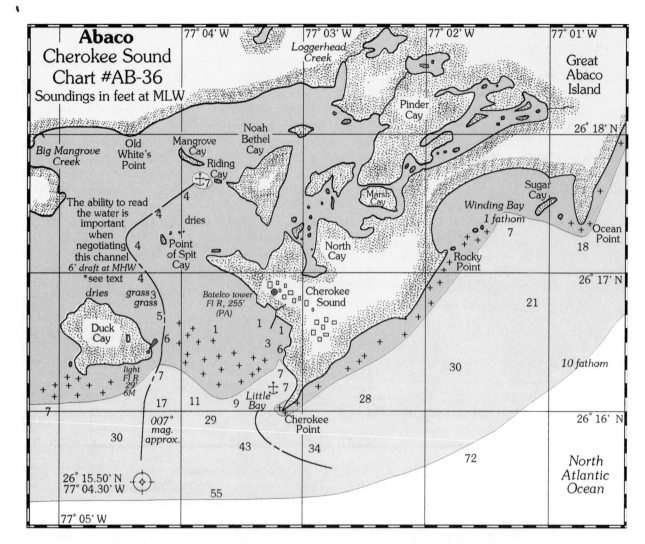

Today, Randolph has passed away and Pete has taken over the foundry. His remarkable castings are exciting pieces and much sought after. His *Pete's Pub* is actually fashioned from deckhouse of the schooner *Langosta* and is probably one of the most popular watering holes in the entire Abacos. When you're here you must visit the very laid-back *Pete's Pub* for food and drinks and visit the *Gallery* to view some of the Johnston's works. The gallery is open from 10:00am to 4:00pm daily except Sundays, more or less.

CHEROKEE SOUND

If approaching Abaco from the south/southeast, from Eleuthera or perhaps Nassau via the North Atlantic Ocean, the first possible anchorage is at Cherokee Sound, about six miles south of Little Harbour. Cherokee boasts one very nice lee anchorage and another anchorage that, although harder to access and almost a mile from town, offers great protection and is fine if you need to ride out a frontal passage. Never attempt to enter either of these two anchorages if there is a heavy sea running, better to continue north and try Little Harbour Bar or North Bar Channel.

If you're approaching Cherokee from the north, say from Little Harbour Bar, keep at least a mile or more off Great Abaco to avoid the treacherous reefs system known as "The Boilers" that lies close in between Little Harbour and Cherokee Sound.

The anchorage in Little Bay is good for winds from northeast through east and is easily entered by rounding Cherokee Point and rounding up to anchor in the lee of Cherokee Point as shown on Chart #AB-36. You will pass between the conspicuous reef that lies between Duck Cay and the mainland as well as the reef that runs WNW from Cherokee Point. Tuck in to the beach as close as your draft allows and enjoy your stay.

Cherokee has no marina but they do have their famous "long dock," probably the longest dock in The Bahamas. It is possible for shallow draft vessels to access the dock via Little Bay, but you must first sound the route in your dinghy or better still, call for a pilot (call *Cherokee Radio* on VHF ch. 16). The water near the dock is only about 1'-2' at MLW. The long dock was almost cut in half by Hurricane Andrew and is still to be rebuilt.

Cruisers wishing to access the better protection offered by the anchorage at Riding Cay must approach the entrance channel east of Duck Cay from the GPS waypoint at 26° 15.50' N, 77° 04.30' W as shown on Chart #AB-36. This waypoint places you approximately ¾ mile south of Duck Cay and about a mile southwest of Little Bay. From the waypoint take up an approximate course of 007° towards the light on Duck Cay. The actual courseline is not that important, what is important is to line up the light on Duck Cay with the western tip of Point of Spit Cay and follow that range until about 150 yards south of Duck Cay avoiding the reef south of Duck Cay. At this point turn to starboard a bit and pass between Duck Cay and the conspicuous reef east of Duck Cay taking the reef to starboard and Duck Cay to port. You'll pass fairly close to Duck Cay, less than fifty yards, and continue north/northeastward. As you come to the conspicuous grassy patch north of Duck Cay you will turn to port on a heading that will bring you to clear Point of Spit Cay well to starboard. At the grassy patch, the shallowest on the route at 3' MLW, you should be able to pick up the dredged channel that will wind around Point of Spit Cay and into the Riding Cay anchorage. The route past Duck Cay can only be done with excellent visibility and is good for less than 6' at high tide so watch the tide carefully when entering and leaving. If you have any doubts about using the channel leading into Riding Cay anchorage call *Cherokee Radio* on VHF ch. 16 and ask for someone to show you in. The Riding Cay anchorage is surrounded by shallow sandbanks on three sides and offers excellent protection even in southwest and westerly winds.

Some folks will tell you that tiny, isolated Cherokee is "The Place! A little piece of heaven down below." No one quite knows for sure how "the place" got its name, but one theory has it that it was named after a local wild cherry tree and according to some very old English sailing charts was shown as "Cherry Cay." Another story details how the first settler was an old Cherokee Indian woman who arrived from North Carolina during the American Revolution. All records of marriages, births, deaths, crop yields and annual rainfall have been forwarded to Nassau since the early 1800's and no journals or diaries have survived to tell us the real history about Cherokee.

Before the Government of The Bahamas installed navigational lights to aid sailing ships, salvaging/wrecking was a very lucrative occupation for many Bahamians and the folks in Cherokee were no different. Then around the turn of the twentieth century boat-building, fishing and sponging soon took over as this little community swelled to over 400 persons (today there are less than a hundred families), making it the largest settlement in Abaco at that time. The residents also made rope from the sisal plant and collected shells which were sent away to be made into buttons as the Depression swept through the Bahamas. Although farming is still carried on in the surrounding fields, and many residents have jobs in Marsh Harbour, the majority of the 100 or so families of Cherokee still make a living from the sea, either by fishing, crawfishing, or as bonefishing guides.

Today you'll find a monument in Cherokee honoring her fishermen and their "Cherokee smacks," most of which were built right here in Cherokee. The old timers in Cherokee can tell you some truly interesting tales of the Cherokee fisherman. A Cherokee fishing smack was a unique vessels that stood out from other island fishing boats; they carried five sails instead of the usual seven. A smack and her crew of nine had none of the modern amenities that cruisers today take for granted. The crews would be gone for up to six weeks at a time earning their pay. The 1950's saw most of these smacks converted into power vessels and gone forever was the hail "Sail ho!" when the returning boats were sighted. The older folks however can still remember when all the smacks were anchored in Riding Cay Channel, a sight the rest of us can only imagine.

If you visit Cherokee by car (see the section *Great Abaco by Car*), you will have to park and walk through the town. In town you'll find a two-room schoolhouse, a Post Office and Library, a laundromat, gas station, a general store, and a *Batelco* office, but no bar or restaurant.

Some of the ladies of Cherokee make some truly beautiful quilts that are traditional bride's gifts and a real find if you can pick one up. Some of the more enterprising ladies of Cherokee have gathered together a collection of old-time recipes and have preserved them in a locally published volume entitled *Abaco Cooks*. This book has been selling well for over ten years and I highly recommend it. All the profits from the book go back into the Cherokee community for special needs.

Cherokee has some of the best bonefishing grounds in the Abacos as well as being on the edge of the North Atlantic Ocean. In the early 1950's, a fishing camp was built on the hill overlooking the sound and Cherokee has since been somewhat of a secret known only to the real fishing enthusiasts. The fishing camp did not survive, but many of its patrons return year after year to enjoy the waters of Cherokee Sound.

HOLE IN THE WALL

At the southern end of Great Abaco Island lies a long thin arm of rock that reaches southeastward into the mouth of the Northeast Providence Channel where it meets the Atlantic Ocean. This point is called Hole in the Wall after the large arch near the southern end of the point and it is one of the least visited sites in Abaco. At one time there were at least three "holes in the wall" as evidenced by their rocky remains on these 80' bluffs. Visitors can actually climb down into the "hole" on a calm day.

A GPS waypoint at 25° 50.50' N, 77° 09.50' W, will place you approximately 1½ nautical miles southeast of Hole in the Wall. From here you can take up a course for Little Harbour Bar, Nassau, Eleuthera, or you can forge westward around Southwest Point to work your way long the southern shore of Great Abaco Island to Sandy Point. Vessels can find temporary shelter on the western shore of Hole in the Wall. Round the southern tip and parallel the shoreline northward and you'll find shelter in the bight below the lighthouse in winds from northwest to east.

Located on higher ground just north of the rugged spit is the Hole in the Wall Lighthouse. Today the light is automated (Fl W eve 10 sec, 168', 19nm) which is a bit of a loss in a sense. It was always an interesting and educational outing to rent a car in Marsh Harbour and travel the 55 or so miles south to the Lighthouse to visit the keepers and their families. The lighthouse is now the home of the *Bahamas Marine Mammal Survey* and we shall discuss that group in a moment. You can still get there by car, but you'll need a high-clearance vehicle. To get there by road take the Great Abaco Highway south and about 12 miles south of Crossing Rocks you'll come to the Sandy Point junction. Take a left here to get to the lighthouse some 15 miles away, about an hour or so each way over a very rough road. Keep an eye out for the rare Bahamian parrot on this route.

As you wander around you will marvel at the absolutely gorgeous view of the surrounding waters that the lighthouse keepers woke up to every morning. If you cross over to the western side of the spit, you will see some small beaches and you can probably get a good view of the hole itself. To the north, by the first bluff, is an old homestead.

Spelunkers will be attracted to the remarkable cave complexes at Hole in the Wall. The largest complex has a small opening just to the right of the road as you approach the lighthouse. At the entrance there is a 10' drop into the initial passage which is a little too low for an adult to stand upright. In just a few feet the passage opens up to a larger passage that takes you into the main cavern with its high domed ceiling and its smattering of dozens of passages leading away from the center. These smaller passages are also fine for exploration and lead to even smaller passages with several having more than one level. Here you'll find stalagmites, stalactites, bats and all the other things that make cave exploration so interesting.

The Government of The Bahamas has now leased the lighthouse keeper's quarters to the *Bahamas Marine Mammal Survey*. Hole in the Wall is one of the prime whale-watching areas of The Bahamas and the *Marine Mammal Survey* is a long-term project whose emphasis is to catalog sightings of whales and dolphins in the Northeast and Northwest Providence Channels. The *Survey* has documented the first previously unpublished sighting of five species in these waters, and has found a resident population of some 90 Atlantic bottlenose dolphins in central Abaco and the northeastern Bahamas. This dolphin population has been photo-identified and their role in the ecosystem of the shallow banks of the islands is being investigated. Several rare species of tropical whales have also been documented in the surrounding waters. Marine mammal sight forms have been distributed throughout The Bahamas in an effort to obtain species distribution data with the help of cruisers and fishermen. You can pick up these forms in most area marinas as well as at the National Trust in Nassau and at the Exuma Park Headquarters at Warderick Wells.

The system seems to be working well as the *Survey* has received over 700 sighting reports from boaters since 1991. The *Survey* has documented the occurrence of 17 different species of dolphins and whales in Bahamian waters, five of which had never been described in the area previously. For instance, in 1995 the *Survey* documented the appearance of killer whales in The Bahamas. The *Survey* photo-identified a female killer whale in the northwestern Bahamas that had previously been sighted in the Gulf of Mexico. If you'd like more info on the *Survey* and their work you can e-mail them at dolphin@oii.net. If you're in Marsh Harbour and desire more information on the *Survey*, contact Brenda Mitchell or Diane Claridge at *Sapodilly's Bar and Grill*. You can reach them on VHF ch. 65 at *Dolphin Research* or *Beluga*.

APPENDICES

APPENDIX A: Navigational Aids

A-1: Lights

Navigational lights in the northern Bahamas should be considered unreliable at best. Their characteristics may differ from those published here and are subject to change without notice. It is not unusual for a light to be out of commission for long periods of time. Listing of lights reads from north to south.

LIGHT	CHARACTERISTICS	COLOR	HT.	RANGE
GRAND BAHAMA				
Sweeting's Cay	Fl ev 5 sec	W	23'	8nm
Bell Channel sea buoy	Fl ev 2 sec	W		7nm
Freeport Lighthouse	FL (3) ev 15 sec	WR	52'	12nm
Freeport – E side of channel	Qk Fl (2)	R		
Freeport – W side of channel	Fl ev 4 sec (2)	G		
Freeport – W jetty	Fl ev 4 sec	G	23'	2nm
Freeport – W jetty	Fl ev 4 sec	G	13'	2nm
Freeport – E Jetty	Fl	R	19'	3nm
Freeport – lower range, 021°	Fxd	G	26'	3nm
Freeport – upper range, 021°	Fxd	G	46'	3nm
Freeport – Borco Oil Term.	Fl (3) ev 7 sec	W		5 nm
Freeport – Borco Oil Term.	Qk Fl	W		
Pinder Point Light	Gp. Fl (3) ev 5 sec	WR	64'	12nm
Riding Point Tower	Fl (airwarning top) Fxd	R	135'	14nm
Settlement Point (West End)	Fl ev 4 sec	W	32'	6nm
Indian Cay	Fl ev 6 sec	W	40'	8nm
THE ABACOS				
Memory Rock	Fl ev 3 sec	W	37'	11nm
Barracuda Shoal	Fl ev 4 sec	W		
Indian Cay Rock	Fl ev 6 sec	W	40'	8nm
Little Sale Cay	Fl ev 3 sec	W	47'	9nm
Carter's Cay	Fl (airwarning) Fxd	R	200'	25nm
Crab Cay (Angelfish Point)	Fl ev 5 sec	W	33'	8nm
Whale Cay	Fl ev 5 sec	W	40'	8nm
Treasure Cay (off entrance)	Fl	W		
Guana Cay	Fl	W	30'	5nm
Man-O-War Cay	Fl	W	30'	5nm
Marsh Harbour	Fl ev 4 sec	G		
Marsh Harbour	Fl	G		
North Parrot Cay	Fl	G		
Elbow Cay Lighthouse Gp.	Fl (5) ev 15 sec	W	120'	15nm
Little Harbour	Fl ev 4 sec	W	61'	10nm
Duck Cay, Cherokee Sound	Fl (unreliable)	R	29'	6nm
Hole in the Wall Lighthouse	Fl ev 10 sec	W	168'	19nm
Rock Point (Sandy Point)	Fl ev 6 sec	W	35'	10nm
Channel Cay (Mores Island)	Fl ev 2.5 sec	W	32'	6nm

A-2: Batelco Towers

Towers over 50' in height have red lights at their tops, either fixed or flashing (Fxd or Fl). Taller towers may have fixed red lights at intermediate levels. Positions are approximate. Listing of towers is from north to south. "B" denotes a *Batelco* tower.

LOCATION	LT.	HT.	LOCATION	LT.	HT.
GRAND BAHAMA			**ABACOS (Continued)**		
Bassett Cove	Fl R	420'	Cedar Harbour	unlit	50'
Eight Mile Rock	FlR	200'	Coopers Town	Fl R	200'
Freeport	FlR	200'	Crossing Rock	unlit	60'
Grand Cay	Fxd R	140'	Green Turtle Cay	Fl R	100'
McLeans Town	Flr	200'	Treasure Cay	Fl R	200'
Pinder's Point	Fxd R	100'	Guana Cay	Fxd R	50'
South Riding Point	FlR	225'	Hope Town	unlit	40'
Sweetings Cay	Fxd R	60'	Man-O-War Cay	unlit	40'
Water Cay	Fxd R	50'	Marsh Harbour-E. shore	Fxd R	255'
West End	FlR	215'	Marsh Harbour-central	Fl R	200'
ABACOS			Dundas Town* (radio)	Fxd R	200'
Walker's Cay	Fl R	250'	Cherokee Sound	Fl R	255'
Grand Cay	Fl R	250'	Mores Island	Fxd R	200'
Fox Town	Fxd R	200'	Sandy Point	Fl R	260'

* The private radio tower at Dundas Town, two miles west of Marsh Harbour, should not be confused with the 200' *Batelco* tower (also Fxd R) on the eastern shore of Marsh Harbour.

APPENDIX B: Marinas

Some of the marinas listed below may be untenable in certain winds and dockside depths listed may not reflect entrance channel depths at low water. For instance, at Man-O-War Cay the entrance channel carries 5' at MLW, while the dock will accommodate 8' at the same tide. Always check with the Dockmaster prior to arrival. All the marinas can handle your garbage disposal problems however some may levy a charge per bag for those who are not guests at their docks. For cruisers seeking services *Nearby* may mean either a walk or short taxi ride away.

MARINA	FUEL	SLIPS	DEPTH	GROCERY	DINING
GRAND BAHAMA					
West End					
Old Bahama Bay	D & G	30	9'	Nearby	Nearby
Lucaya					
Bahama Bay	D & G	20	7'	Nearby	Nearby
Lucayan Marina Vlg.	D & G	150	9'-12'	Nearby	Yes
Port Lucaya	D & G	160	8'	Nearby	Yes
Ocean Reef Yacht Cl.	None	52	6'	Nearby	Nearby
Running Mon Marina	D & G	60	9'	Nearby	Nearby
Xanadu Beach	D & G	77	8'	Nearby	Nearby
Deep Water Cay					
Deep Water Cay Club	None	2	5'	None	Yes
ABACOS					
Walker's Cay					
Walker's Cay Marina	D & G	75	4½'-6'	Limited	Yes
Grand Cays					
Rosie's Place	D & G	15	5'	Limited	Yes
Spanish Cay					
Spanish Cay Marina	D & G	75	8'	Limited	Yes
Green Turtle Cay					
Abaco Yacht Services	None	6	6½'	Nearby	Nearby

Black Sound Marina	None	15	7'	Nearby	Nearby
Bluff House Club/Marina	D & G	20	4'	Nearby	Yes
Green Turtle Club/Marina	D & G	35	5½'	Nearby	Yes
Other Shore Club & Marina	D & G	15	5½'	Nearby	Nearby
Robert's Cottages and Dock	None	3	6½'	Nearby	Nearby
Treasure Cay					
Treasure Cay Marina	D & G	150	7'	Nearby	Yes
Guana Cay					
Guana Beach Resort	D & G	22	6'	Nearby	Yes
Orchid Bay Marina	D & G	32	7½'	Nearby	Nearby
Man-O-War Cay					
Man-O-War Marina	D & G	60	7'	Yes	Nearby
Marsh Harbour					
Admiral's Yacht Haven	None	10	5'-7'	Nearby	Yes
Boat Harbour Marina	D & G	160	6'	Yes	Yes
Conch Inn Marina	D & G	75	7'-9'	Yes	Yes
Harbour View Marina	D & G	36	6'	Nearby	Yes
Mangoes Marina	None	25	6'-7'	Nearby	Yes
Marsh Harbour Marina	D & G	57	7'	Nearby	Yes
Triple J Marina	D & G	26	5'-7'	Nearby	Nearby
Elbow Cay					
Club Soleil	D & G	6	7½'	Nearby	Yes
Hope Town Hideaways	None	12	7'	Nearby	Nearby
Lighthouse Marina	D & G	6	6'	Nearby	Yes
Sea Spray Resort & Marina	D & G	24	6'	Nearby	Yes

APPENDIX C: Service Facilities

As with any place, businesses come and go, sometimes seemingly overnight. Certain entries on this list may no longer exist by the time this is published. All telephone numbers are area code 242 unless otherwise noted.

FACILITY	LOCATION	TEL. #	VHF CALL ch.16
AUTO RENTALS			
A & A Car Rentals	Marsh Harbour	367-2148	
A & P Auto Rentals	Marsh Harbour	367-2655	
A & W Travel	Green Turtle Cay	365-4140	
A & W Travel	Hope Town	366-1000	
A & W Travel	Man-O-War Cay	365-6002	
Alison's Car Rentals	Treasure Cay	365-8193	
Cornish Car Rentals	Treasure Cay	365-8623	
Covenant Car Rentals	Murphy Town, Grt. Abaco	367-4007	
Jensen Edgecomb	Treasure Cay		*Jensen Edgecomb*
Flamingo Car Rentals	Marsh Harbour	367-4787	
H & L Rentals Shell Station	Marsh Harbour	367-2840	
Laysue Rentals	Marsh Harbour	367-4414	*Triple J Marina*
Mckenzie's Car Rental	Treasure Cay	365-8849	
Reliable Car Rentals	Abaco Towns	367-3015	
Thrifty Car Rental	Freeport, Grand Bahama	352-9308	
V & R Car Rentals	Marsh Harbour	367-2001	
Veronica's Car Rentals	Marsh Harbour	367-2725	
Wilmac Rent A Car	Airport, Great Abaco	367-4313	
BOAT RENTALS & CHARTERS			
Abaco Bahama Charters-Sail	Hope Town		*Abaco Bahama Charters*
Blue Wave	Marsh Harbour		*Blue Wave Rentals*
David Albury	Man-O-War Cay	365-6059	

FACILITY	LOCATION	TEL. #	VHF CALL ch.16
BOAT RENTALS AND CHARTERS (CONTINUED)			
Wilmac Rent A Car	Airport, Great Abaco	367-4313	
C & C Rentals	Treasure Cay	365-8582	*C & C*
Dame's Boat Rentals	Green Turtle Cay	365-4247	
Dave's Boat Rentals	Hope Town, Elbow Cay	366-0029	*Dave's Dive Shop*
Donny's Rentals	Green Turtle Cay	365-4119	
Florida Yacht Charters	Marsh Harbour	367-4853	
Hope Town Marina	Hope Town	366-0003	*Hope Town Marina*
Island Marine	Parrot Cay	366-0282	*Island Marine*
Lazy Sue Rentals	Marsh Harbour	367-4414	
Lighthouse Charters-Sail	Hope Town	366-0154	*Lighthouse Marina*
J.I.C. Boat Rentals	Treasure Cay	365-8465	*J.I.C.*
Donnie Maura-day sails	Hope Town	366-0154	
The Moorings-Sail	Marsh Harbour	800-535-7289	
R & A Rentals and Tours	Treasure Cay		*R & A*
Rainbow Rentals	Elbow Cay	367-4602	*Rainbow Rentals*
Rich's Rentals	Marsh Harbour	367-2742	
Roberts Hardware & Marine	Green Turtle Cay	365-4249	*Roberts Marine*
Russell Rentals	Hope Town	366-0358	
Sea Horse Marine	Hope Town	366-0023	
Sea Horse Rentals	Marsh Harbour	367-2516	
Sea Spray Resort & Marina	White Sound, Elbow Cay	366-0065	*Sea Spray*
HOTELS, INNS			
Abaco Beach Hotel & Resort	Marsh Harbour	367-2158	
Abaco Inn	White, Sound, Elbow Cay	366-0133	
Abaco Towns by the Sea	Marsh Harbour	367-2221	
Airport Motel	Airport, Great Abaco		
Ambassador Inn	Marsh Harbour	367-2022	
Atlantic Beach Resort	Grand Bahama	373-1444	
Bahama Grand	Grand Bahama	352-6025	
Bahama Inn	Grand Bahama	325-6648	
Bahama Princess	Grand Bahama	352-6721	
Banyan Beach Club	Treasure Cay	365-8111	
Bell Channel Inn	Grand Bahama	373-1053	
Benny's Place	Hope Town	366-0061	
Bluff House Club & Marina	Green Turtle	365-4247	*Bluff House*
Castaways Resort	Grand Bahama	352-6682	
Channel House Resort	Grand Bahama	373-5405	
Club Fortuna Beach	Grand Bahama	373-4000	
Club Soleil Resort	Hope Town, Elbow Cay	366-0003	*Club Soleil*
Coco Bay Club	Green Turtle	365-5464	
Conch Inn Marina & Hotel	Marsh Harbour	367-4000	*Conch Inn*
Grand Bahama Beach	Grand Bahama	373-1333	
D's Guest House	Marsh Harbour	367-3980	
Different of Abaco	Abaco	366-2150	
Gillam Bay House	Green Turtle Cay	365-4321	
Green Turtle Club	Green Turtle Cay	365-4271	
Guana Beach Resort	Great Guana Cay	365-5133	
Guana Seaside Village	Great Guana Cay	365-5106	
Hope Town Harbour Lodge	Hope Town, Elbow Cay	366-0095	*Hope Town Harbour Lodge*
Hope Town Hideaways	Hope Town, Elbow Cay	366-0224	
Hope Town Villas	Hope Town, Elbow Cay	366-0030	
Island Bay Motel	Little Grand Cay	359-4476	*Love Train (Ch. 68)*

FACILITY	LOCATION	TEL. #	VHF CALL ch.16
BOAT RENTALS AND CHARTERS (CONTINUED)			
Island Breezes	Marsh Harbour	367-3776	
Island Seas	Grand Bahama	373-1271	
Lighthouse Hotel	Hope Town, Elbow Cay	366-0154	
Linton's Beach Cottages	Green Turtle Cay	365-4003	
Lofty Fig Villas	Marsh Harbour	367-2681	
Marsh Harbour Airport Hotel	Marsh Harbour	367-3658	
New Plymouth Inn	Green Turtle Cay	365-4161	
Ocean Reef Yacht Club	Grand Bahama	373-4662	*Ocean Reef Yacht Club*
Oeisha's Resort and Rest.	Sandy Point, Aba co	366-4139	
Pelican Beach Villas	Marsh Harbour	367-3600	
Pelican Cay Hotel	Lucaya, Grand Bahama	373-7616	*Lucayan Marina Village*
Pete and Gay's Guest House	Sandy Point, Abaco	366-4045	
Port Lucaya Resort	Grand Bahama	373-6618	*Port Lucaya Marina*
Running Mon Marina	Grand Bahama	352-6834	*Running Mon Marina*
Royal Islander	Grand Bahama	351-6000	
Royal Palm Resort	Grand Bahama	352-3462	
Schooner's Landing	Man-O-War Cay	365-6072	
Sea Spray Resort & Marina	White Sound, Elbow Cay	366-0065	
Silver Sands Hotel	Grand Bahama	373-5700	
Spanish Cay Inn	Spanish Cay	365-0083	*Spanish Cay*
Sun Club Resort	Grand Bahama	352-3462	
Taino Beach Resort	Grand Bahama	373-5640	
Tangelo Hotel	Wood Cay	365-2222	
Treasure Cay Beach Hotel	Treasure Cay	365-8535	*Treasure Cay*
Tree House	Green Turtle Cay	365-4258	
Turtle Hill Resort	Elbow Cay	366-0557	
Walker's Cay Hotel & Mar.	Walker's Cay	800-Walkers	*Walker's Cay*
Xanadu Beach	Grand Bahama	352-6783	*Xanadu Marina*
DIESEL REPAIR/PARTS			
Asterix	Marsh Harbour	367-3166	*Asterix*
Bradford Yacht & Ship	Freeport, Grand Bahama	352-7711	*Bradford Yacht & Ship*
Pinder's Marine and Auto	Marsh Harbour	367-2274	
Roberts Marine	Green Turtle Cay	365-4249	*Roberts Marine*
Sea Services Boat Harbour	Marsh Harbour	367-6805	
ELECTRONICS-MARINE			
Bahamas Elect. Lab. Co., Inc.	Freeport, Grand Bahama	352-2286	
Bradford Yacht & Ship	Freeport, Grand Bahama	352-7711	*Bradford Yacht & Ship*
Triple J Marina	Marsh Harbour, Abaco		*Triple J*
Wellington Pinder	Hope Town	366-0106	
HAUL OUT			
Abaco Yacht Services	Green Turtle Cay	365-4033	*Abaco Yacht Services*
Bradford Yacht & Ship	Freeport, Grand Bahama	352-7711	*Bradford Yacht & Ship*
Edwin's Boat Yard	Man-O-War Cay	365-6007	*Edwin's Boat Yard*
HULL REPAIR/PAINTING			
Abaco Yacht Services	Green Turtle Cay	365-4033	*Abaco Yacht Services*
Albury Brothers	Man-O-War Cay	365-6086	
Bradford Yacht & Ship	Freeport, Grand Bahama	352-7711	*Bradford Yacht & Ship*
Edwin's Boat Yard	Man-O-War Cay	365-6007	*Edwin's Boat Yard*
Winer Malone	Bay St., Hope Town		
MARINE SUPPLIES			
Abaco Hardware	Marsh Harbour	367-2827	
Abaco Yacht Services	Green Turtle Cay	365-4033	*Abaco Yacht Services*

FACILITY	LOCATION	TEL. #	VHF CALL ch.16
MARINE SUPPLIES (CONTINUED)			
Adnil Marine Supplies	Freeport, Grand Bahama	352-1856	
B & D Marine Ltd.	Marsh Harbour	367-2522	*B & D*
Boat Harbour Marine Store	Marsh Harbour		*Boat Harbour Marina*
Bradford Yacht & Ship	Freeport, Grand Bahama	352-7711	*Bradford Yacht & Ship*
Dolphin Marine	Green Turtle Cay	365-4262	*Dolphin Marine*
Edwin's Boat Yard	Man-O-War Cay	365-6007	*Edwin's Boat Yard*
Green Turtle Club	Green Turtle Cay	365-4271	*Green Turtle Club*
National Marine	Marsh Harbour	367-2326	
Man-O-War Marina	Man-O-War Cay	365-6013	*Man-O-War Marina*
Man-O-War Hardware	Man-O-War Cay	365-6011	
Roberts Hardware & Marine	Green Turtle Cay	365-4249	*Roberts Marine*
Standard Hardware	Marsh Harbour	367-2660	
Triple J Marina	Marsh Harbour	367-2163	*Triple J Marina*
OUTBOARD REPAIR			
Abaco Outboard-*Yamaha*	Marsh Harbour	367-2452	*Abaco Outboard*
Abaco Yacht Serv.-*Yamaha*	Green Turtle Cay	365-4033	*Abaco Yacht Services*
Adnil Mar. Supplies-*Yamaha*	Freeport, Grand Bahama	352-1856	
Albury Brothers	Man-O-War Cay	365-6086	
B & D Marine Ltd.-*Suzuki*	Marsh Harbour	367-2522	*B & D*
Dolphin Marine-*OMC*	Green Turtle Cay	365-4262	*Dolphin Marine*
Hope Town Marina-*Nissan*	Hope Town	366-0003	*Hope Town Marina*
Island Marine-*OMC*	Parrot Cay	366-0282	*Island Marine*
Lighthouse Marina-*Yamaha*	Hope Town	366-0154	*Lighthouse Marina*
Man-O-War Marina	Man-O-War Cay	365-6013	*Man-O-War Marina*
National Marine-*Mercury*	Marsh Harbour	367-2326	
Outboard Shop-*OMC*	Marsh Harbour	367-2703	*Outboard Shop*
Roberts Hrd. & Marine-*OMC*	Green Turtle Cay	365-4249	*Roberts Marine*
Sea Horse Marine-*OMC*	Hope Town	366-0023	*Sea Horse Marine*
PROPANE			
Abaco Gas-Corner Value	Marsh Harbour	367-2250	
Harbour View Grocery	Hope Town	366-0033	
Curry's Food Store	Green Turtle Cay	365-4171	
Man-O-War LP Gas	Man-O-War Cay	365-6057	
Sid's Food Store	Green Turtle Cay	365-4055	
SAIL REPAIR			
Edwin's Boat Yd.-Jay Manni	Man-O-War Cay	365-6171	*Edwin's Boat Yard*
Phillip's Sails	Nassau, New Providence	393-4498	

APPENDIX D: GPS Waypoints

Caution: GPS Waypoints are not to be used for navigational purposes. GPS waypoints are intended to place you in the general area of the described position. All routes, cuts, and anchorages must be negotiated by eyeball navigation. The author and publisher take no responsibility for the misuse of the following GPS waypoints. There are places throughout the northern Bahamas, the inshore route west of Tilloo Cut for instance, where some Skippers would feel comforted by GPS waypoints. Waypoints along any tight passage offer a false sense of security and any navigator who uses waypoints to negotiate a tricky passage instead of piloting by eye is, to be blunt, a fool and deserving of whatever fate befalls him or her. Waypoints are listed from north to south. Latitude is "**North**" and longitude is "**West**." Datum used is WGS84.

DESCRIPTION	Latitude	Longitude
SOUTH FLORIDA		
Hillsboro Inlet	26° 15.19'	80° 04.55'
Ft. Lauderdale/Port Everglades	26° 05.57'	80° 05.40'
Miami – Government Cut	25° 45.70'	80° 05.80'
Cape Florida	25° 38.74'	80° 07.70'
Angelfish Creek	25° 19.35'	80° 12.60'
BERRY ISLANDS		
Great Stirrup/Slaughter Harbour entrance - ½ nm N	25° 49.60'	77° 55.66'
Great Stirrup/Panton Cove entrance - ½ nm NE	25° 49.40'	77° 53.30'
Great Harbour Cay - entrance to eastern anchorage	25° 46.03'	77° 49.41'
Devil's Hoffman Anchorage - ¼ nm east of	25° 36.56'	77° 43.49'
Little Harbour/Frozen Alder Anchorage entrance - ½ nm W	25° 33.93'	77° 42.50'
Little Whale Cay - ¼ nm east of entrance to anchorage	25° 26.77'	77° 45.13'
Frazier - Hogg/Bird Cay	25° 23.45'	77° 51.05'
Chub Cay - 1 nm south of and on the 35° range	25° 23.90'	77° 55.08'
NEW PROVIDENCE		
Nassau Harbour - W entrance	25° 05.33'	77° 21.35'
NEW PROVIDENCE TO ELEUTHERA		
Little Pimlico Island - ½ nm SW of	25° 18.10'	76° 53.60'
Fleeming Channel - ¼ nm N of channel entrance	25° 16.00'	76° 55.30'
Fleeming Channel - ¼ nm S of channel entrance	25° 15.50'	76° 54.50'
Douglas Channel - 1 nm NW of	25° 10.00'	77° 05.50'
Douglas Channel - 1 nm SE of	25° 07.80'	77° 03.00'
Chub Rock - ¼ nm N of	25° 06.85'	77° 14.60'
ELEUTHERA		
Pilot pickup point N of Ridley Head Channel	25° 34.50'	76° 44.30'
Ridley Head Channel - N waypoint	25° 34.00'	76° 44.30'
Ridley Head Channel - S waypoint, just off Ridley Head	25° 33.54'	76° 44.33'
Spanish Wells Harbour - just E of pilings at eastern entrance	25° 32.60'	76° 44.35'
Spanish Wells Harbour - just S of pilings at western entrance	25° 32.10'	76° 45.40'
Royal Island - ½ mile S of entrance	25° 30.50'	76° 50.73'
Egg Island Cut - 1 nm WNW of Cut	25° 29.60'	76° 54.40'
Wreck of the *Arimora* - ½ nm SW	25° 27.74'	76° 54.06'
Current Rock - ½ nm NW of	25° 24.80'	76° 51.42'
Current Cut - ½ nm WNW of western entrance	25° 24.41'	76° 47.48'
Current Cut - 1 nm SW of eastern entrance	25° 22.94'	76° 46.61'
Current Island - ½ nm SW of southwestern tip	25° 18.45'	76° 51.29'
Little Pimlico Island - ½ nm SW of	25° 18.10'	76° 53.60'
GRAND BAHAMA		
Indian Cay Channel – eastern entrance to channel	26° 46.37'	78° 57.15'
Indian Cay Channel, Barracuda Shoal – ¼ nm S of	26° 45.65'	78° 58.30'

DESCRIPTION	Latitude	Longitude
Indian Cay Channel – ¼ nm SW of western entrance to channel	26° 42.80'	79° 00.60'
West End – ½ nm W of entrance channel to marina	26° 42.23'	79° 00.15'
Dover Sound – 1½ nm NW of entrance channel to GLWW	26° 38.40'	78° 39.70'
Peterson Cay – ½ nm SE of	26° 32.60'	78° 30.65'
Grand Lucayan Waterway - ¾ SSE of jetties at southern entrance	26° 31.30'	78° 33.33'
Freeport Harbour – 1 nm SSW of entrance jetties	26° 30.10'	78° 47.05'
Bell Channel - 1 nm SE of entrance channel	26° 29.95'	78° 37.70'
Xanadu Channel – ½ nm SW of entrance channel	26° 29.00'	78° 42.40'
Madioca Point - ½ nm SE of entrance channel to *Running Mon*	26° 29.00'	78° 41.31'
Silver Cove - ¾ nm SE of entrance channel	26° 29.00'	78° 39.35'
THE BIGHT OF ABACO		
Northwest Passage – N waypoint	26° 53.90'	77° 58.15'
Northwest Passage – S waypoint	26° 52.83'	77° 58.15'
Randall's Cay – ¼ nm NW	26° 51.60'	77° 32.90'
Crab Cay – ½ nm SE of, entrance to route to Spence Rock	26° 50.70'	77° 52.40'
Randall's Creek – ¼ nm W of mouth	26° 50.00'	77° 31.50'
Spence Rock – ½ nm SSW of, entrance to route to Crab Cay	26° 48.70'	77° 51.40'
Basin Harbour Cay – ¼ nm SW of entrance to harbour	26° 47.75'	77° 30.10'
Norman's Castle – ¾ nm W of	26° 43.25'	77° 27.75'
Big Joe Downer Cay – ¾ nm W of anchorage at Amos Bight	26° 36.90'	77° 26.90'
Woolendean Cay – ¾ nm W of	26° 34.00'	77° 25.00'
Mores Island – ½ nm NW of	26° 20.55'	77° 35.20'
Mores Island – ½ nm W of Hard Bargain anchorage	26° 19.10'	77° 35.50'
Channel Cay – 2 nm SW of channel to Mores Island	26° 14.00'	77° 40.00'
Castaway Cay (Gorda Cay) – ½ nm WSW of cruise ship harbour	26° 04.50'	77° 32.90'
Sarah Wood Bars – entrance to Bight of Abaco from Sandy Point	26° 04.10'	77° 27.60'
Sandy Point – ¼ nm W of anchorage off settlement	26° 01.10'	77° 24.70'
Rocky Point – 1½ nm W of Rocky Point and clear of shoals	25° 59.60'	77° 25.80'
ABACO		
Walkers Cay – ½ nm N of entrance W of Seal Cay (Seal Cay Cut)	27° 16.20'	78° 21.55'
Walker's Cay – beginning of staked route over sandbar	27° 14.00'	78° 24.20'
Grand Cays – ¼ nm S of entrance channel to harbour	27° 12.60'	78° 18.80'
Strangers Cay Channel – N waypoint	27° 12.33'	78° 09.80'
Double Breasted Cays – ½ nm S of	27° 10.85'	78° 16.40'
Strangers Cay Channel – S waypoint	27° 10.50'	78° 10.50'
White Sand Ridge – ½ nm west of	27° 08.00'	79° 11.00'
Strangers Cay – ½ nm SSW of anchorage	27° 07.10'	78° 06.70'
Moraine Cay Channel – N waypoint	27° 05.00'	77° 14.00'
Carters Cay Bank, route across bank from east – ¼ nm E of start	27° 04.25'	77° 58.75'
Carters Cays – 1 nm SSW of Gully Cay	27° 03.80'	78° 01.15'
Little Sale Cay – ½ nm NW of northwestern tip	27° 03.20'	78° 10.90'
The Fish Cays – ½ nm SW of	27° 01.90'	77° 50.20'
Moraine Cay – ½ nm S of anchorage	27° 01.80'	77° 46.25'
Allan's-Pensacola Cay – ½ nm WSW of entrance to anchorage	26° 59.20'	77° 42.20'
Great Sale Cay – ¼ nm W of Northwest Harbour	26° 58.50'	78° 14.70'
North Spanish Cay Channel, outer waypoint	26° 58.40'	77° 31.90'
Great Sale Cay – 1 nm SE of Tom Johnson Harbour	26° 58.15'	78° 10.45'
North Spanish Cay Channel, inner waypoint	26° 57.90'	77° 32.70'
Fox Town – ½ nm NW of Hawksbill Cays	26° 57.00'	77° 48.80'
South Spanish Cay Channel, outer waypoint	26° 56.55'	77° 28.85'
Crab Cay – ¼ nm N of Angelfish Point	26° 56.10'	77° 36.40'
Spanish Cay – ½ nm WSW of marina	26° 56.10'	77° 32.10'
South Spanish Cay Channel, inner waypoint	26° 56.00'	77° 29.50'

DESCRIPTION	Latitude	Longitude
Mangrove Cay – ½ nm NW of	26° 55.50'	78° 37.50'
Memory Rock – 2¼ nm S of	26° 54.75'	79° 05.75'
Powell Cay – ½ nm W of anchorage	26° 54.25'	77° 29.50'
Coopers Town – ½ nm NE of	26° 52.70'	77° 30.10'
Manjack Cay – ¾ nm SW of anchorages	26° 48.80'	77° 22.80'
Green Turtle Cay – ½ nm W of anchorage off New Plymouth	26° 45.70'	77° 20.35'
Treasure Cay – ¼ nm SE of entrance channel	26° 39.53'	77° 17.00'
Whale Cay Passage, outer N waypoint	26° 43.70'	77° 14.10'
Whale Cay Passage, outer S waypoint	26° 42.90'	77° 12.60'
Whale Cay Passage, inner N waypoint	26° 42.80'	77° 15.60'
Great Guana Cay Harbour	26° 39.50'	77° 06.90'
North Man-O-War Channel – outer waypoint	26° 38.00'	77° 01.30'
North Man-O-War Channel – inner waypoint	26° 37.00'	77° 01.90'
Leisure Lee – ¼ nm NE of entrance	26° 36.90'	77° 15.20'
South Man-O-War Channel – outer waypoint	26° 36.10'	76° 58.65'
South Man-O-War Channel – inner waypoint	26° 35.60'	76° 59.10'
Man-O-War Cay – 200 yards S of entrance channel to harbour	26° 35.30'	77° 00.22'
Marsh Harbour – ¼ nm NW of Outer Point Cay	26° 33.60'	77° 04.40'
Hope Town Harbour – ¼ nm W of entrance channel	26° 32.65'	76° 58.10'
Boat Harbour Marina – ¼ nm SE of entrance	26° 32.40'	77° 02.50'
White Sound, Elbow Cay – ¼ nm WNW of entrance channel	26° 31.10'	76° 59.00'
Tilloo Cut – ¼ nm W of	26° 29.80'	76° 58.55'
Witch Point – ½ nm ESE of Witch Point Shoal	26° 29.50'	77° 01.25'
Cormorant Cay – ¼ nm SE of anchorage	26° 27.45'	77° 02.75'
Tilloo Pond – ¼ nm W of entrance to pond	26° 27.00'	77° 00.50'
Snake Cay – ¼ nm SE of	26° 26.90'	77° 02.70'
Tilloo Bank, Middle Channel – N waypoint	26° 25.90'	77° 01.10'
Tilloo Bank, Middle Channel – S waypoint	26° 25.38'	77° 00.20'
North Bar Channel – ½ nm WNW of	26° 23.60'	76° 59.00'
North Bar Channel – ½ nm ESE of	26° 23.45'	76° 58.10'
Little Harbour – ½ nm N of entrance channel	26° 20.10'	76° 59.95'
Little Harbour Bar – ½ nm SE of opening between reefs	26° 19.75'	76° 59.20'
Cherokee Sound – ¾ nm S of entrance channel to anchorage	26° 15.50'	77° 04.30'
Hole in the Wall – 1½ nm SE of	25° 50.50'	77° 09.50'

APPENDIX E: Tidal Differences

All tides mentioned in this guide are based on Nassau tides. Times of tides in other locations throughout The Bahamas vary from a few minutes to a few hours before or after Nassau tides. Times and heights are affected by local conditions, the season, and the phase of the moon. The tidal differences in this table are to be used as a general guideline only. Actual times may vary from times shown in this table. Time is "B" for before Nassau, and "L" for later than Nassau

LOCATION	LAT. N	LON. W	TIME HW	TIME LW
Allan's-Pensacola, Abacos	26° 59'	77° 40'	35 min. L	45 min. L
Freeport, Grand Bahama	26° 31'	78° 46'	same	same
Green Turtle Cay, Abacos	26° 46'	77° 18'	5 min. L	5 min. L
Memory Rock, Abacos	26° 57'	79° 07'	24 min. L	29 min. L
Pelican Harbour, Abacos	26° 23'	76° 58'	26 min. L	31 min. L
Walker's Cay, Abaco	27° 16'	78° 24'	1 hr. 25 min. L	1 hr. 25 min. L

APPENDIX F: Logarithmic Speed Scale

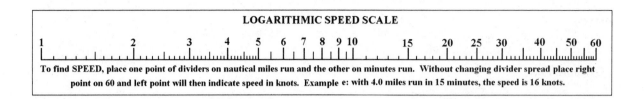

APPENDIX G: Depth Conversion Scale

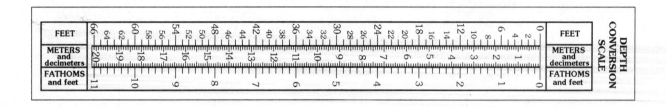

APPENDIX H: Metric Conversion Table

Visitors to The Bahamas will find the metric system in use and many grocery items and fuel measured in liters and kilograms. As a rule of thumb, a meter is just a little longer than a yard and a liter is very close to a quart. If in doubt use the following table.

1 centimeter (cm) = 0.4 inch	1 inch = 2.54 cm
1 meter (m) = 3.28 feet	1 foot = 0.31 m
1 m = 0.55 fathoms	1 fathom =1.83 m
1 kilometer (km) = 0.62 nm	1 yard = 0.93 m
1 km = 0.54 nautical nm	1 nautical mile =1.852 km
1 liter (l) = 0.26 gallons	1 gallon = 3.75 l
1 gram (g) = 0.035 ounce	1 ounce = 28.4 g
1 metric ton (t) = 1.1 tons U.S.	1 pound = 454 g

APPENDIX I: Weather Broadcast Frequencies

Frequencies sometimes change with little notice and may differ by the time of publication.
All frequencies are upper sideband except where noted.

Voice Broadcasts
NMN
Coast Guard Portsmouth, VA

AREA		TIME UTC	FREQ. KHz
Offshore Forecast	W. Cental N. Atl., Car., SW N. Atl., Gulf of Mexico	0330	4426, 6501, 8764
Offshore Forecast	same as above plus the offshore waters east of New England	0930	4426, 6501, 8764
		1600, 2200	6501, 8764, 13089

AREA	TIME UTC	FREQ. KHz
High Seas Forecast-N. Atl, Car., Gulf	0500	4426, 6501, 8764
	1130, 2330	6501, 8764, 13089
	1730	17314

CW Broadcasts

STATION	AREA	TIME UTC	FREQ. KHz
WNU-Slidell, LA	SW. N. Atl. & Car. Gulf of Mexico	0350, 0950	478, 4310, 8570, 12826.5
		1550, 2150	17117.6, 22575.5
WCC-Chatham, MA	**High Seas**-Atl., Car., Gulf of Mexico	1250, 1650	4331, 6376, 8586 8630, 13033 16972

AMTOR/SITOR (FEC)

STATION	AREA	TIME UTC	FREQ. KHz
NMF-Boston, MA	**High seas**-Atl., Car., Gulf	0140, 1630	6314, 8416.5 12579, 16806.5
WCC-Chatham, MA	**High seas**-Atl., Car., Gulf	0440, 1240, 1640	4216.5, 6324 8424
	Offshore-New Eng., W Centl. N. Atl., SW N Atl.		8426.5, 12589.5 12598, 16817 16825
	Car., & Gulf of Mexico		22386.5 (ATOR-LSB and 1.4 KHz higher)
WNU-Slidell, LA	**Offshore**-SW N Atl., Car., Gulf of Mexico	0350, 0950	4210.5, 6327 8425.5
		1550, 2150	12588.5, 16834.5

WEATHERFAX

STATION	TIME UTC	FREQ. KHz
NAM-U.S. Navy, Cutler, ME	0000-1200 only	3357
	1200-0000 only	10865
	24 hours	8080, 15959 20015
NMF-U.S. C.G., Boston, MA	24 hours	6340.5, 9110, 12750
NMG-U.S.C.G., New Orleans, LA	24 hours	4317.9, 8503.9 12789.9

NAVTEX

STATION	TIME UTC	FREQUENCY	FORECAST
NMA-Miami, FL	0000, 0400, 0800, 1200, 1600, 2000	518 KHz	SW N. ATL. & Car., coastal Florida
NMF-Boston, MA	0045, 0445, 0845, 1245, 1645, 2045	518 KHz	Offshore New England
NMG-New Orleans,LA	0300, 0700, 1100, 1500, 1900, 2300	518 KHz	Offshore Gulf, Coastal Gulf
NMN-Chesapeake,VA	0130, 0530, 0930, 1330, 1730, 2130	518 KHz	W. Cntl. N. Atl.
NMR-San Juan, PR	0200,0600,1000, 1400, 1800, 2200	518 KHz	SW N. ATL. & Car., W. Cntl. N. Atl.
ZBM-Bermuda	0100, 0500, 0900, 1300, 1700, 2100	518 KHz	SW N. ATL. & Car., W. Cntl. N. Atl.

TIME

STATION	FREQUENCY
WWV-Ft. Collins, CO	2.5, 5, 10, 15, 20, 25 MHz
WWVH-Kekaha-Kawai, HI	2.5, 5, 10, 15, 20 MHz.

The National Bureau of Standards broadcasts voice time signals continuously 24 hours a day and storm alerts at 8 minutes after the hour.

REFERENCES
AND SUGGESTED READING

Abaco, The History of an Out Island and its Cays; Steve Dodge, White Sound Press, 1995

Artist on his Island; Randolph W. Johnston, Assisted by Denny Johnston, Little Harbour Press, 1975

A Birder's Guide to the Bahama Islands; Anthony M. White, American Birding Assoc., Inc., Colorado Springs, Colorado, 1998

A Cruising Guide to Abaco; Steve Dodge, White Sound Press, 1999

A Cruising Guide to the Caribbean and the Bahamas; Jerrems C. Hart and William T. Stone, Dodd, Mead and Company, New York, 1982

A Cruising Guide to the Exumas Cays Land and Sea Park; Stephen J. Pavlidis with Ray Darville, Night Flyer Enterprises, U.S.A., 1994

A History of the Bahamas; Michael Craton, San Salvador Press, Ontario, Canada, 1986

American Practical Navigator; Nathaniel Bowditch, LL.D., DMA Hydrographic Center, 1977

Cruising Guide to the Abacos and the Northern Bahamas, Second Edition; Julius M. Wilensky, Westcott Cove, Stamford, CT, 1980

Dictionary of Bahamian English; John A. Holm, Lexik House Pub., Cold Springs, NY, 1982

On and Off The Beaten Path; Stephen J. Pavlidis, Seaworthy Publications, Inc., Port Washington, WI, 1997

Out Island Doctor; Dr. Evans W. Cottman, Hodder and Stoughton, London, 1963

Reptiles and Amphibians of The Bahamas; Bahamas National Trust, 1993

Sailing Directions for the Caribbean Sea; Pub. #147, Defense Mapping Agency, #SDPUB147

Secrets of the Bahamas Family Islands 1989; Nicolas Popov, Dragan Popov, & Jane Sydenham; Southern Boating Magazine, May 1989

The Aranha Report on the Abaco Islands; Land and Surveys Dept., Nassau, N.P., Bahamas, 1925

The Bahamas Handbook; Mary Moseley, The Nassau Guardian, Nassau, Bahamas, 1926

The Bahamas Rediscovered; Nicolas and Dragon Popov, Macmillan Press, Ltd., London, 1992

The Ephemeral Islands, A Natural History of the Bahamas; David G. Campbell, MacMillan Education, 1990

The Exuma Guide; Stephen J. Pavlidis, Seaworthy Publications, Inc., Port Washington, WI, 1995

The Ocean Almanac; Robert Hendrickson, Doubleday, New York, 1984

The Turks and Caicos Guide; Stephen J. Pavlidis, Seaworthy Publications, Inc., Port Washington, WI, 1999

The Yachtsman's Guide to the Bahamas; Meredith Fields, Tropic Isle Pub., 1999

Index

About The Author

Stephen J. Pavlidis has been cruising in The Bahamas aboard his 40' sloop *IV Play* since the winter of 1989. In January of 1990, he began cruising and living in the Exumas. He met Ray Darville, the new Warden of the Exuma Cays Land and Sea Park in February of 1993. Ray soon drew him into a working relationship with the Park as a volunteer Deputy Warden. In this role he quickly gained an intimate knowledge of the waters of the Exumas. Realizing that The Exuma Cays Land and Sea Park deserved a bit more recognition than is given in even the best guides to the area, he and Ray produced *A Cruising Guide to the Exuma Cays Land and Sea Park.* The favorable response to that publication in turn led to *The Exuma Guide.* The excellent response to that work has in turn led to the complete coverage of the central and southern Bahamas in *On and Off the Beaten Path, A Guide to the Central and Southern Bahamas.* While cruising the Southern Bahamas, Steve began to frequent the Turks and
Caicos Islands. Steve fell in love with South Caicos and through exploration, discovered that the entire island group offered much more to the visiting boater than the sparse coverage given by other publications would lead one to believe. Therefore, Steve wrote *The Turks and Caicos Guide,* which became an immediate success. Now with the release of *The Abaco Guide,* Steve's coverage of the entire Bahamas and Turks and Caicos Region is complete. Steve, N4UJP, is a member of the *Waterway Radio and Cruising Club.*

Jack Blackman

Jack Blackman designed and painted the cover for this guide. Jack has had a varied and successful career as an artist and designer. His fine art studies were obtained from *The School of Fine Arts* at *Columbia University* and *The Art Students League* in New York City. Jack's talents have involved many disciplines, such as designing sets for the Broadway stage, network television, and as Art Director for various major motion pictures. Several years ago Jack sailed his cutter *Sea Rogue* to The Bahamas, where he fell in love with the brilliant colors of the islands and their waters. Since then, his watercolors have been inspired by the graceful lines of racing sloops, time worn facades of Out Island buildings, and the warm, honest Bahamian people at work and play. Having had a number of successful exhibits, many of Jack's paintings reside in private and corporate collections internationally. His original works and reproductions are well represented in local galleries. Jack has a studio in the Berry Islands where he paints daily, completing commissions and new works for his next show.